Foundations of Art Therapy Supervision

Creating Common Ground for Supervisees and Supervisors

Yasmine J. Awais and Daniel Blausey

NEW YORK AND LONDON

First published 2021
by Routledge
52 Vanderbilt Avenue, New York, NY 10017

and by Routledge
2 Park Square, Milton Park, Abingdon, Oxon, OX14 4RN

Routledge is an imprint of the Taylor & Francis Group, an informa business

© 2021 Taylor & Francis

The right of Yasmine J. Awais and Daniel Blausey to be identified as authors of this work has been asserted by them in accordance with sections 77 and 78 of the Copyright, Designs and Patents Act 1988.

Library of Congress Cataloging-in-Publication Data
Names: Awais, Yasmine J., author. | Blausey, Daniel, author.
Title: Foundations of art therapy supervision : creating common ground for supervisees and supervisors / Yasmine J. Awais, Daniel Blausey.
Description: New York, NY : Routledge, 2020. | Includes bibliographical references and index.
Identifiers: LCCN 2020009541 (print) | LCCN 2020009542 (ebook) | ISBN 9781138212145 (hardback) | ISBN 9781138212152 (paperback) | ISBN 9781315451176 (ebook)
Subjects: MESH: Art Therapy–organization & administration | Interprofessional Relations
Classification: LCC RC489.A7 (print) | LCC RC489.A7 (ebook) | NLM WM 450.5.A8 | DDC 616.89/1656–dc23
LC record available at https://lccn.loc.gov/2020009541
LC ebook record available at https://lccn.loc.gov/2020009542

ISBN: 978-1-138-21214-5 (hbk)
ISBN: 978-1-138-21215-2 (pbk)
ISBN: 978-1-315-45117-6 (ebk)

Typeset in Times
by River Editorial Ltd, Devon, UK

Visit the eResources:
https://www.routledge.com/9781138212152

"Supervision is the cornerstone of clinical training. Yasmine J. Awais and Daniel Blausey draw on their 20-year relationship that began as supervisor and supervisee to offer an extraordinary book that showcases the dynamic, complex, and contextual nature of art therapy supervision for both the supervisor and supervisee. *Foundations of Art Therapy Supervision* is a strong synthesis of theory, ethical, legal, and practice guidelines and clinical material for art therapy supervisors and supervisees. The heart of this volume, however, is the importance of mutual learning that is ongoing and requires cultural humility to explore how the supervisor and supervisee's intersecting personal and professional identities are ever present in the supervision room, influencing dynamics related to power and privilege, topics that are discussable (or not), and ultimately the therapeutic relationship between therapist and client."

Tamara R. Buckley, Associate Professor, Counselor Education, School of Education, Hunter College, City University of New York. Co-author, The Color Bind: Talking (and Not Talking) About Race at Work

"Yasmine J. Awais and Daniel Blausey have written an art therapy supervision text, much needed in art therapy. The book offers guidance to supervisees and supervisors to contextualize supervision as a conscious and thoughtful experience, one that is imbedded in a cultural context exploring theories of social and cultural differences. Focusing on mentorship, leadership, cultural humility and mutual learning, the book offers various anecdotal examples of how supervision is a complex process when issues of race, class, gender, sexuality and disability intersect. Of particular importance, they stress, is a critical understanding of ethical and legal responsibility of art therapists when involved in dual relationships, confidentially, and art work created in the art therapeutic context. Theirs is a timely book."

Savneet Talwar, Professor, Master of Arts in Art Therapy and Counseling, School of the Art Institute of Chicago. Author, Art Therapy for Social Justice: Radical Intersections

"Clearly built upon their 'mutually supportive supervisory alliance', Yasmine Awais and Daniel Blausey provide for us – through valuable historical and theoretical perspectives, and thought-provoking personal reflections and narratives – insights into the identity-enhancing, complex interrelationship between the supervisor and supervisee; and they do so with deftness and respect. Thank you to the authors for this unique and enriching collaborative venture that belongs in every professional's library."

Dave Gussak, Professor and Graduate Art Therapy Program, Florida State University, and Project Coordinator, Florida State University/Florida Department of Corrections, Art Therapy in Prisons Program. Co-editor, The Wiley Handbook of Art Therapy

"With the partnership of these authors, their shared vision of supervision as a collaborative professional growth relationship, and its organization of chapters highlighting supervisor and supervisee perspectives, this text is gift to the profession of art therapy. The most important contributions are the chapters devoted to theoretical constructs which refuse to let cultural identity and lived experiences remain unacknowledged in the development of art therapists and art therapists-in-training. Indeed, addressing the difficult work and meaningful opportunities inherent in working with difference is the cornerstone of the book, and is no less than imperative within the context of contemporary mental health services and the building of therapeutic relationships."

Gaelynn P. Wolf Bordonaro, Director of the
Emporia State University Art Therapy Program and Professor
in the Department of Counselor Education

Foundations of Art Therapy Supervision

Foundations of Art Therapy Supervision serves as a reference guide for art therapists who have found themselves in supervisor roles without prior training and supervisees hoping to learn what to expect from the supervision relationship, and illustrates how to receive and provide clinical art therapy supervision.

Written by two art therapists with over 35 years of collective supervision experience, this new resource includes a framework for providing effective supervision in the classroom and in the field, case studies and art-based supervisory exercises, and guidance for new professionals seeking certification or licensure. Chapters weave the authors' supervision experience with a significant literature review, and feature explanations on how professional identities (art therapist, psychotherapist, counselor, supervisor, supervisee, administrator, educator, etc.) and personal identities (gender, race, sexuality, etc.) influence the supervisory and therapeutic relationships.

This book will teach supervisees how to make the most of their experience while simultaneously providing a comprehensive reference for practicing supervisors.

Yasmine J. Awais, MAAT, ATR-BC, ATCS, LCAT, LPC, is a doctoral candidate in Social Welfare at the Graduate Center, City University of New York. Awais has published and presented nationally and internationally on supervision, cultural humility, and competency. Her research interests center diversity in the creative arts therapies and in higher education.

Daniel Blausey, MA, ATR-BC, ATCS, LCAT, is a New York City-based art therapist in private practice providing art therapy, psychotherapy, and supervision. He has presented nationally and internationally on supervision, adult survivors of sexual trauma, and sex-positive clinical practices.

Contents

PART 3
Embracing and Working with Differences 119

PART 4
Locations, Places, and Spaces: Supervision Formats 173

Illustrations

Color Plates

Figures

Boxes

Tables

Preface

Just as the therapist–client relationship is the cornerstone of therapy, the relationship between the supervisor and supervisee is key to supervision. By collaborating on a book together, negotiating our relationship, honoring our differences, and sharing our experiences, we offer a multilayered perspective to supervision. We address the inherent power differentials in supervision, which we feel can best be done by looking simultaneously through the supervisee's and supervisor's eyes (and may not be so effective when only written from one perspective). Our life experiences and journeys to art therapy and supervision drastically differ (as shared in our positionality statements below), yet we have come to overlap remarkably in intent, expectation, and ability to acknowledge and appreciate each other's intersectional identities.

We have been working on this book for four years. Over the course of this time we have grown so much. Part of the difficulties with writing a book about supervision is the more we experience supervision (as a supervisor and as a supervisee), the more we learn. This book may never be truly finished. We offer this book to readers as a way to conceptualize supervision as a learning opportunity from the perspectives of both supervisor and supervisee, looking at on- and off-site supervision, on and off campus, while one individual is in formal training as an art therapist and the other is considered a professional. We wrote this book to provide a framework for ourselves, for current supervisors and supervisees, and for those who are thinking about this process.

About Our Supervisory Relationship, as Told by Yasmine

The clinical team that I joined was comprised of a variety of psychotherapists trained in art, dance/movement, drama, and music therapies; social work; mental health counseling; master's-level interns of various professions; and one part-time psychiatrist. The team was also diverse regarding racial and ethnic backgrounds, language, gender, sexual orientation, and citizenship. This team was reflective of New York City, the overall staff at the organization, and the young people we worked with.

As with the organizational life of many non-profits, Daniel's position changed shortly after I was hired. The incoming counseling supervisor was a gay-identified, white male therapist newly arrived from the Midwest. After three years, the supervisor left. I was promoted to Clinical Supervisor and Daniel was promoted to Director of Counseling Programs. Daniel's new position oversaw two units: one was responsible for intakes, crises, and drop-in services, and the other was the group that I led as Clinical Supervisor.

Daniel and I worked together for approximately six years at this organization, with our relationship shifting from supervision of clinical work to supervision of supervision. We eventually went our separate ways to pursue opportunities working in different non-profit agencies, teaching in master's-level art therapy programs, private practice and consultation, and moving to and working in new locales (Daniel to Colorado and myself to Saudi Arabia), before each of us returned to New York. Throughout this time, we kept in touch through our board and professional work.

Years later, in 2014, we were independently asked if we were interested in pitching book ideas based on our expertise as noted in the American Art Therapy Association (AATA) conference proceedings. When we realized the same editor approached us both, we immediately thought about collaborating on art therapy supervision. Together, we proposed our idea – a book on supervision – written collaboratively by a former supervisor and supervisee – for supervisors and supervisees.

Yasmine's Positionality Statement

I identify as a straight, cisgender, able-bodied multiethnic Asian (South Asian and South East Asian), East Coast American female. Constantly aware of difference, my brown-skinned body never fit into the upper-middle-class white neighborhood of my youth, or, subsequently, other personal and professional spaces I have inhabited. While much of my clinical work has engaged with diverse teams and clients, my educational experiences (compulsory to higher education) were predominately white women teachers in public schools. As I have moved up professionally, from new clinician to professor, the spaces I have occupied have grown more white. As I write this today, I am a professor and a student, a partner in an interracial marriage, and a daughter of immigrants of different ethnicities and religions. I have a full-time job, I have health insurance, I am a homeowner and a member of the middle class.

I originally became interested in supervision after having two key negative experiences. These instances shaped my views on how my positionality impacted the supervisory relationship, particularly the influence of organizational structure, gender, and communication styles. The first incident occurred during my art therapy internship. As a young woman, I was distressed when a male client was masturbating in my group. When I told my supervisor what happened, I felt dismissed when the concern was "if the client finished" and not how I was feeling. My feelings of being violated turned into hurt and anger, and I became verbally aggressive. As a result, my individual supervision became group supervision – three art therapy supervisors supervising me. When I brought this incident to my school, I was not supported. During a collage workshop with David Henley, I created a response art piece to the incident (see Color Plate 1). I remember carefully cutting, applying so much pressure that my hands hurt – I wanted to make sure it was perfect. It was created on colored mat board, which allowed the piece to have structure and sturdiness. It is a reminder that I still have, 20 years later, to why I continue to be invested in supervision and listening to the experiences of my supervisees. The second incident happened when I was a professional art therapist (see Chapter 7). What was difficult for me was not simply the incidents themselves, but realizing that the supervisors that I held so high in regard were not who I wanted or needed them to be.

As a result, I sought out as much supervision training and educational experience as possible. These trainings were outside of the field of art therapy – advanced trainings by social workers in the specialization of child welfare, and training for middle managers working in non-profit organizations. At the same time, as a staff art therapist at a non-profit, community-based youth organization, I was supervising graduate-level art therapy interns, and was then promoted to supervise staff therapists across disciplines (i.e., music, dance/movement, and drama therapists; social workers; mental health counselors; and psychiatrists).

Eventually, I provided consultation for non-profit organizations, supervising bachelors through master's-level counselors and therapists who were working with underserved populations. As my consulting practice grew, licensure became the norm across states, resulting in required supervision hours for clinicians. I focused my supervision practice on clinicians who were interested in diversity issues in their clinical work. This proved to be an amazing experience – I had the chance to learn about different settings and populations thorough the experiences of my supervisees. Child life, early intervention, trauma for infants and toddlers (0 to 3), and older adults are just a few examples of groups that I learned about as a supervisor. The majority of my consultation practice occurred outside of the site where therapy was occurring. I also had the opportunity to supervise therapists individually, in groups, and with some therapists both individually and in group settings.

As I write this preface, I am currently providing classroom group supervision to master's-level art therapy and counseling students. I enjoy seeing students work through the struggles and celebrations of learning the craft of being an art therapist, working with colleagues, understanding systems, and problem solving. I also supervise therapists and counselors who are working towards their credentials, including licensure. Like my graduate students, the professionals I supervise are learning. However, a key difference is these professional supervisees are seeking me out as their supervisor, rather than being assigned to my course.

Daniel's Positionality Statement

At present, I identify as a queer/gay, cisgender, able-bodied, East Coast white man of mainly European (Western and Central) descent. Raised as a child on a small family farm in the Midwest, the majority of my peers reflected the whiteness of my skin, shared a family-farm/working-class status and Lutheran religion, and had heavily involved extended families. Art therapy is a second career for me, after previously spending seven years as an illustrator and art director at advertising agencies in the Midwest. Currently, I am an art therapist in private practice, an art therapy educator, a homeowner, solidly middle class, and a partner in a long-term, same-sex, interracial marriage.

A tentative interest in supervision began during graduate school at my second internship, when I secured art therapy supervision from a contracted art therapy supervisor to complement my on-site youth development internship supervision. In this setting, in addition to learning from the typical supervisor-as-expert model, I was able to gain much by witnessing and engaging with the art therapy supervisor as *learner*. The on-site supervisors confidently maintained the expertise of the population, yet welcomed the opportunity to grasp how the art therapy process supported clients' mental health. Meanwhile, the contracted supervisor firmly held her art therapy capability while also bringing a proper curiosity to better understanding the population we worked with, in order to increase her own clinical proficiency and supervisory capacity. The significance of supervision, and my own growing passion for becoming a supervisor, quickly intensified when supervising an art therapy graduate student for the first time.

When I first met Yasmine at the AATA conference in Orlando (1999), I was roughly five years into my art therapy career. At the time, I was a clinical supervisor at a comprehensive youth agency in New York City, where I became the Director of Counseling Programs a few years later. I had the privilege to develop and lead a dynamic and diverse team of traditional mental health practitioners and creative art therapists, as well as an internship training program. I was the first director at the agency to be an art therapist. My path was not always smooth, or well supported with the needed supervisory training.

My next career move entailed a larger agency and larger team (50–60 members) with more layers between the actual clinical work and me. This role entailed the supervision of associate and assistant directors, coordinators, and select direct care staff. Supervision required a balance of program management, mid-manager-level development, and increasing staff expertise to raise the quality of client experiences. My position provided supervision to clinical supervisors as well as staff therapists across disciplines (i.e., creative arts therapists, social workers, psychologists, nurse practitioners, and psychiatrists), and included program development and management responsibilities. In addition to seeing clients for art therapy in my private practice, I also continue to provide campus group supervision to master's-level art therapy students and professionals in the field.

My intent in supervision is to provide a secure space within the mutual unfolding of theory and practice for a series of intertwining discoveries that shape the therapist identity. I firmly believe that a productive supervisor not only holds the space to acknowledge and works through the inherent privileges in the relationship, but also holds the expertise in a manner readily shared yet not freely dispersed. A supervisee gains little when a supervisor simply rests within their expertise doling out nuggets of insights. A dynamic supervisory relationship challenges not only the supervisee but the supervisor as well.

Acknowledgements

To Our Supervisors

We could not have written this book without our supervisors, both formal and informal. We have learned so much from those we wanted to emulate and those we felt could have done better. Without these experiences, we would not have been inspired to write this book. A special thanks and much gratitude to Ani Buk, who supervised each of us early on in our art therapy journeys – Daniel as a graduate student and Yasmine during her first art therapy position.

To Our Supervisees

Supervision is nothing without our supervisees. We have become stronger, more competent, and humbler due to all of you. Of course, supervision is nothing without the people you work with – the patients, clients, family members, individuals, and communities. Much appreciation to supervisees and workshop participants who allowed us to include their artwork in this text – Julia Anderson, Jessica Benston, Julie Gotthold, Erica Bucci, ToniAnn Eisman, Katie Gentile, Arianna Kendra, Kristy Leone, Lauren Messina, Adele Minton, Erica Ochsenreither, Christiana Son, Kristyn Stickley, Danielle Szulanski, Christina Taylor, and Therese Zakrzwski. We specifically want to thank our supervisees who also contributed vignettes – Blair Chase, Cindy Gordon (who we both were fortunate enough to supervise at different points in her career), Julie Gotthold, Emily Reim Ifrach, and Anna Jackson. Through supervision, we have had the chance to indirectly work with those you have worked with, and for that we are grateful.

Our Writing Team

We are thankful to Routledge for believing in our project and vision. Thank you to Amanda Devine, our editor at Routledge, for supporting us on this journey that may have taken a few more years than originally proposed. This book could not have been realized without the additional support of so many other behind the scenes people, including Grace

McDonnell, Editorial Assistant at Routledge, and the very detailed Andrew Melvin. We also have much gratitude for Emily Austin, a thoughtful and amazing editor who gave us the final outside perspective and push we needed to finish this book. Special thanks to Becky Asch, Trina Dow, and K.C. Wuebbling for providing additional commentary. We also value the additional perspectives and professional expertise from our co-authors outside of art therapy, Karen Myers and Stephanie Brooks. We would like to honor Hamilton and Spike!, two of our furriest supporters and most adorable distractions, who crossed over the rainbow bridge during the writing of this book.

Yasmine's Additional Acknowledgements

In addition to our collective thanks, I could not have asked for a better supervisor, colleague, and writing partner in Daniel. Thank you for being patient with my writing style and contradictions! I appreciate our writing retreats and how our relationship has grown stronger after working together on this project. Also, special thanks to Frank Delano, who showed me that supervision is a relationship, provided me with my first supervision training, and mentored me when I was a novice supervisor and trainer. I still share *If I Could Supervise My Supervisor* to this day. Finally, this book would not have been possible without the support of David Geiger, who lovingly asked over five years when the book would be finished. It's finished.

Daniel's Additional Acknowledgements

Tremendous gratefulness to Yasmine for being an engaged and inspiring supervisee as I gained my footing as a supervisor. More significantly, thank you for being a thought-provoking colleague, friend, and writing partner over the last 20 years. Much appreciation for your ability to encourage, challenge, and reflect in the midst of this project that allowed us to become stronger as writers and deepened our friendship. Lastly, to Gerry Valentine, much gratitude for your unwavering support, love, and commitment to this book and our journey together.

Authors

Yasmine J. Awais, MAAT, ATR-BC, ATCS, LCAT, LPC, is a doctoral candidate in Social Welfare at the Graduate Center, City University of New York (CUNY), and is a Presidential Research Fellow. She is a board-certified registered art therapist and certified supervisor (ATR-BC, ATCS), licensed creative arts therapist in New York (LCAT), and licensed professional counselor in Pennsylvania (LPC). Yasmine obtained her Master of Arts in Art Therapy (MAAT) from the School of the Art Institute of Chicago; MA in Psychology from CUNY, where she was awarded the Kenneth Clark Award for Social Justice; and a certificate from Columbia University's Institute for Not-for-Profit Management at Columbia Business School's Middle Management Program. She has presented extensively on supervision and multicultural and cross-cultural clinical practice. Yasmine's research interests center social justice and diversity in the creative arts therapies and in higher education.

Daniel Blausey, MA, ATR-BC, ATCS, LCAT, is a board-certified and registered art therapist, art therapy certified supervisor, and a licensed creative arts therapist in New York. He obtained his master's (Art Therapy) from New York University, a certificate from the International Trauma Studies Program at New York University, and a certificate from the Sexual Abuse Treatment and Training Institute. Daniel maintains a private practice in New York City, where he provides art therapy, psychotherapy, and contracted clinical supervision. In addition to supervision, his areas of focus are DE&I (diversity, equity, and inclusion), sex positivity, and the impact of traumatic events throughout the life span, including childhood sexual abuse. Previously he held roles as a non-profit senior manager with over 20 years of experience in youth development, mental health/substance abuse services, and creative arts therapy programming. In these positions he gained extensive supervisory experiences with accountability for direct clinical and administrative supervision of senior departmental staff, managers, clinical teams, and interns. Artistically, Daniel often explores identity through the psychological complexity of the human figure by examining themes of darkness, whimsy, pain, and resiliency.

Contributors

Stephanie Brooks, PhD, LCSW, LMFT, is a clinical professor in the College of Nursing and Health Professions at Drexel University. She is the Senior Associate Dean for Health Professions and Faculty Affairs and Couple and Family Therapy PhD Program Director. Dr. Brooks is an American Association for Marriage and Family Therapy (AAMFT) Approved Supervisor and Clinical Fellow and the Executive Program Consultant for the AAMFT Minority Fellowship Program. Dr. Brooks' clinical and scholarly interests include: supervision and training, cultural diversity, social justice, Person of the Therapist Training, addiction, and behavioral health. Dr. Brooks maintains a small private practice in Philadelphia.

Karen Myers, MSW, JD, is an associate professor in the Social Work department at James Madison University (JMU). With a background in public interest law and social work, she brought over 15 years of practical experiences to her current position. She currently teaches practice classes in the Bachelor of Social Work program at JMU, including Skills for Generalist Social Work Practice and Mezzo Practice. She incorporates diversity awareness activities and critical self-reflection into all of the courses she teaches. She enjoys using qualitative research methods to examine diversity issues, specifically related to the LGBTQIAP+ community. She is committed to continuing to explore ways in her teaching, research, and service to enhance social justice by challenging power imbalances and calling for institutional accountability. She also believes deeply in self-care practices and is a certified yoga and Bodyflow instructor.

Introduction and Intent

Foundations of Art Therapy Supervision: Creating Common Ground for Supervisees and Supervisors illustrates how to receive and provide clinical art therapy supervision. Like many other mental health professionals, art therapists may find themselves in a supervisory role based on their experience as a clinician, instead of through formalized training or guidance on how to be a supervisor. Likewise, if how to be *in* supervision is not fully addressed in their formal education, supervisees, and supervisors who do not engage in their own supervision, may lack the ability to fully contribute to the supervisory process. When we first conceived of this book, there were few books written specifically for art therapists: we found one that is out of print (Malchiodi & Riley, 1996) and one from art therapists based in the United Kingdom (Schaverien & Case, 2007). Given the paucity of available resources, art therapists interested in furthering knowledge in supervision utilized books from other disciplines (see Sweitzer & King, 2018), supplemented by art-therapy-related works. Fortunately, since we have begun this collaborative writing journey, Routledge has published two books on supervision that we respect – one specific to diversity (Hardy & Bobes, 2016) and one on art-based supervision (Fish, 2016).

So, why the need for another book on supervision, let alone one on art therapy supervision? What unique perspectives do we offer?

Together, we have more than 35 years of collective supervision experience. We have gained so much from our supervisory relationships and experiences. We wrote this book to help other supervisors and supervisees get the richest experience possible out of supervision. For us, this includes bringing an awareness of how our professional identities (e.g., art therapist, psychotherapist, counselor, supervisor, supervisee, administrator, educator) and personal identities (e.g., male, female, white, multiethnic Asian, straight, queer, cisgender, able-bodied) influence the supervisory and therapeutic relationships. We started our professional relationship as supervisee and supervisor in 2000, which has grown into a mutual respect, as colleagues and as friends. Since then, we have presented on supervision together and separately, been guest speakers for each other's classes, and relied on each other for peer consultation for a variety of matters. We believe our mutual understanding and appreciation for each other's sometimes contrasting and often intersecting approaches to clinical and supervisory work provides us with knowledge that we can share. This knowledge is amplified by acknowledging our differing social locations and identity privileges, and a distinct desire to change the supervision experience of art therapists.

Book Layout

Part 1: How to Get the Most Out of Supervision

The book is structured into four content parts. The first, *How to Get the Most Out of Supervision*, lays the foundation for this book, including reasons for and expectations of art therapy supervision, along with best practices for both supervisees and supervisors. While there is an inherent power differential in the supervisory relationship, since one holds the role of supervisor and one of supervisee (see the exceptions in peer supervision and consultation groups), we believe that best practices hold both the supervisor *and* supervisee as accountable for the relationship.

Part 2: The Business and Administrative Sides to Supervision

Ethical and legal matters are addressed in Part 2. With the assistance of Karen Myers, who comes from the disciplines of social work and law, we look at scope of practice, the unique challenges of art therapists surrounding credentialing and licensing, dual relationships, contracted supervision, and confidentiality. Furthermore, art therapists hold the additional responsibility of the ethical and legal issues regarding artworks created by clients, including the implications of sharing these products.

Part 3: Embracing and Working with Differences

A key component of supervision for us as authors is *Embracing and Working with Differences*, the title of Part 3. Similar to our practice with clients, we understand that the social location and identities of the supervisor and supervisee influence the relationship. The importance of not only understanding, but also naming and addressing differences across supervisee and supervisor are addressed. We attend to identities of race, ethnicity, gender, sexual orientation, religion, age, socioeconomic status, and abilities that hold power or agent status and those that are subjugated or hold target status. This is done by borrowing from critical race theory, understanding the impact of colonialism in our work, and paying attention to feminist epistemologies. In addition to individual differences within the tripartite relationship of supervisor, supervisee, and client (which includes the supervisor–supervisee, art therapist–client, and supervisor–client relationships), and systemic differences (e.g., community–agency, administration–staff), we are also concerned about identity of discipline. How to negotiate when the art therapist is supervised by a non-art therapist? Similarly, how do art therapists supervise those who come from other fields while not going beyond our scope of practice?

Part 4: Locations, Places, and Spaces: Supervision Formats

Finally, Part 4 breaks down the different formats of supervision: individual, group, and distance supervision. In *Locations, Places, and Spaces: Supervision Formats*, we acknowledge that although methods may have similar overall goals (e.g., objective feedback, educational purposes) there are unique differences which are helpful to identify. We clearly outline what these are so both supervisees and supervisors better manage expectations, whether someone is supervising or being supervised on-site (i.e., where the art therapy is taking place) or off-site.

Other Structural Elements

While the spirit of our book is based on our desire for others to learn from our various experiences as the clinician, supervisor, supervisee, and educator, we also situate this book in theory and knowledge based in the literature, drawing from contemporary supervision models in art therapy, psychology, counseling, social work, and related helping professions theories. Our aim is broad and foundational – we wish to assist supervisees in learning to manage up and achieve the most out of supervision, and also support supervisors who wish to gain a framework on how to provide effective supervision to students in the classroom, students in the field, new professionals seeking certification or licensure, seasoned professionals, and those supervising across disciplines. We also provide vignettes and artwork from actual supervision experiences to illustrate supervision concepts.

We conclude each chapter with a summary and practice prompts, including art experientials that can be utilized in supervision or help the reader explore the topic in more detail. A glossary is included at the end of this book, defining key terms. While foundational, we envision this book to be one that is utilized in art therapy group supervision courses, for those receiving supervision, and for those who supervise therapists (whether or not they are art therapists). Quite simply, we wrote a book we wish to share with our own supervisees and supervisors. We hope it can be used as a map for those who are taking their own journey through supervision.

References

Fish, B. J. (2016). *Art-based supervision: Cultivating therapeutic insight through imagery.* New York, NY: Routledge.

Hardy, K. V., & Bobes, T. (Eds.). (2016). *Culturally sensitive supervision and training: Diverse perspectives and practical applications.* New York, NY: Routledge.

Malchiodi, C. A., & Riley, S. (1996). *Supervision and related issues: A handbook for professionals.* Chicago, IL: Magnolia Street Publishers.

Schaverien, J., & Case, C. (Eds.). (2007). *Supervision of art psychotherapy: A theoretical and practical handbook.* New York, NY: Routledge.

Sweitzer, H. F., & King, M. A. (2018). *The successful internship: Personal, professional, and civic development in experiential learning* (5 ed). Boston, MA: Cengage.

Part 1

How to Get the Most out of Supervision

The act of art therapy supervision is complex. This section aims to orient the reader by providing a shared language and foundational understanding of what supervision entails for both supervisors and supervisees. Our purpose is to encourage the formation and maintenance of a meaningful and dynamic relationship to art therapy supervision that highlights an intentional awareness and attention to race, gender, and other differences. This section, *How to Get the Most Out of Supervision,* contains three chapters:

- What is Art Therapy Supervision? Reasons and Expectations;
- What Supervisors Need to Know about Supervision; and
- What Supervisees Need to Know about Supervision.

In Chapter 1, *What is Art Therapy Supervision? Reasons and Expectations*, we provide a working definition of the topic, review history on the beginnings of supervision, consider a supervision framework, outline three key areas of supervision, and clarify the roles and responsibilities of the supervisor and supervisee. We also consider the crucial role of artmaking – no other type of supervision grapples with the implicit role of art. In Chapter 2, *What Supervisors Need to Know about Supervision,* we explore best practices of the supervisor. This includes understanding ideal supervisor qualities and ensuring art is incorporated in supervision sessions – the art of the clients, the art of the supervisee, and the art of the supervisor. Finally, Chapter 3, *What Supervisees Need to Know about Supervision,* focuses on how to get the most out of supervision, including an exploration of ideal qualities of supervisees. For the supervisee who has less structural power in the relationship, we identify strategies on how to bring artmaking to supervision. Each chapter in *How to Get the Most out of Supervision* includes practice prompts for readers who are supervisors or supervisees. We hope these prompts invite a fuller exploration of how to get the most out of supervision.

1 What Is Art Therapy Supervision?

Reasons and Expectations

Introduction

Clinical practice can be categorized as occurring in two broad settings: public-institutional settings and private practice. The private practice setting tends to be more homogeneous, with clusters of clinically prepared master's- or doctoral-level clinicians. The public domain of clinical practice tends to be more diverse – assorted clinicians with divergent credentials – and yet their responsibilities and roles overlap and converge. In both of these settings, administrators and supervisees sometimes narrowly view clinical supervisors as gatekeepers of the organization's policies and procedures. In other words, managers in public-institutional settings often see an on-site supervisor's primary supervisory responsibility as administrative, prioritizing the organization's mission via policies and procedures over the educational or supportive supervisory aspects of developing clinicians and their work. With balance, we believe the cultural context of these settings can provide something magical for the client, therapist, and supervisor. In particular, the isomorphic nature of the supervisor-and-supervisee relationship can foster creativity and professional growth that in turn may facilitate quality client care.

The aim of this chapter is to give the reader a working definition of supervision. We explain what supervision is, including some history of the beginnings of clinical supervision. The roles and responsibilities of the supervisor and supervisee are also clarified. Ultimately, our aim for this chapter, in conjunction with the rest of this book, is to provide a framework and foundation for the practice of supervision.

Just as importantly, we want to create an enthusiasm for forming a deeper, dynamic relationship to supervision. Supportive, thoughtful supervisory relationships multiply the benefits of supervision. A genuinely effective supervisor creates a reassuring and supportive environment for the art therapist's field experience. Reliable and accountable supervision supports not only the art therapist, but also directly influences the experiences of the people engaging in art therapy. Supervision can be an instrumental experience of mentorship, leadership, humility, mutual learning, and "figuring things out together" in the most challenging and enlightening of ways. Learning is mutual in supervision. A good supervisor openly expects to learn from the supervisee and continually discovers how to be a better supervisor. This openness increases skills in the supervisor. Supervisees have a greater likelihood of becoming equally strong supervisors when they are actively engaged in the supervisory process.

As seen in Daniel's story (see Vignette 1.1), it is common for clinicians to become supervisors due to their time in the field, whether they have had training in the practice of supervision or not. This is not unique to art therapy and has been documented in other behavioral health professions (Hoge, Migdole, Farkas, Ponce, & Hunnicutt, 2011). We aim to disrupt this tradition by providing current and future supervisors a framework for best practices. Becoming a supervisor should be a conscious, thoughtful, and educated experience.

Vignette 1.1 Daniel's First Supervisee

My first art therapy supervisory role was as an on-site internship supervisor for a graduate student. At the time, I had been an art therapist for four years. As the only art therapist on staff, I was encouraged and supported by the agency I worked for, and the graduate program of the student, to bring in an art therapy intern. Despite this support, I deliberated whether I was ready and experienced enough for the commitment. However, there were many benefits of accepting of an art therapy intern: the agency increased the potential for the provision of art therapy services, and I discovered the role of being an art therapy supervisor and created a new art therapy internship placement.

The intern was an established artist: white, female, and, surprisingly, several years older than me. At first the age difference was somewhat intimidating to me. Nonetheless, it quickly became an asset as the intern's natural inquisitiveness, comfortableness with her own vulnerability, and eagerness to learn fed a quickly built alliance. Transparency, especially my own ability to say, "I don't know," was pivotal. The alliance was based on mutual respect and understanding of what the other provided and the reciprocated "Let's figure this out together" approach.

The success of this internship paved the way for a robust creative arts therapy internship program implemented over the next decade to include art, drama, music, and dance movement interns.

The Landscape of Supervision

The Oxford English Dictionary defines *supervision* as "The action or function of overseeing, directing, or taking charge of a person, organization, activity, etc.; supervisory responsibility" ("Supervision", 2019). When we further break down the word, we find two parts – *super* and *vision*. *Super* refers to being "above, on top (of), beyond, besides, in addition" ("Super", 2019) while *vision* is "Something which is apparently seen otherwise than by ordinary sight" ("Vision", 2019). Having someone who is outside of yourself, someone with more experience and an outside perspective, can help one see things that may be overlooked. This is because it is not possible to see all aspects of a situation, particularly when you are learning. Learning by observing and doing is the hallmark of clinical training, and supervision – required for trainees and new professionals – is a key component of this process.

Supervision has evolved over time, moving away from a model where two clinicians discussed a case (and the psychology of the client) and towards a more triadic relationship between the supervisor, supervisee, and client (Watkins, 2011). This does not mean that all three persons are in the room together, but that the relationship between all three individuals is considered. See Figure 1.1 for a visual representation of this tripartite relationship. As you can see from this simplified illustration, the relationship extends beyond just these three players into the community. Furthermore, like social work, psychotherapy has acknowledged that the location of the therapy, meaning the administrative aspects of where psychotherapy takes place, influences the practice of supervision (Watkins, 2011).

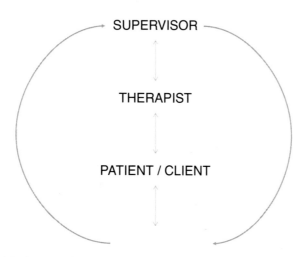

Figure 1.1 The impact of supervision.

There are a variety of reasons a supervisor or supervisee engages in supervision:

- To process what actually occurs in sessions so the therapist can do better clinical work;
- To fulfil a requirement for education or employment;
- To "give back" to the profession;
- To obtain national credentials and state-level licensure;
- To obtain support during a job change, when developing a private practice, or for specific case consultation; and
- To become a better supervisor (i.e., supervision of supervision).

Regardless of the reasons why therapists participate in supervision, we believe effective supervision requires a fundamental understanding of the complexity and act of supervision that goes beyond a well-informed definition.

The Practice of Supervision

The act of supervision is complex, and has been defined and described in a variety of ways. The oversight of clinical work has been described as "the act of managing, directing, controlling, guiding, inspecting, or providing oversight" (Hoge et al., 2011, p. 187). This oversight is often broken down into two categories: administrative (or task assistance) and emotional support (Hoge et al., 2011). Watkins (2011) identifies five common aspects of psychotherapy supervision in his review of the literature:

1. It is educative.
2. It is distinct from therapy.
3. It is distinct from consultation.
4. While components overlap with teaching, psychotherapy, and consultation aspects, supervision is a separate endeavor.
5. "Supervision is a distinct intervention" (Watkins, 2011, p. 59).

Kadushin and Harkness (2014) identified not two but three components of supervision – *administrative*, *educational*, and *supportive*. While we understand there are overlaps in these concepts, we use these three key areas throughout the book as they break down the elements of supervision in a clear manner. Administration, education, and support are crucial to any supervising process, regardless of the theoretical orientations of supervision or who is being supervised. See Figure 1.2 for a visual depiction as originally published in Delano (2001), which looks at the three components of supervision overlapped onto the tripartite relationship of the supervisor, supervisee, and client.

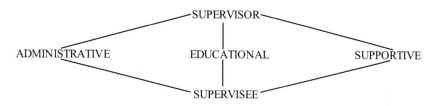

Figure 1.2 Three aspects of supervision in relation to the supervisor and supervisee. Reprinted by permission of Frank Delano (2002).

Key Area 1: Administrative

This aspect of supervision may be the most difficult one for art therapists to grasp, as we tend to focus on the relationship between art therapist and client, not the client and their environment (i.e., family systems, community, etc.), or the art therapist and their work environment. This is a growing understanding that, in addition to attending to the individual psychodynamics of the patient/client, part of the clinical work of therapists is to attend to the systems that affect and shape the client. This is evident to art therapists working in communities (see Allen, 2007; Hocoy, 2007; Timm-Bottos, 2011) and other settings. Furthermore, as art therapists are increasingly trained to also be counselors, many seek licensure and jobs that are geared towards counseling or even case management. Regardless of how much art therapy is being conducted, there are always administrative components to consider: documentation, scheduling, and compliance.

Documentation

Documenting the art therapy – the work done in session – often consumes more time than the art therapy itself. Documentation includes progress notes (both on paper and electronically), creating and updating treatment plans, and visual documentation of artwork created in session. Artwork documentation is unique to the practice of art therapy and challenging because of ethical concerns. Some of the most challenging concerns involve maintaining confidentiality and maintaining records for the appropriate amount of time as determined by the agency or state. It is not always realistic to hold original artwork created by clients for years due to storage issues, and art therapists may choose to photograph the artwork created. With digital photography, artwork can easily be documented and stored electronically or printed. In some facilities, photography is not allowed, or the art therapist may not have access to a camera. In such cases, the art therapist documents the artwork in the progress note by recreating the client image or describing the artwork in words.

Scheduling

The scheduling of daily tasks, which include seeing individual clients, group sessions, supervision, documentation, treatment team meetings, and personal time off, are a part of administration. Creating schedules becomes complicated when working in a treatment team, particularly when multiple groups run simultaneously. The setting itself also impacts how one manages one's time. For example, art therapists in a school setting often have to decide when student clients must be "pulled out" of class or if they are to "push in" to a class to run a group. How does an art therapist decide when is the ideal time to schedule their work? Or does the art therapist have a choice?

Compliance

A third aspect of administrative duties is compliance. This includes professional credentials, practice and licensing laws, and compliance with workplace policy and procedures. Art therapy professionals must comply with national accreditation (i.e., the Art Therapy Credentials Board, or ATCB) and keep up to date with current (and changing) state title protection and licensing laws. State-level title protections exist to protect consumers from fraud by outlining specific criteria for determining who is allowed to use an "art therapist" title. State by state, criteria differ depending on art therapy licensure. For example, an agency may not require a clinician to hold a degree or license in art therapy, yet state law may require individuals to hold a specific license, appropriate credentials, or certifications to call themselves an art therapist. For more information on credentials as administered by the ATCB, see Chapter 4, *Navigating Professional Identity: Credentials, Representation, and Relationships*. Other aspects of compliance the art therapist must adhere to are the mission statement of the place of work and any accreditation standards the agency or hospital must abide by (e.g., Commission on Accreditation of Rehabilitation Facilities [CARF], Joint Commission). Annual reviews fall under compliance, but can also fall under educational (see below) if done with consideration of the supervisee's career goals. Professional development may also be considered administrative and/or educational when scheduling time away for training and conferences: administrative if taking courses that are required, educational if seeking learning about topics that the therapist is truly interested in (which may include required courses).

Key Area 2: Educational

Education, commonly called clinical supervision, is the second component of supervision. "Educational supervision is concerned with teaching the knowledge, skills, and attitudes necessary" to interact with clients (Kadushin &

Harkness, 2014, p. 117). Virtually all that has been written about supervision in the art therapy literature focuses on the educational or clinical components. The educational aspect of supervision tends to examine how arts expression represents the psychodynamics of the individual, group, family, or community who are utilizing art therapy. Some examples of how art therapy supervision has been described:

- The use of artmaking and art in supervision (Deaver & Shiflett, 2011; Fish, 2012, 2017; McNamee & McWey, 2004; Miller, 2012);
- Journaling (Deaver & McAuliffe, 2009);
- The benefits of group supervision (Linesch, Holmes, Morton, & Shields, 1989); and
- And the different phases of art therapy supervision (Wilson, Riley, & Wadeson, 1984).

Components of the art therapy supervisee's education include skills for learning about their clients, more general educational aspects of therapy, the clinical work itself, and skills for self-awareness and self-reflection. Skills for learning about the client include obtaining knowledge and assessing the functioning of the individuals that the supervisee works with (i.e., persons with particular medical or mental health diagnoses, individuals seeking services for a specific social issue, problem, or concern, etc.). There are also more universal educational aspects of therapy that supervisees seek support for, such as case conceptualization, understanding of countertransference, building communication, and the overall supervisory relationship, as well as the clinical work itself (i.e., assessing, diagnosing, treating, and ongoing evaluation). The integration of theory and clinical observation, and subsequently the transformation of theoretical knowledge and the emotional response to the therapy, are also aspects of educational components of supervision. Finally, self-awareness (Kadushin & Harkness, 2014; Sanders, 2016) and self-reflection (Deaver & Shiflett, 2011) are skills that are addressed in the education component of the supervisor–supervisee relationship. Educational supervision also helps the clinician to attend to the verbal and non-verbal responses of the client. Note that emotional responses, self-awareness, and self-reflection overlap with supportive aspects of supervision.

Key Area 3: Supportive

The supportive aspects of supervision focus on work-related stress and the emotional responses of the supervisee. Burn out, compassion fatigue, and vicarious traumatization are all potential (or inevitable) hazards of clinical work (see Newell & MacNeil, 2010). While it is arguable that providing solid administrative and educational supervision also provides support, paying special attention to stress reduction as a separate function of supervision is worthwhile. In fact, the field of social work makes this aspect of supervision explicit in the National Association of Social Workers (NASW) Standards for Social Work Practice in Child Protection (1981, cited in Kadushin & Harkness, 2014).

Artmaking, art therapy, and art interventions by art therapists have been utilized to prevent or ameliorate burnout in nurses (Repar & Patton, 2007) and caregivers (Camic, Tischler, & Pearman, 2014; Murrant, Rykov, Amonite, & Loynd, 2000; Potash, Chan, Ho, Wang, & Cheng, 2015; Reid & Hartzell, 2013; Salzano, Lindemann, & Tronsky, 2013). Because artmaking has been used to reduce job-related stress for those who are in caring roles, we strongly encourage artmaking for art therapists themselves in and around the supervisory session. Early in his supervisory career, Daniel prioritized artmaking as a way to address the potential for burnout and being overwhelmed not only from his own clients but those of his supervisees as well. The artmaking took the form of 30-second responses to longer pieces that transformed greatly over time. *Up in Arms* (see Color Plate 2) spans nearly ten years of paints, pastel, and mixed media on printmaking paper. The multilayered art holds the history, struggle, and evolution of wisdom acquired. The use of artmaking by supervisors can serve as a supportive function as well as an educational one. For a text dedicated completely to arts-based supervision, please see the work of Barbara Fish (2017).

Differences between Supervision and Therapy

There often is a parallel process that teaches the therapist how to attend to and honor the intrinsic emotional experiences in relation to others and how to use this information therapeutically. There can be transference and countertransference in supervision and in therapy. While both supervision and therapy involve a relationship built on trust and understanding, there are differences, which are clearly outlined by Dixon (2004). We have created a table to map Dixon's outline with the American Art Therapy Association's (AATA's) definition of art therapy to explicate the parallels and differences of clinical art therapy, educational or clinical supervision, and supportive and administrative supervision (see Table 1.1).

The primary differences are in the goals and intended outcomes. While art therapy goals are holistically focused on the client, supervision goals are ultimately designed to enhance a client's experience and potential for reaching positive outcomes by enhancing the supervisee's attention, skills, and scope. Specifically, the purpose of art therapy is to "improve or restore functioning and sense of personal well-being" (ATCB, 2020, para 4) while the goal of clinical supervision is to best serve the client through enhanced professional performance of the therapist. Supervision involves a triadic process (i.e., supervisor, supervisee/therapist, and client),

Table 1.1 Differences between the practice of art therapy and clinical supervision

	Therapy	Supervision[1]		
	Clinical Art Therapy[2]	Educational (Clinical) Supervision	Supportive Supervision	Administrative Supervision
Goals and Purpose	Improve or restore functioning and sense of personal well-being of a client	Improve clinical skills of the supervisee through a triadic process (i.e., supervisor, supervisee/therapist, and client) to strengthen client outcomes	Reduce work-related stress and lessen pressure of supervisee's emotional responses to clinical work (i.e., burnout, compassion fatigue, and vicarious traumatization)	Assure compliance with documentation, scheduling, professional credentials, practice and licensing laws, workplace policy and procedures
Outcome	Based on client needs, which may include: exploration of feelings, reconciling emotional conflicts, fostering self-awareness, managing behaviors and additions, developing social skills, improving reality orientation, reducing anxiety, increasing self-esteem	"Enhanced proficiency in knowledge, skills, and attitudes essential to effective job performance including skills for self-awareness and self-reflection" (Dixon, p. 2)	Ability to identify and implement strategies for work-related pressures that foster self-care in response to clinical work	Consistent use of approved formats, policies, and procedures
Time Frame	Self-paced; tends to be longer-term or open-ended	"Short-term and on-going" (Dixon, p. 2)		
Agenda	Based on client needs	"Based on service mission and design" (Dixon, p. 2)		"Based on agency needs" (Dixon, p. 2)
Format	• Individual • Triadic • Group • Family	• Individual • Dyad • Group • Peer		• Individual • Team meetings

(Continued)

Table 1.1 (Cont.)

	Therapy	Supervision[1]		
	Clinical Art Therapy[2]	Educational (Clinical) Supervision	Supportive Supervision	Administrative Supervision
		• Distance • Educational and supportive focused trainings		
Location	• In-patient (includes hospitals, prisons, residential treatment facilities) • Schools and social service agencies • Community-based • Private practice	• On-site • Off-site (i.e., on-campus, private practice, telesupervision/distance)		On-site

which includes administrative and compliance components to adhere to location-specific policies and procedures. In addition to compliance, supervision also provides didactic experiences to supervisees to become better art therapists, and addresses related work stress in an empathic and strategic manner.

History

In contemporary practice, supervision is a way to monitor and reflect on clinical practice through consultation with a more experienced professional (Schaverien & Case, 2007). Supervision is intentionally imbedded in the culture of art therapy education training and ongoing practice, including licensure and in some cases even the maintenance of credentials.

However, tracing the origins of supervision is difficult. Art therapy is young as a formalized field. Many specific educational training programs and associations were first established in the 1970s. The texts on art therapy supervision often assume the practice of supervision as typical because the authors were supervised themselves. Case (2007) remarked that art therapy supervision borrowed from existing fields such as social work and psychology for two primary reasons: models were already established, and supervisors of art therapists came from these established professions. A history of art therapy supervision is not well documented, so we are drawing from related disciplines for origins. We feel it is important to acknowledge the history of supervision and not blindly accept its importance. It goes without saying we believe supervision is important (writing this book is evidence of that!), but having historical context helps us understand why we continue to utilize supervision, and also how to name the vital aspects of supervision.

It appears supervision began in the field of social work. The Charity Organization Society (COS) was established in 1878. Part of its mission was to help volunteer workers – "agency visitors" – manage their work stress (Tsui, 1997). There is evidence of earlier forms of supervision – church workers in Madison, Wisconsin, in 1788, for example. Regardless of the exact date of formalized supervision, there is agreement that supervision originated with the purpose of overseeing volunteers. While the administrative, educational, and supportive functions were considered vital to supervision by COS, Tsui (1997) argued the administrative function was most likely the primary function of supervision in the beginning. Part of the function of supervision was to provide emotional support to address the high turnover rate of volunteers, and since the volunteers lacked formalized training, there were some educative aspects as well. However, Tsui (1997) points out that agency visitors were originally upper-class individuals coming from privilege, and supervision did not begin until volunteers were recruited from the middle and working classes. Supervision seems to have developed in response to this class divide, part of an administrative function to keep volunteers in check and the class hierarchy in place. While supervision is now seen as a vital component for clinical education, this original hierarchy continues to persist today, especially when supervisors do not understand or acknowledge their inherent power in the relationship.

The year 1896 marked the first formalized supervisory training outside of the agency, when six-week summer training was offered to students of New York's COS. In 1904, the first one-year social work program began. Tsui (1997) chronicles the eventual shift that moved social work from the agency to the university in the 1920s. At the university, an educational process was developed to learn the values, knowledge, and skills of practice. This coincided with Freud's psychoanalytic movement and his corresponding organization, the Wednesday Psychological Society, which involved consultations on cases (White & Winstanley, 2014). "[In the 1920s] Max Eitingon proposed that a psychoanalyst in training should undergo *supervised* psychoanalysis sessions" at the Berlin Psychoanalytic Institute (Urlic and Brunori, as cited in White & Winstanley, 2014, p. 10, emphasis added). However, it is noted that Freud included regular supervision and case consultation during his weekly meetings while he was training analysts, starting in 1902 (Watkins, 2011).

The influence of psychoanalytic theory became imbedded in the practice of supervision. Supervision began to mirror many aspects of the therapeutic process, such as the importance of the didactic relationship and confidentiality (Tsui, 1997). Similarly, the relationship between supervisee and supervisor has been recognized as being as important to the act of supervision as the relationship between the therapist and the client in the endeavor of psychotherapy (Watkins, 2011).

As education became more formalized, professionalization followed. In 1956 the NASW was formed. The establishment of journals is another form of legitimizing professions, and in 1961 *Counselor Education and Supervision* was established. In 1983 a second journal dedicated to supervision, *The Clinical Supervisor*, was launched.

We overlaid key historical points in time from the history of art therapy with the history of supervision to further contextualize the work (see Figure 1.3). The timeline highlights supervision as an instructive point in the establishment of new fields (e.g., social work, psychotherapy, art therapy). Later, as the professions progress, the significance of supervision reappears as a more pertinent topic, worthy of journals, books, research, licensure, and accreditation. In order to pinpoint when the burgeoning profession of art therapy began to be formalized, you may wish to consider when the first art therapy courses were offered by a university. This occurred in 1959 at the University of Louisville (Gussak & Rosal, 2016), over 60 years after the first social work training program. However, the term "art therapy" was coined in the 1940s by Adrian Hill in Britain (Hogan, 2001). Around the same time, Naumberg was hired by New York State Psychiatric Institute in 1941 (Junge, 2010). The topic of art therapy was discussed at the National Association for the Prevention of Tuberculosis conference in 1946. After the establishment of courses, professionalization quickly occurred, with the formation of a journal in 1961, the first degree program at Hahnemann (now Drexel University) in 1967, and an association in 1969, followed by a conference in 1970. During this period of professionalization, the establishment of guidelines occurred, including educational requirements for practitioners. In these requirements, much of the theoretical and clinical educational foundations were based from the established fields of social work, psychiatry, and psychoanalysis, as noted in the timeline. In 2009, the ATCB (2009) gave a distinction for supervisors by the creation of the Art Therapy Certified Supervisor (ATCS). Books specifically on art therapy supervision were published: *Art-based Supervision: Cultivating Therapeutic Insight Through Imagery* (Fish, 2017), *Supervision of Art Psychotherapy: A Theoretical and Practical Handbook* (Schaverien & Case, 2007), and *Supervision and Related Issues: A Handbook for Professionals* (Malchiodi & Riley, 1996).

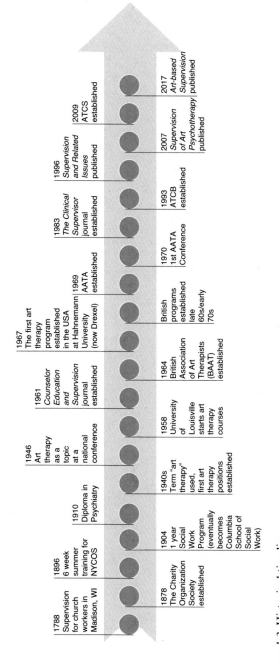

Figure 1.3 Historical timeline.

Considering Theoretical Approaches

Choosing and implementing a theoretical approach for supervision is highly individual, and this overview only begins to briefly highlight a few of the various options. It is incredibly important to research these approaches, as we believe supervisory interactions are more valuable when based in identified theories and approaches, as opposed to blindly moving forward. Some models are universal while others can be very focused to specific populations such as The Queer People of Color Resilience-Based Model of Supervision (Singh & Chun, 2010), A Model for Art Therapy–Based Supervision for End-of-Life Care Workers in Hong Kong (Potash et al., 2015), and Social Constructivist Supervision (Chang, Hays, & Milliken, 2009). The population-specific models build on the earlier works about supervision (Chang et al., 2009; Falender, 2018; Leddick, 1994; Stoltenberg, 1981; Watkins & Wang, 2014) where "developmental, orientation-specific, and integrated" (Leddick, 1994, p. 1) emerged as the three broad theoretical approaches. These, and select others, are covered below.

Irrespective of the model, approach, or theory chosen, incorporating Kadushin and Harkness' three key areas (administrative, educational, and support) is crucial.

Developmental Models

In developmental models, the supervisor considers a sequence of stipulated phases of interventions (Bambling, 2014, p. 451) to complement the supervisee's developing art therapy expertise. There are usually four developmental phases – Introductory, Intermediate, Proficient, and Advanced therapists (Stoltenberg, 1981; Stoltenberg & McNeil, 2010). See Chapter 7, *Disciplinary Differences: When Your Supervisor Is Not an Art Therapist*, for more information on the developmental phases.

To promote optimal supervisee growth, Purswell and Stulmaker (2015) argue a supervisor's ability to identify and implement valuable art-based interventions is enhanced not only by assessing a supervisee's overall attributes, but also by being in tune with an understanding and sensitivity of the development of the supervisee. Barrett and Barber (2005) explain developmental approaches as:

> a systematic way to determine what skills might prove more difficult or anxiety-provoking for a trainee, why such anxiety may occur, and how to vary their interventions such that confrontation, direction, guidance, task assignment, or other supervisory approaches better influence therapist learning and strengthen the supervisory relationship.
>
> (p. 181)

Competency-Based Supervision

Holloway described competency-based supervision as the zeitgeist of modern supervision, an approach that emphasizes supervisor competency and readiness (in Falender, 2018, p. 1243). A meta-theoretical approach, competency-based supervision is guided by stage-appropriate competency standards for knowledge, skills, and attitudes, and set apart through the unique attention to the "art of supervision, including emotional response and personal factors" (Falender, 2018, p. 1243). For clarity, Falender (2018) expands upon personal factors, emotional reactivity, and use of the self in the context of competency-based supervision. Personal factors, shaped by professional learning and worldviews, balance our essential beliefs regarding others, ethical values, and ourselves. Emotional reactivity, the act of experiencing, processing, and organizing emotions resulting from the therapist role and work, requires a thoughtful management plan developed in supervision. The plan requires identifying the triggers of "self-insight and differentiation, increasing empathy, anxiety management, and case conceptualization" (Falender, 2018, p. 1243), which Falender identifies as the "use of self". Addressing the emotional reactivity helps keep the therapist client focused, emotionally present, and engaged.

For further learning: Falender and Shafranske (2007) precisely define competency-based clinical supervision, consider views of competence as a construct, and address the variety of ethical, legal, and contextual practical issues that arise from this model. Fouad et al. (2009) introduce core foundational and functional competencies (p. S5) within three stages of professional growth. Falender, Burnes, and Ellis and others delve into multiculturalism and cross-cultural supervision within the context of the competency benchmarks (Falender, Ellis, & Burnes, 2013; Foo Kune, & Rodolfa, 2013; Ladany, Mori, & Mehr, 2013; Westefeld & Rasmussen, 2013; Wong, Wong, & Ishiyama, 2013).

Orientation-Specific Models

As supervisors, art therapists may apply an orientation-specific supervision approach adapted and clearly defined from their psychotherapy theory of choice. Through this lens, the supervision process is implemented through a particular model of psychotherapy to best facilitate the studying and practice of an exact psychotherapy theory and model (e.g., mindfulness or humanistic) (Watkins & Scaturo, 2013, p. 76). It is commonly acknowledged that the intent and process of thoughtfully implementing theory in an engaging supervisory manner is more important than which theory or theories resonate the most with an individual. However, incongruities may occur when a supervisor functions from a theoretical approach in supervision that differs from the supervisee's practice. Variations may include differing vocabulary, integration of the artmaking processes and related dialogue, and practice between the supervision session and the clinical work. These differences can somewhat defeat the intent of an orientation-specific approach. If theoretical differences exist, it is important to discuss in advance how they will be handled.

Integrated Models

An integrated approach often combines orientation-specific theory with developmental elements and additional elements for a more eclectic, yet purposeful, approach. Watkins and Scaturo (2013) present a three-part learning-based model that intermixes alliance-building and maintenance, educational interventions, and learning/relearning in a way that can be implemented across theories. This proposed integrated model was prompted by the absence of an "educationally grounded, common language model of psychotherapy supervision" (p. 89) to encompass these basic fundamentals. Developmental Relational Theory (DRT) is another integrated example, which combines Relational Cultural Supervision, cognitive and narrative theories, and the Enneagram Personality Typology. Compassion, clarity of awareness, and relational connection are intersecting hallmarks of DRT that "highlights how a person's use of power, as well as feedback delivery and receptivity, can result in compassionate empowerment, isolative disconnection, or manipulative relational abuse" (Duffey, Haberstroh, Ciepcielinski, & Gonzales, 2016, pp. 406–407).

Psychoanalytical/Psychodynamic Models

Freud wrote very little about supervision. However, the seeds of his brief expressions are evident in psychodynamic models (Eagle & Long, 2014, p. 472). Max Eitingon formalized this paradigm – known interchangeably as the Berlin, Eitingon, or Eitingon–Freud model – in the 1920s with the advocacy of Karen Horney. Eitingon's model stipulated three interrelated parts for preparing psychoanalytic practitioners: (1) psychoanalytical theoretical instruction and conception, (2) supervised practical treatment/analysis of clients, and (3) personal experience with psychoanalysis (Eagle & Long, 2014; Watkins, 2013). Eitingon specified the supervisor and the therapist are two different people, allowing the supervisor to focus on the supervisee's clients, and the therapist on the supervisee's personal issues. Eagle and Long (2014) describe key areas of psychodynamic/psychoanalytic psychotherapy supervision as:

1. The evaluative component of supervision and the supervisee's vulnerability to narcissistic injury.
2. The supervisor's role in engaging with trainee countertransference and differentiation of training and treatment roles.

3. The triadic nature of the supervisory relationship and understanding of parallel process dynamics (p. 479).

Some concerns with this model are the inherent hierarchy, focus on undeveloped therapists in training, and the connection with psychoanalytical institutes (Eagle & Long, 2014; Watkins, 2013). However, new developments in psychoanalytical supervision continue to expand the model by exploring elements such as culture, intersectionality, and cultural humility (Eagle & Long, 2014; Rodriguez, Cabaniss, Arbuckle, & Oquendo, 2008; Tummala-Narra, 2004; Watkins & Hook, 2016).

Cognitive Behavioral Supervision

In Cognitive Behavioral Supervision (CBS), an effective supervisor applies a structured framework mirroring Cognitive Behavioral Therapy (CBT) (Pilling & Roth, 2014; Reiser, 2014) "with the goal of providing clients with good care where client progress and outcomes are measured" (Iwamasa, Regan, & Sorocco, 2019, p. 321). Reiser (2014) worked in collaboration with Derek L. Milne to create a definition of CBT supervision that highlights a structured agenda with a problem-oriented approach that includes cognitive case conceptualization, collaboration with active participation, CBT-specific frameworks, clinical observations, and use of empirically supported methods (p. 495). We have expanded this framework below with considerations for art therapists.

- Utilize a structured, collaborative cognitive therapy supervision agenda (Pilling & Roth, 2014; Reiser, 2014). As art therapists, integrating art interventions, the review of art products, and making art into the agenda are essential.
- Problem-oriented approach: assumes a dynamic, practical, and "problem-oriented approach to enhance the learning process" (Reiser, 2014, p. 495).
- Cognitive case conceptualization: explored through art processes, "case discussion (i.e., symbolic learning) and diagrammatic CBT formulations (i.e., iconic learning)" (Reiser, 2014, p. 495).
- Collaborative with active participation: supervisees are "active participants" (Pilling & Roth, 2014, p. 30) collaboratively engaging in cognitive therapy techniques such as Socratic questioning, capsule summaries, guided discovery, role-playing, and behavioral rehearsal with corrective feedback (Iwamasa et al., 2019; Pilling & Roth, 2014; Reiser, 2014).
- Self-examination: supervisors must "be willing and able to examine their own values, beliefs, attitudes, and worldview" (Iwamasa et al., 2019, p. 328) through introspection, artmaking, and identifying blind spots "before attending to personal and interpersonal dynamics affecting therapy and supervision" (Reiser, 2014, p. 495).

- A good supervisor:

  - Teaches, demonstrates, and provides resources for professional knowledge and skills by varying long-established CBT models to embody culturally pertinent content modifications based on client cultural characteristics "beneficial for a wide variety of clients, including those in distress due to racism or discrimination" (Iwamasa et al., 2019, p. 318).
  - Educates on evidence-based procedures.
  - Incorporates audio, video, or live observation of the supervisee's clinical work for evaluation and to provide formal feedback and guidance for further development (Iwamasa et al., 2019; Pilling & Roth, 2014; Reiser, 2014).
  - Utilizes empirically supported methods, and makes use of psychometric tools to monitor the supervisee's clinical effectiveness, using patient's responses for corrective feedback, and so on (e.g., the Beck Depression Inventory).

Feminist Multicultural Supervision

As a starting point, Feminist Multicultural Supervision (FMS) can be defined by a consciousness of and consideration for the contextual and sociocultural processes of the supervisory process (Arczynski & Morrow, 2017; Porter & Vasquez, 1997). This approach is strengthened by a "mutual and reflexive" (Porter & Vasquez, 1997, p. 161) synergetic alliance cultivated through respectful communication established through authentic, truthful, transparent, and straightforward engagements. Inclusive in nature, FMS honors an awareness of "boundaries, hierarchies, gender, race, and diversity of all kinds" (Arczynski & Morrow, 2017 p. 192). In their research on attending to power and diversity in clinical supervision, Green and Dekkers (2010) clarify FMS by connecting the writings of Porter and Vasquez (1997) with Szymanski (2003) to identify four categories for feminist supervisory practices: (1) collaborative relationships, (2) power analysis, (3) diversity and social context, and (4) feminist advocacy and activism. We explore these categories below within the perspective of art therapy.

Collaborative Relationships

Porter and Vasquez (1997) clarify a collaborative relationship does not infer parity within the supervisory relationship and "to portray supervisory relationships as egalitarian denies power where it exists and obscures the nature and purpose of supervisory relationships" (p. 164). In art therapy supervision, a collaborative relationship can be established through the artmaking process as well as verbal interactions.

A collaborative relationship is not stifling; rather, it purposely encourages and establishes space for "mutual respect and mutual feedback" (Green & Dekkers, 2010, p. 305) while acknowledging the inherent hierarchy between supervisor and supervisee without being overly directive.

Power Analysis

Regardless of the supervisory setting and role, the supervisor holds power as they are in a "position of power and can influence the clinical, social, and professional development of supervisees" (Green & Dekkers, 2010, p. 294). The application of power through words and the artmaking process provides a tremendous opportunity to shape and maintain the alliance. Supervisors need to evaluate, recognize, and intentionally apply their power in supervision. For continued development, supervisors would benefit from "diligent self-reflection" and collegial discussions to review their use of power (Green & Dekkers, 2010; Porter & Vasquez, 1997).

Diversity and Social Context

Leah Gipson (2015) raises critical consciousness by supporting students to acknowledge personal privilege; however, this is simply a single action. Gipson stresses that art therapy education, and in particular the art therapy classroom, "can become a place where anti-Black racism and other forms of systemic violence are contested, making practices of freedom and social justice essential to our profession" (p. 144). Likewise, whether group or individual supervision, this is a critical factor to be embraced. To meet expected supervisee learning outcomes, the research by Green and Dekkers (2010) suggests a best practice for supervisors is "to attend to power and diversity through the use of feminist practices" (p. 307).

Feminist Advocacy and Activism

Raising awareness and encouraging advocacy and activism through the supervisory role can be accomplished in many ways. It may be through "the promotion of social activism, ethics, and lifelong self-examination and professional development" (Porter & Vasquez, 1997, p. 161), attempting legislative change, designating related readings, or exploring the societal context of intersectionality and social location of clients and supervisees (Arczynski & Morrow, 2017; Green & Dekkers, 2010; Nelson et al., 2006; Porter & Vasquez, 1997). One way to ensure that supervisees and supervisors are aware of current actions and events is to make room to resource-share during the supervision session.

Takeaways

- It is valuable to name and acknowledge personal and professional motivations and/or requirements that may compel you to actively supervise others or participate in supervision as a supervisee.
- Tracking reactions, performance, and comfort levels within the three components of supervision (educational, supportive, and administrative) provides a comprehensive understanding of current functioning to strategize striving for success in all components of supervision.
- Distinguish and maintain a clear boundary between supervision providing emotional support for a supervisee conducting clinical work and their personal therapy.
- Supervision is best received through researching, assessing, and implementing a clearly defined model, whether that is developmental or theory-based, or includes an integrated approach. Some models are widely applicable while others can be specifically designed for focused populations of supervisors or populations.

Practice Prompts

Venn Diagram for Considering the Three Key Areas of Supervision

A Venn diagram is a visual representation utilizing circles to identify relationships between concepts. A key aspect is how the circles overlap and intersect. Following the suggestions below, create a Venn diagram for yourself, considering the three key areas of supervision – administrative, educational, and supportive. Create a circle for each of the three areas of supervision. Pay particular attention to how or if the circles overlap and the potential impact on your supervision. You may decide to share it with your supervisor or supervisee in your next session. Alternatively, student trainees may share their diagram with their school-based group supervisor.

- **For supervisees:** Create a Venn diagram that shows your needs in the administrative, educational, and supportive aspects of supervision. Write, draw, collage, or otherwise visually depict what you require, need, desire, and/or currently receive in each circle. What aspects are missing? Are there areas which you pay more attention to than others? Would you be willing to share this with your supervisor? What do you hope would be gained by doing so? If you do not wish to share this with your on-site supervisor, would you share this with your on-campus group supervisor (if a student) or your off-site supervisor (if you are seeking external supervision)? Can you share your Venn diagram with colleagues?
- **For supervisees:** Create a Venn diagram that contains two overlapping circles: one that contains the supervisory needs that are currently

being met, the other that contains needs that are not. Where the circles intersect, identify what areas are partially met. In supervision, consider with your supervisor how and when the partially and presently unmet needs may be addressed.

- **For supervisors:** Create a Venn diagram that contains the administrative, educational, and supportive roles you provide. What areas do you avoid or wait for your supervisee to bring up? What areas do you tend to bring up during every supervisory session? Your Venn diagram may not be three evenly drawn intersecting circles and should reflect your current supervisory style (i.e., areas you pay more attention to should be larger than those you spend less time with). Would you share this with your supervisee? Why, or why not? What areas would you like to focus on more? Where can you find support in graining these skills?

Create Response Art in Reaction to the Chapter

Take a few moments and sit in stillness, bring awareness to any reactions you may be experiencing from the reading of this chapter, and when you are ready take ten minutes to create response art. Create spontaneously and minimize censorship. After the ten minutes are completed, spend a minute or so responding with a written stream of consciousness witnessing the art. Take a few moments to process the response art and the witness writing.

- What would it be like if you shared this artwork and/or witness writing with your supervisor or supervisee? How does reviewing your artwork connect with your clinical work?

Notes

1 Adapted from Dixon (2004).
2 From ATCB (2020). *What is art therapy?*

References

Allen, P. B. (2007). Wielding the shield: The art therapist as conscious witness in the realm of social action. In F. Kaplan (Ed.), *Art therapy and social action* (pp. 72–85). Philadelphia, PA: Jessica Kingsley Publishers.

Arczynski, A. V., & Morrow, S. L. (2017). The complexities of power in feminist multicultural psychotherapy supervision. *Journal of Counseling Psychology, 64* (2), 192–205. doi:10.1037/cou0000179

ATCB. (Fall, 2009). *ATCB Review.* Retrieved from www.atcb.org/resource/pdf/Newsletter/Fall2009.pdf

ATCB. (2020). What is Art Therapy? Retrieved from www.atcb.org/Public/WhatIsArtTherapy

Bambling, M. (2014). Creating positive outcomes in clinical supervision. In C. E. Watkins & D. L. Milne (Eds.), *Wiley international handbook of clinical supervision* (pp. 445–457). Chichester, UK: John Wiley & Sons.

Barrett, M. S., & Barber, J. P. (2005). A developmental approach to the supervision of therapists in training. *Journal of Contemporary Psychotherapy, 35*(2), 169–183. doi:10.1007/s10879-005-2698-8

Camic, P. M., Tischler, V., & Pearman, C. H. (2014). Viewing and making art together: A multi-session art-gallery-based intervention for people with dementia and their carers. *Aging & Mental Health, 18*(2), 161–168. doi:10.1080/13607863.2013.818101

Case, C. (2007). Review of literature on art therapy supervision. In J. Schaverien & C. Case (Eds.), *Supervision of art therapy: A theoretical and practical handbook* (pp. 11–27). London, UK: Routledge.

Chang, C. Y., Hays, D. G., & Milliken, T. F. (2009). Addressing social justice issues in supervision: A call for client and professional advocacy. *The Clinical Supervisor, 28*(1), 20–35.

Deaver, S. P., & McAuliffe, G. (2009). Reflective visual journaling during art therapy and counselling internships: A qualitative study. *Reflective Practice, 10*(5), 615–632. doi:10.1080/14623940903290687

Deaver, S. P., & Shiflett, C. (2011). Art-based supervision techniques. *The Clinical Supervisor, 30*(2), 257–276. doi:10.1080/07325223.2011.619456

Delano, F. (2001). If I could supervise my supervisor: A model for child and youth care workers to own their own supervision. *Journal of Child and Youth Care, 15*(2), 51–64.

Dixon, G. D. (2004). Clinical supervision: A key to treatment success. Retrieved from www.attcnetwork.org/explore/priorityareas/wfd/getready/docs/Beacon004.pdf

Duffey, T., Haberstroh, S., Ciepcielinski, E., & Gonzales, C. (2016). Relational-cultural theory and supervision: Evaluating developmental relational counseling. *Journal of Counseling & Development, 94*(4), 405–414.

Eagle, G., & Long, C. (2014). Supervision of psychoanalytic/psychodynamic psychotherapy. In C. E. Watkins & D. L. Milne (Eds.), *Wiley international handbook of clinical supervision* (pp. 471–492). Chichester, UK: John Wiley & Sons.

Falender, C. A. (2018). Clinical supervision – the missing ingredient. *American Psychologist, 73*(9), 1240–1250. doi:10.1037/amp0000385

Falender, C. A., Burnes, T. R., & Ellis, M. V. (2013). Multicultural clinical supervision and benchmarks: Empirical support informing practice and supervisor training. *The Counseling Psychologist, 41*(1), 8–27.

Falender, C. A., Ellis, M. V., & Burnes, T. R. (2013). Response to reactions to major contribution: Multicultural clinical supervision and Benchmarks. *The Counseling Psychologist, 41*(1), 140–151.

Falender, C. A., & Shafranske, E. P. (2007). Competence in competency-based supervision practice: Construct and application. *Professional Psychology: Research and Practice, 38*(3), 232–240.

Fish, B. J. (2012). Response art: The art of the art therapist. *Art Therapy: Journal of the American Art Therapy Association, 29*(3), 138–143. doi:10.1080/07421656.2012.701594

Fish, B. J. (2017). *Art-based supervision: Cultivating therapeutic insight through imagery.* New York, NY: Routledge.

Foo Kune, N. M., & Rodolfa, E. R. (2013). Putting the benchmarks into practice: Multiculturally competent supervisors – effective supervision. *The Counseling Psychologist, 41*(1), 121–130.

Fouad, N. A., Grus, C. L., Hatcher, R. L., Kaslow, N. J., Hutchings, P. S., Madson, M. B., ... Crossman, R. E. (2009). Competency benchmarks: A model for understanding and measuring competence in professional psychology across training levels. *Training and Education in Professional Psychology, 3*(4S), S5–S26. doi:10.1037/a0015832

Gipson, L. R. (2015). Is cultural competence enough? Deepening social justice pedagogy in art therapy. *Art therapy, 32*(3), 142–145.

Green, M. S., & Dekkers, T. D. (2010). Attending to power and diversity in supervision: An exploration of supervisee learning outcomes and satisfaction with supervision. *Journal of Feminist Family Therapy, 22*(4), 293–312.

Gussak, D., & Rosal, M. L. (2016). *The Wiley handbook of art therapy.* Chichester, UK: Wiley-Blackwell.

Hocoy, D. (2007). Art therapy as a tool for social change: A conceptual model. In F. Kaplan (Ed.), *Art therapy and social action* (pp. 21–39). Philadelphia, PA: Jessica Kingsley Publishers.

Hogan, S. (2001). *Healing arts: The history of art therapy.* London, UK: Jessica Kingsley Publishers.

Hoge, M. A., Migdole, S., Farkas, M. S., Ponce, A. N., & Hunnicutt, C. (2011). Supervision in public sector behavioral health: A review. *The Clinical Supervisor, 30*(2), 183–203. doi:10.1080/07325223.2011.604276

Iwamasa, G. Y., Regan, S. P., & Sorocco, K. H. (2019). Culturally responsive cognitive behavior therapy clinical supervision. In G. Y. Iwamasa & P. A. Hays (Eds.), *Culturally responsive cognitive-behavioral therapy: Practice and supervision* (pp. 317–332). Washington, DC: American Psychological Association. doi:10.1037/0000119-013

Junge, M. B. (2010). *The modern history of art therapy in the United States.* Springfield, IL: Charles C. Thomas Publisher.

Kadushin, A., & Harkness, D. (2014). *Supervision in social work.* New York, NY: Columbia University Press.

Ladany, N., Mori, Y., & Mehr, K. E. (2013). Effective and ineffective supervision. *The Counseling Psychologist, 41*(1), 28–47.

Leddick, G. R. (1994). Models of Clinical Supervision. ERIC Digest. Retrieved from https://files.eric.ed.gov/fulltext/ED372340.pdf

Linesch, D. G., Holmes, J., Morton, M., & Shields, S. S. (1989). Post-graduate group supervision for art therapists. *Art Therapy: Journal of the American Art Therapy Association, 6*(2), 71–75. doi:10.1080/07421656.1989.10758869

Malchiodi, C. A., & Riley, S. (1996). *Supervision and related issues: A handbook for professionals.* Chicago, IL: Magnolia Street Publishers.

McNamee, C. M., & McWey, L. M. (2004). Using bilateral art to facilitate clinical supervision. *The Arts in Psychotherapy, 31*(4), 229–243. doi:doi:10.1016/j.aip.2004.06.007

Miller, A. (2012). Inspired by El Duende: One-canvas process painting in art therapy supervision. *Art Therapy: Journal of the American Art Therapy Association, 29*(4), 166–173. doi:10.1080/07421656.2013.730024

Murrant, G., Rykov, M., Amonite, D., & Loynd, M. (2000). Creativity and self-care forcaregivers. *Journal of Palliative Care, 16*(2), 44–49.

Nelson, M. L., Gizara, S., Hope, A. C., Phelps, R., Steward, R., & Weitzman, L. (2006). A feminist multicultural perspective on supervision. *Journal of Multicultural Counseling and Development, 34*(2), 105–115.

Newell, J. M., & MacNeil, G. A. (2010). Professional burnout, vicarious trauma, secondary traumatic stress, and compassion fatigue: A review of theoretical terms, risk factors, and preventative methods for clinicians and researchers. *Best Practices in Mental Health, 6*(2), 57–68.

Pilling, S., & Roth, A. D. (2014). The competent clinical supervisor. In C. E. Watkins, Jr. & D. L. Milne (Eds.), *Wiley international handbook of clinical supervision* (pp. 20–37). Chichester, UK: Wiley.

Porter, N., & Vasquez, M. (1997). Covision: Feminist supervision, process, and collaboration. In J. Worell & N. G. Johnson (Eds.), *Psychology of women book series. Shaping the future of feminist psychology: Education, research, and practice* (pp. 155–171). Washington, DC: American Psychological Association. doi:10.1037/10245-007

Potash, J. S., Chan, F., Ho, A. H., Wang, X. L., & Cheng, C. (2015). A model for art therapy–based supervision for end-of-life care workers in Hong Kong. *Death Studies, 39*(1), 44–51. doi:10.1080/07481187.2013.859187

Purswell, K. E., & Stulmaker, H. L. (2015). Expressive arts in supervision: Choosing developmentally appropriate interventions. *International Journal of Play Therapy, 24*(2), 103–117. doi:10.1037/a0039134

Reid, S., & Hartzell, E. (2013). Art therapy with a group of dementia caregivers: Exploring wellbeing through social support and creative expression. *Alzheimer's & Dementia, 9*(4), P485. doi:10.1016/j.jalz.2013.05.991

Reiser, R. P. (2014). Supervising cognitive and behavioral therapies. In C. E. Watkins & D. L. Milne (Eds.), *Wiley international handbook of clinical supervision* (pp. 493–517). Chichester, UK: Wiley.

Repar, P. A., & Patton, D. (2007). Stress reduction for nurses through arts-in-medicine at the University of New Mexico Hospitals. *Holistic Nursing Practice, 21*(4), 182–186. doi:10.1097/01.HNP.0000280929.68259.5c

Rodriguez, C. I., Cabaniss, D. L., Arbuckle, M. R., & Oquendo, M. A. (2008). The role of culture in psychodynamic psychotherapy: Parallel process resulting from cultural similarities between patient and therapist. *American Journal of Psychiatry, 165*(11), 1402–1406.

Salzano, A. T., Lindemann, E., & Tronsky, L. N. (2013). The effectiveness of a collaborative art-making task on reducing stress in hospice caregivers. *The Arts in Psychotherapy, 40*(1), 45–52. doi:10.1016/j.aip.2012.09.008

Sanders, G. J. (2016). *Art Response to Confusion, Uncertainty, and Curiosity During Group Art Therapy Supervision* (Doctoral dissertation, Notre Dame de Namur University).

Schaverien, J., & Case, C. (Eds.). (2007). Supervision of art psychotherapy: A theoretical and practical handbook. New York, NY: Routledge.

Singh, A., & Chun, K. Y. S. (2010). "From the margins to the center": Moving towards a resilience-based model of supervision for queer people of color supervisors. *Training and Education in Professional Psychology, 4*(1), 36–46. doi:10.1037/a0017373

Stoltenberg, C. D. (1981). Approaching supervision from a developmental perspective: The counselor-complexity model. *Journal of Counseling Psychology, 28*(1), 59–65.

Stoltenberg, C. D., & McNeil, B. W. (2010). *IDM supervision: An integrative developmental model for supervision counselors and therapists* (3rd ed.). New York, NY: Routledge.

Super. (2019). In *Oxford English Dictionary*. Retrieved from https://www-oed-com. ezproxy2.library.drexel.edu/view/Entry/194186?rskey=SaJ15G&result=20#eid

Supervision. (2019). In *Oxford English Dictionary*. Retrieved from www.oedcom. ezproxy2.library.drexel.edu/view/Entry/194558?redirectedFrom=supervision&

Szymanski, D. M. (2003). The feminist supervision scale: A rational/theoretical approach. *Psychology of Women Quarterly*, *27*(3), 221–232.

Timm-Bottos, J. (2011). Endangered threads: Socially committed community art action. *Art Therapy: Journal of the American Art Therapy Association*, *28*(2), 57–63. doi:10.1080/07421656.2011.578234

Tsui, M. S. (1997). The roots of social work supervision: An historical review. *The Clinical Supervisor*, *15*(2), 191–198. doi:10.1300/J001v15n02_14

Tummala-Narra, P. (2004). Dynamics of race and culture in the supervisory encounter. *Psychoanalytic Psychology*, *21*(2), 300–311.

Vision. (2019). In *Oxford English Dictionary*. Retrieved from https://www-oed-com. ezproxy2.library.drexel.edu/view/Entry/223943?rskey=CHDBhZ&result=1#eid

Watkins, C. E., Jr. (2011). Psychotherapy supervision since 1909: Some friendly observations about its first century. *Journal of Contemporary Psychotherapy*, *41*(2), 57–67. doi:10.1007/s10879-010-9152-2

Watkins, C. E., Jr. (2013). The beginnings of psychoanalytic supervision: The crucial role of Max Eitingon. *The American Journal of Psychoanalysis*, *73*(3), 254–270.

Watkins, C. E., Jr., & Hook, J. N. (2016). On a culturally humble psychoanalytic supervision perspective: Creating the cultural third. *Psychoanalytic Psychology*, *33*(3), 487–517.

Watkins, C. E., Jr., & Scaturo, D. J. (2013). Toward an integrative, learning-based model of psychotherapy supervision: Supervisory alliance, educational interventions, and supervisee learning/relearning. *Journal of Psychotherapy Integration*, *23*(1), 75–95.

Watkins, C. E., & Wang, D. C. (2014). On the education of clinical supervisors. In C. Edward Watkins, Jr. & D. L. Milne, *The Wiley international handbook of clinical supervision* (pp. 177–203). Chichester, UK: John Wiley & Sons.

Westefeld, J. S., & Rasmussen, W. (2013). Supervision: The importance and interaction of competency benchmarks and multiculturalism. *The Counseling Psychologist*, *41*(1), 110–120.

White, E., & Winstanley, J. (2014). Clinical supervision and the helping professions: An interpretation of history. *The Clinical Supervisor*, *33*(1), 3–25. doi:10.1080/07325223.2014.905226

Wilson, L., Riley, S., & Wadeson, H. (1984). Art therapy supervision. *Art Therapy: Journal of the American Art Therapy Association*, *1*(3), 100–105. doi:10.1080/07421656.1984.10758761

Wong, L. C. J., Wong, P. T. P., & Ishiyama, I. F. (2013). What helps and what hinders in cross-cultural clinical supervision: A critical incident study. *The Counseling Psychologist*, *41*(1), 66–85. doi:10.1177/0011000012442652

2 What Supervisors Need to Know about Supervision

Introduction

This chapter explores how to become a supervisor. The structure we provide in this chapter is particularly important for first-time supervisors. We begin with appreciating essential supervisor competencies and qualities; move towards recognizing important tasks, goals, roles, and interventions; explore conflict and acknowledge counterproductive incidents in supervision; and discuss ways to develop realistic expectations from both your supervisees and yourself (Barrett & Barber, 2005; Sweitzer & King, 2018).

The overarching framework of this chapter utilizes Kadushin and Harkness' (2014) three components of supervision – administrative, educational, and supportive – and Feminist Multicultural Supervision (FMS).

What It Takes: Supervisor Competencies and Qualities

In order to create and support the supervisory alliance needed to achieve multilayered functions such as the assessment, development, and oversight of the supervisee, it is essential for the supervisor to embody the following competencies and qualities. It is beneficial for the supervisor to understand base-level competencies and ideal supervisor qualities, which reinforce supervisory best practices. The following section details base-level competencies and clarifications and lists ideal supervisor qualities. These lists describe "what it takes" to be an effective supervisor.

Base-Level Competencies

This essential set of base-level competencies is the requisite knowledge, attitude, skills, and values for providing direct services (Milne & Watkins, 2014; Watkins & Wang, 2014):

- Form and maintain collaborative relationships through supervisor identity.
- Recognition of diversity, equity, and inclusion.

- Knowledge and skill base of contemporary supervision practices.
- Model professional and ethical behaviors.
- Evaluate performance, identify competency issues, and provide feedback.

Collaborative Relationships through Supervisor Identity

As in psychotherapy, research on supervision has indicated the relational aspect between the supervisor and the supervisee is critical for success (American Psychological Association [APA], 2014; Gaete & Ness, 2015; O'Donovan, Halford, & Walters, 2011). This is achieved through clearly defined roles and expectations (Inman et al., 2014) that are best supported through a strong supervisor identity. Therefore, the ability to cultivate, establish, and sustain a strong, collaborative supervisory alliance enhances the probability of stronger satisfaction outcomes. From their 2017 study, Arczynski and Morrow found that "Participants honored their supervisees' and their own clinical approaches by holding back their own thoughts and drawing out supervisees' views" (2017, p. 198). The honoring of supervisees' viewpoints assists in establishing the supervisory alliance. A supervision contract (described in more detail in Chapter 4, *Navigating Professional Identity*), particularly one that is created collaboratively, is one tool that fosters alliance through boundaries and defined expectations to reinforce the relationship (Falender, 2014; Watkins, 2017). When things go awry, and they will, the supervisor often relies on the supervision contract and the strength of the relationship to identify, address, and repair potential strains and ruptures within the alliance.

Diversity, Equity, and Inclusion

In the simplest of terms, a supervisor must acknowledge the essentialness of diversity while embracing its inextricable nature to supervision (APA, 2014). Due to the significance and consequence of this topic, Part 3, *Embracing and Working with Differences*, discusses this in much greater detail with more information and strategies on working with differences between supervisor, supervisee, and clients. However, in this chapter we raise the importance of how supervisory power is "moderated by social locations, depending on the degree to which supervisees accepted or rejected internalized values and beliefs from the dominant culture" (Arczynski & Morrow, 2017, p. 196). This requires art therapy supervisors to understand their own social locations in light of privilege and oppression. For example, art therapist Owen Karcher (2017) reflected on his personal positions of power (e.g., race, education, citizenship status, and size) contrasted with experienced oppression of marginalized identities (e.g., a queer, transmasculine person with a mixed-class background; p. 126).

This systematic contemplation allows for a comprehensive view of what an individual carries into therapeutic and supervisory relationships.

Karcher (2017) propounded eight actionable intentions to practice art therapy in a more socially just approach. Many of these intentions are analogous to the FMS categories as described in Chapter 1. In Table 2.1, we propose how art therapy supervisors can create their own actions by mapping Karcher's intentions for clinicians onto FMS practices.

Table 2.1 Connections between social-justice-oriented art therapy, FMS practices, and actions for art therapy supervisors

Karcher's Eight Actionable Items (Arczynski & Morrow, 2017)	*FMS Practices* (based on findings from Arczynski & Morrow, 2017)	*Actions for Art Therapy Supervisors*
Critical self-reflection of your "identities and places of privilege" (p. 127)	Power analysis: acknowledge the supervisory relationship has an intended and intrinsic hierarchy. Work to create a space of shared respect and reciprocal feedback	Reflectivity
Serve all clients with dignity and respect. Explicit attention to language, experiences, and experiences navigating oppressive systems of care (e.g., medical, mental health)	Collaborative relationships	Engagement, commitment, and investment. Positive regard and acceptance. In art therapy supervision, a collaborative relationship can be established through the artmaking process as well as verbal interactions
Attune to barriers that cause distress, such as "policies, forms, and interpersonal interactions" (p. 127)		Empathy and sensitivity
Understand your impact on others holding "different beliefs, identities, and experiences" (p. 127)	Diversity and social context	Warmth, support, genuineness, and boundaries
Acknowledge "all violence and oppression is interconnected, and that liberation, health, and wellness depend on the liberation, health, and wellness of all" (p. 127)		Empathy and sensitivity

(*Continued*)

Table 2.1 (Cont.)

Engage in current events, systematic change including legislative activity	Feminist advocacy and activism	Engagement, commitment, and investment
Attend formal (i.e., training, readings) and informal learning activities (i.e., speaking with colleagues)	Feminist advocacy and activism	Respect, openness, and concreteness
Utilize the arts "to imagine a world free from societal oppression, trauma, and harm. Bring this vision to each session" (p. 127)		Cultivate positive expectations and hope

Knowledge and Skills

Continuing education commitments for licensure and accreditation often create opportunities to acquire up-to-date education and skills relevant to supervision. However, these requirements do not override the need to foster a supervisor's self-motivated quest for ongoing professional development, or the need for supervisors to be unbiased, to engage in continued reflection, and to be "open-minded, to engage in continued reflection" (Cummings, Ballantyne, & Scallion, 2015, p. 158). Wilson, Riley, and Wadeson (1984) remind supervisors to act as "a model of the reflective, thoughtful art therapist" – to encourage a continuous cycle of self-assessment to review approaches, interventions, and outcomes (p. 100). Professional competence has been described as the "habitual and judicious use of communication, knowledge, technical skills, clinical reasoning, emotions, values, and reflections, in daily practice for the benefit of the individual and community being served" (Epstein & Hundert, 2002, p. 226). Accordingly, it is important for supervisors to seek and obtain current knowledge in the area in which supervision is provided (APA, 2014; Borders et al., 2014) in order to integrate up-to-date knowledge, and retain expertise and competence while discarding superseded information (Mann & Merced, 2018, p. 100).

Professional and Ethical Behaviors

A supervisor must embrace and demonstrate professional behavior that models ethical values and actions, appropriate boundaries, and self-care (Mann & Merced, 2018), while maintaining adherence to relevant jurisdictional laws and regulations (APA, 2014). Art therapists are also guided by the American Art Therapy Association's (AATA) aspirational *Ethical Principles for Art Therapists* (2013) and the Art Therapy Credentials Board's (ATCB) consequential *Code of Ethics, Conduct, and Disciplinary Procedures* (2018) in addition to licensure- and location-based responsibilities. Conversely, it is requisite for supervisors to encourage and nurture a supervisee's *often overlooked* capacity for self-care, in order to prevent burnout and boost the personal heath of the supervisee, while continuing to recognize the need to implement a personal self-care regimen (O'Donovan et al., 2011).

Professional ethics for art therapists are explored further in chapters 5 and 7; however, the following briefly introduces the AATA and ATCB ethical expectations.

The AATA (2013) *Ethical Principles for Art Therapists* recognize aspirational values and principles based on core ideals that affirm basic human rights with a two-pronged goal. Within these "non-binding guidelines", the *Responsibility to Art Therapy Students and Supervisees* section specifically addresses the supervisor's ethical responsibilities (AATA, 2013).

The ATCB's *Code of Ethics, Conduct, and Disciplinary Procedures* (2018) moves beyond the aspirational and outlines violations that have consequences. The ATCB holds the power to "decline to grant, withhold, suspend, or revoke the credentials of any person who fails to adhere to the Standards of Ethics and Conduct" (Part I, Section 3). The code is written in two parts and five sections. While supervisors of art therapists should be familiar with the entire code, the *Responsibility to Students and Supervisees* section details ethical responsibilities required in supervision. The section covers topics such as fostering professional growth, maintaining high standards of scholarship, instructing with accurate and current scholarly information, and acknowledging power and privilege within the supervisory relationship (ATCB, 2018).

Performance, Competency, and Feedback

Supervisors should provide accurate, reliable, and knowledgeable feedback on their supervisee through clearly defined formats and routine plans. The ability to evaluate and judiciously provide feedback provides an avenue for supervisors to identify and build upon strengths as well as addressing competency problems (APA, 2014; Borders et al., 2014). Just a few of the many matters requiring direct feedback include specific therapeutic situations, how to meet job-specific expectations (e.g., number of client-contact hours), and professionalism in the workplace (e.g., dress code, client boundaries). The supervisor literally acts as a gatekeeper for the profession by providing "formative and summative feedback" through evaluations of the supervisee's performance (Mann & Merced, 2018, p. 102).

Best practices for feedback include conveying meaningful feedback in a consistent manner, at regular intervals, and in a confidential space. Instead of using a polarizing binary approach reduced to positive and negative, we encourage supervisors to embrace a continuum of feedback. A continuum makes the practice of feedback much less daunting, and reframes negative feedback into an engaging dialogue that is challenging, thought-provoking, and stimulating. For positive feedback, which is often superficial, the use of a continuum provides a moment for deeper reflection and comprehension. Cook, McKibben, and Wind (2018) identified that supervisees found supervisors to hold the "most power in identifying interventions to use with clients, setting goals for supervision, and providing feedback about clinical skills in supervision" (p. 188). To mitigate this power differential, and normalize the experience of feedback, it is important to inform the supervisee in advance on the delivery and value of feedback. Furthermore, objective and timely feedback is key.

Objective Feedback

Typically based on specific and behaviorally defined criteria, objective feedback guides supervisees with less bias, less distortion, and fewer subjective opinions. It is therefore less confusing to the supervisee, and guides them to the appropriate areas for adjustment or for the development of new behaviors.

Timely Feedback

In addition to benefiting from a systematic approach, providing timely feedback allows for a more immediate and opportune dialogue, where the supervisee can readily begin to comprehend the issues, and enables the supervisor to quickly support and motivate the efforts for change. Delayed feedback misses a window of awareness that may grant a deeper reflection and perception of the situation. This immediacy also helps to "maintain motivation and hope for change despite an unsuccessful outcome" (Freeman, 1985, p. 8). When attempting to alter behaviors, it is quite normal to have early successes followed by an ebb and flow of intensity and attention to further growth. Thus, the balance between the installation of hope, increased expectations, regular reviews and discussions, and opportunities to practice new skills, is critical to support change.

Clearly Understood

Regardless of whether you are sharing positive or challenging feedback, the message needs to be balanced, clear, specific, and credible (Freeman, 1985).

- Balanced feedback does not favor critiques weighted to one side. For example, providing only positive and vague feedback (i.e., *great job, you're the best*) gives the supervisee little to reflect upon or understand what is positive about the work.
- Providing clear and well-timed feedback allows space for the identification of effective therapeutic interventions (i.e., art material choice, theory integration) and to better recognize areas for improvement (i.e., developmental level and art therapy intervention). Ambiguous feedback presents an opening for the message to be misinterpreted, disregarded, or simply ignored.
- To enhance delivery and assimilation of feedback, consider specific art-based methods or other techniques such as role-playing, empty-chair work, or response writing to better receive feedback.
- Feedback is often perceived as more credible when the supervisor is credentialed and demonstrates expertise in the relevant area, and the feedback is given at a time when the supervisee is more accepting in order to effectively integrate the information.

Additionally, empathetic approaches by the supervisor to convey challenging feedback in response to concerns spurred by a supervisee's self-reports or a supervisor's direct observation often builds trust and may allow a supervisee to take more risks.

(Freeman, 1985, pp. 9–10)

Reciprocal Feedback

Effective feedback generates a more nuanced and mutual dialogue that begins, not ends, with the initial communication. This mutuality approach offers the supervisee opportunity to seek clarification, share another perspective, and reflect on topics shared in the feedback (Freeman, 1985). When supervisors actively foster and receive feedback from the supervisee, they can model appropriate ways to clarify and incorporate feedback. This avoids a controlling and rigid authoritarian style that inhibits communication.

The exact tools and methods utilized for assessment and feedback are determined by setting, purpose, and supervisory style. Supervisors can use a number of methods to assess the work of their supervisees. Whatever methods are employed, the goal is to maximize and normalize the opportunity to be as helpful and specific as possible. To do so, monitoring needs to be transparent, contain no surprises, and cover both focuses for improvement and areas of accomplishment related to objectives and proficiencies (Falender, 2014). In summary, "it is important to give frequent formative (i.e., regular and ongoing) feedback in addition to summative evaluation (e.g., a formal final evaluation at the end of a practicum placement), and try to do so at each supervision meeting"

(Cummings et al., 2015, p. 160). Some methods and tools that are often used to assess performance and competency are direct observation, video and audio recordings, process notes (also known as process recordings), clinical or progress notes, visual journals, and annual reviews.

Direct Observation

The most proximal way to see a supervisee's work is through directly observing – physically being in the room viewing an individual or group session conducted by a supervisee. The supervisor remains exclusively in an observation role, minimizing the intrusion. The observer-awareness factor is often lessened for participants in a group setting and can be heightened in an individual session. Though potentially intrusive, this eyewitness view of the session provides invaluable data and can capture the nuances of what is transpiring throughout the session. Beneficial post-session discussion relies on accurate recall by the supervisor and the supervisee. Other options for live observation include two-way mirrors or live video. In some settings, the supervisor has the opportunity to provide "live" feedback through audio devices for minimal disruption.

Video and Audio Recordings

Some academic and professional settings have the accommodations for video recording, allowing for post-session review. This accuracy advantage literally eliminates the need for recalling word choice, timing, implementation of interventions, body language, and further critical data depicted in video, freeing focus to what transpired in the session. There is power in the ability to press pause, rewind, review, and reflect on particular segments of the session. Like artwork, the recording becomes another presence in the room providing a distanced, albeit potentially anxiety-provoking, review of the session. There are locations that do not allow for video recordings of sessions, such as prisons. In these facilities, sometimes audio recordings are permitted. Like video recordings, they can be reviewed post-session.

Process Notes

This is a deep type of reflection specifically designed to provide structure for therapists to share with a supervisor what was experienced objectively and subjectively during and after the session. This typically includes: presenting information and history, observation and description of the art therapy process, the art therapist's reflection on their inner process, interpreting and assessing the session, and summary/goals. See Appendix A for a sample process note structure.

Clinical Notes

While clinical notes are usually taken for the purposes of tracking individual and group therapy, they can also be used to provide feedback to supervisees. On-site supervisors often review clinical notes for compliance purposes, or, in the case of students or unlicensed clinicians, a supervisor may "sign off" on notes. If your supervisee is working at a location where there is no specific note-taking format, it may be helpful to provide a format such as SOAP and DAP. SOAP stands for *subjective* (what the therapist feels is occurring), *objective* (what the therapist observes), *assessment* (the therapist's assessment of the session), and *plan* (which can include next session[s], treatment goals, etc.). DAP refers to: *data* (what occurred in the session; this can include subjective and objective information), *assessment* (again, what the therapist makes of the session), and *plan* (next steps for treatment). These formats also help clarify the amount and intent of the information being documented to further protect confidentiality, as the art therapist has to be very intentional in what information is being shared, and not simply write anything and everything which occurred in the session.

Visual Journals

Visual journals, which utilize both text and images, are an intimate way to process observations, transference, countertransference, and emotional reactions. For students, this is also an opportunity to explore class discourse and the larger internship experience. Journal entries can be powerful departure points for class discussion or private risk-taking revelations. Doodles, drawings, magazine clippings, photographs, and paintings are just a few forms of visual imagery that may share the journal pages with poetry, free writing, free association, and witness writing. These creative elements are offered to increase clarity of the event, and strengthen the supervisee's therapist identity, while expanding their understanding and comprehension of art therapy.

Annual Reviews

This tool is used for trainees as well as professionals. They can be stressful to the reviewee – reviews or evaluations can be seen as a judgment, and can influence a grade, a salary, or even professional standing. At their worst, they can be conducted because they are required, with minimal to no feedback. Annual reviews can be used to effectively support and guide a supervisee at any stage of their art therapy career. This can be best done if the supervisor and supervisee work on the review together and discuss strengths, areas of improvement, points of disagreement, and future goals.

Ideal Supervisor Qualities

The ideal supervisor exemplifies countless worthy qualities. We share a few of significance that are relevant across sites and populations. Some qualities that we describe in more detail:

- Engagement, commitment, and investment.
- Positive regard and acceptance.
- Warmth, support, genuineness, and boundaries.
- Empathy and sensitivity.
- Reflectivity.
- Respect, openness, and concreteness.
- Cultivating positive expectations and hope.

Engagement, Commitment, and Investment

Supervisors should value the training therapist and validate their supervisee as a unique individual of varied intersections, including culture, viewpoints, pursuits, and styles of learning. The supervisor can demonstrate the value of the supervisee through a consistent supervision time and space and a consistent format, by being routinely accessible and, when unavailable, providing a competent back-up. Emotional investment, establishing interest, and expressing enthusiasm are further realized through a supervisor's approachability, attentiveness, constructive feedback, getting to know the supervisee, and willingness to repair any ruptures in the alliance (Beinart, 2014, p. 264). The supervisor can further demonstrate investment by understanding and incorporating the notion that

> Intersectionality, power, and relational safety provide a foundation for a critical postcolonial supervision framework ... [while] ... [s]tructured dialogue, reflection, and action around similarities and differences relative to power, privilege, and oppression are the scaffoldings toward equity and justice in supervision and clinical work.
>
> (Hernandez-Wolfe & McDowell, 2014, p. 34)

Positive Regard and Acceptance

A psychotherapist's ability to deliver positive regard is meaningfully linked to positive therapeutic outcomes success (Farber & Doolin, 2011; Kirschenbaum & Jourdan, 2005; Rogers, 1977). Positive regard is actively demonstrating the capability and consistency to be supportive, accepting, and affirming in a manner that is experienced by another. Farber and Doolin (2011) have recommendations for clinical practice, which we have adapted for relevance to the supervisory relationship:

- The supervisors' displays of positive regard strongly affects positive change in the supervisee.
- The withholding of positive regard is not promoted.
- Expression of caring and positive regard may facilitate the supervisee to grow and fulfill personal capacity.
- Positive regard may bridge differences in the supervisory relationship.
- The supervisor expresses positive feelings to affirm the supervisee's worth.
- The supervisor should monitor positive regard and vary it depending on the supervisee's need.

Warmth, Support, Genuineness, and Boundaries

Ideally, we believe a supervisor personifies warmth, exemplifies genuineness, and offers stable support to enhance the supervision setting. Similar to positive regard, warmth, support, and genuineness should not be misconstrued to mean saccharine, mawkish, or conflict-avoidant. Our intent is for the supervisor to hold the supervision space with underlying affection, dignity, enthusiasm, and identifiable limitations. Lanyado describes this role as one in which "the supervisor helps the therapist to 'hold' difficult and disturbing experiences, and this enables the therapist in turn to hold the difficult and disturbing experiences being expressed by the patient" (2016, p. 109). This conflux of ideals, buoyed by strong yet flexible boundaries, shapes the potential for discerning disclosure, and fosters the opportunity to raise pertinent questions and sustain meaningful discussions.

This cannot be accomplished without acknowledging the power dynamics.

> Supervisory relationships, by definition, include an evaluative component, and an early focus on supervisee personal issues, before a sense of safety has been established, may undermine the development of a sense of shared trust and the development of a robust supervisory alliance.
> (Angus & Kagan, 2007, p. 375)

Boundaries are critical to forming a framework to hold supervisee self-disclosures such as sharing of mistakes, missteps, and vulnerable thoughts, which allow the supervisor to gently confront and provide direct feedback. Cook et al. (2018) found supervisees "perceived themselves as possessing the most power on maintaining healthy boundaries with their supervisors, a willingness to feel vulnerable in supervision, and feeling empowered in supervision" (p. 188).

Empathy and Sensitivity

When experienced in the supervisory relationship, empathy and sensitivity can empower the supervisee with a sense of trust and confidence that is carried through the therapeutic session with clients. It is important to understand that the role of empathy and sensitivity play out differently in supervision as opposed to therapy.

> The focus of therapy is the elaboration of the client's story and the client's acquisition of new self-knowledge and skills to live a fuller, more satisfying life. In contrast, both supervisee and supervisor are focused on establishing a helping relationship with the client. The supervisee's personal development is in the service of providing a better outcome for the client, not an end in itself.
>
> (Angus & Kagan, 2007, pp. 374–375)

Reflectivity

For the supervisor, self-reflection within the supervisory experience is twofold. First, the supervisor draws on "self-reflections related to learner interactions to appraise thoughts, emotions, and behavior, and how each affects the learner's experience in supervision" (Curtis, Elkins, Duran, & Venta, 2016, p. 134). This type of reflectivity creates a considerate, yet specific view of the gestalt to better understand how to proceed with an optimal learning interaction. The supervisor's ability to demonstrate reflection advances a supervisee's potential for reflectivity through role modeling. "During supervision, the reflective process creates the space and climate for supervisees to reflect on feedback in a manner that is formative (i.e., facilitates the professional development of the counselor-in-training) and generative of multiple perspective taking" (Stinchfield, Hill, & Kleist, 2007, p. 173). "This combination of experience and reflection within the supervision session can then become part of the conscious awareness of the supervisee when he or she returns to the clinical situation" (Lanyado, 2016, p. 110). The gift of reflectivity is in the ability to invoke multiple perspectives to better understand the supervisory and client relationships.

Respect, Openness, and Concreteness

Robbins (2007) explains that when supervision is done well, the supervisor "creates opportunities for openness and communication, and the development of a holding, safe and trusting relationship" (p. 160). As a supervisor, the ability to embody respect, openness, and concreteness demonstrates a certain investment and vulnerability demonstrated by a supervisor's "emotional investment in the relationship, getting to know the supervisee, [and being] emotionally open, for example, sharing strengths and weaknesses, self-disclosure" (Beinart, 2014, p. 267). In addition to the mutual respect desired between supervisor and supervisee, expressing value for the process of supervision, fellow colleagues, and, especially, clients, sets a welcoming tone. Beinart also promotes possible actions, for the supervisor or the supervisee, such as honing the ability to "connect emotionally, be open, honest and willing to engage. Demonstrate enthusiasm and responsiveness. Reflect on learning and be open about any difficulties" (p. 267).

Supervisors, "particularly with new students, [need] to create an atmosphere in which revelation of ignorance and error is gently received, carefully supported and non-judgmentally welcomed" (Wilson et al., 1984, p. 101). "The atmosphere is non-judgmental, grounded and yet maintains boundaries. The supervisor provides a container for primitive affects that are stirred up both in the artwork as well as in the therapeutic relationship" (Robbins, 2007, p. 160).

Preferably, the supervisor will model the ability to engage, with interest and sensitivity, and to connect emotionally, with sincerity. This should all be done directly. In order to concretize the process, we suggest providing clear expectations, delivering precise feedback, and leaving little room for misunderstandings regarding what is non-negotiable. This concreteness solidifies the professional boundary, allowing space to provide feedback within the authority and shelter of the supervisory role. Unwarranted couching and other potentially apologetic distractions, such as "I really hate giving feedback" or "please don't get mad at me, but I have to give you this feedback", take away from the normalcy of receiving feedback in supervision.

Cultivating Positive Expectations and Hope

During anticipated bouts of uncertainty regarding identity and development as an art therapist, creating and upholding optimism within the mindset of the supervisee is fundamental. This clinical and personal doubt often parallels session crises, and can overwhelm the supervisee. It is often necessary to bolster trust and fortify hope in the art therapy process as a viable means to address client outcomes. This is a time, as noted by Lanyado (2016), "that there can be a turning point which emerges from times of despair and crisis in the therapeutic process" (p. 107). Installation of hope, one of Yalom's 11 therapeutic factors, encourages the therapist to understand that "faith in a treatment mode can in itself be therapeutically effective" (Yalom & Leszcz, 2005, p. 4). A supervisor has the opportunity and obligation to nurture, demonstrate, and extend belief in the therapeutic process, not only for the supervisee but also for the direct benefit of the client.

Becoming a Supervisor

Becoming an on-site supervisor for a graduate-level art therapy student is a natural path for a first-time supervisor. Certain concrete requirements should be considered before taking on the responsibility of supervising.

When supervising on-site students, the art therapy supervisor should ensure they have the proper space (therapeutic and administrative), ample art materials, adequate client-contact hours, support from the immediate team, and sustainability for continued client care once the placement ends so that clients are not left without services. Additional considerations for supervising both students and professionals are time, emotional capacity, and skill set.

It is critical to understand the learning opportunities afforded by each art therapy opportunity, through the unique combination of site and population(s) served. Consider the type of supervisory experience you can provide (e.g., individual, group, individual and group) and whether it is best suited for a novice intern who is having their first field experience, a more advanced student completing a final internship, an early career professional seeking credentials or licensure, or an advanced professional. The decision to become a supervisor should not be taken lightly, nor reached under unnecessary pressure (e.g., persuasion from a work setting or educational institution) or without proper planning and training.

Although a supervisor learns a tremendous amount from each supervisee, an advanced proficiency as an art therapist is a basic requirement. Supervisors should also have a commitment to self-reflection and self-criticism "by actively and aggressively working on improving ... professional skills and understanding. We believe that only experiences that are combined with such self-criticism can bring about development" (Vec, Vec, & Žorga, 2014). Before choosing to supervise, explore your motivation and intent for this undertaking. Consider generating art as part of this decision-making process. If a choice is made to supervise, plan thoughtfully and thoroughly, and commit to actively participate, and perhaps even consider supervision for your supervisory activities.

Task and Goals

Supervisors and supervisees benefit when a clear-cut structure of tasks and goals are implemented and followed. "Relational development, role orientation, needs assessment, plan development/evaluation, and monitoring are integral components of any effective supervision process" (Watkins, 2017, p. 146). This format, inspired by Watkins (2017), is simply a base that includes a solid orientation and supervision definition, supports development of a supervisory alliance, highlights the importance of an initial assessment, generates a supervision plan, and promotes strategic, ongoing revision of the supervision plan.

Orientation and Education

Within the supervisory context, it is important to provide supervisees an education that incorporates a broader definition of supervision and a site-specific orientation with a detailed and nuanced initiation and training appropriate to the setting. This education ought to build a broad awareness and appreciation for the implicit power differential, communicate that a supervisor's primary responsibility is the protection of the client and the public, and, in addition, act as a gatekeeper of the profession to ensure that only suitable candidates enter or remain in the field (Falender, 2014; Watkins, 2017). The supervisor also needs to delve into site-specific minutia. This may include general orientations and training to better understand site-particular protocols such as procedures for day-to-day functioning, expectations in case of emergencies, and social media policies. This type of education also provides the opportunity to teach risk assessment skills (e.g., danger to self or others) and client and intern safety factors (e.g., developmentally appropriate art materials). Often overlooked, small details such as the location of the coat closet and the restroom go a long way to create a more gratifying learning environment.

Supervisory Alliance

As in therapy, a strong relationship is beneficial. In our view, developing and cultivating a strong relationship or supervisory alliance with your supervisee is not optional. We understand that this takes work! When comparing trainee therapists' ability to maintain and build alliances, Ybrandt, Sundin, and Capone (2016) found the alliance to the client was more stable than to the supervisor, which experienced more fluctuation, suggesting supervisees may have difficulty navigating the multilayered relationship, primarily the teacher and evaluator roles. This complexity suggests a special emphasis needs to be placed on fostering the supervisory alliance; sometimes, simply checking in openly and honestly to ask your supervisees, "As a supervisor, what can I do better?" or "What might I be missing in what you need from me?" We can also turn to art to foster this relationship.

Art can bring intention and attention to establish and nurture the supervisory alliance. To better explore and facilitate the dynamic between a supervisor and supervisee, McNamee and McWey (2004) introduced an experiential bilateral art protocol that stimulated new insights and made parallel processes more overt for discussion. This process created ensuing relationship shifts. "Bilateral art is an art therapy intervention that engages both dominant and non-dominant hands in the process of creating images in response to opposing cognitions or feelings" (p. 230). Inspired by the artistic struggle of *el duende*, which is an art-based approach to student supervision that embraces painting on a single canvas all through the semester, Miller (2012) created an art-based approach to apply in the academic, group supervision setting, combining "clinical insight with archetypal awareness arising from painting on a single canvas throughout the internship semester" (p. 166). In addition to enhancing the supervisory alliance, this approach presents opportunities to explore multiple relationships simultaneously, including clients and peers. Similarly, Fish (2012) reminds us "there are as many ways to employ art imagery as there are therapists willing to engage it and situations to inspire artistic response. We don't know the limits of our artwork's potential" (p. 142).

Assessment

A mutually supportive supervisory alliance provides a trusted footing to assess and identify supervisee learning deficits, needs, strengths, and assets, while supporting the self-assessment of competencies by the supervisee (Falender, 2014; Watkins, 2017). Time-specific performance reviews are a common type of assessment used for coaching, training, and staff development that facilitates dialogue specific to job performance. The review establishes levels of functioning, identifies strengths, defines areas of needed growth, sets performance objectives, and creates a career development plan.

In an academic-based setting, time-specific marks include mid-term evaluations and final semester reviews. In work settings, reviews fluctuate depending on the supervisor and the setting. One common configuration that supports the standard annual review includes three reviews within the first year of hire. They include a new hire or probationary review completed after the first three months of employment followed by a six-month review. This timing allows for the supervisee to receive and engage in perspicuous feedback within the first six months. In some settings, the annual review date is determined from the anniversary start date while other settings have a specific date when all annual performance reviews are completed. In each case, best practices encourage supervisees' access to the performance criteria that will be evaluated.

Although it is the ultimate responsibility of the supervisor to complete the written review, it is invaluable to have direct input from the supervisee. It is often advantageous to have the supervisee complete the written review as supplemental material to inform the final review. The ability to self-assess is critical for growth-related insight, and the supervisee's viewpoint provides a deeper and concentrated reflection of their own level of functioning.

Supervision Plan

A plan can be developed within the framework of the normative, restorative, and formative tasks. In order to address identified themes for growth and the means to nurture current competencies, plans should include personalized goals and objectives. After implementation of the supervision plan, the supervisor and supervisee should evaluate, review, and revise the plan routinely and often. The ongoing and transparent assessment and evaluation minimizes supervisors' appraisal surprises. Each updated plan should provide tracking, documentation, and consistency. This is different from a formalized evaluation; however, evaluations often include goal-setting.

Supervisory Roles

Training as a supervisor is as important as training to be a therapist. At first, when engaging in the role of supervisor, there can be well-warranted emotions of excitement, anxiety, and fear. Supervision has clearly defined roles distinct from therapy (Borders et al., 2014; Mann & Merced, 2018; Watkins, 2017), even with the tremendous overlap of clinical proficiencies. Thus, it is important to have a better understanding of the role, intervention, and tasks positioned within a theoretical framework, in order to best approach supervision.

Watkins (2017) identified six supervisory role categories: educator, monitor, coach, therapist, collegial peer, and consultant (Hess, 2008; 1980). These roles often accompany the standard supervisory interventions of case conceptualization, teaching, providing feedback, and modeling discussion (Watkins, 2017). The roles are determined by the intervention needed in the moment to best serve the supervisee. These six roles can be easily mapped onto the three components of supervision (administrative, educational, and supportive), which we have done visually as a way of further understanding this concept (see Figure 2.1).

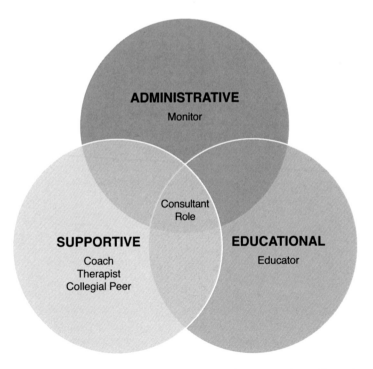

Figure 2.1 Six supervisory roles mapped onto the three supervisory dimensions.

Educator

Activities may include treatment planning, diagnosis, interventions, documentation, and ethical concerns (Borders et al., 2014; Mann & Merced, 2018). For instance, the educator values and seizes teachable moments, capitalizing on the combination of timing, spontaneity, and circumstance to better exemplify what is being taught. In addition, while in the educator role, the supervisor may identify space for the art process to be seamlessly incorporated, and respond to therapeutic and supervisory sessions.

Monitor

The monitor role maintains focus on client treatment. It also simultaneously safeguards care by acting as the gatekeeper for the profession (Cheon, Blumer, Shih, Murphy, & Sato, 2009; Mann & Merced, 2018; Purswell & Stulmaker, 2015) by creating "explicit plans for addressing competency problems or the unsuitability of the supervisee for the profession" (APA, 2014, p. 25). Ethical violations and general ineptness are monitored. However, this does not diminish the supervisee's ability to take risks and make mistakes – an effective supervisor will encourage such practices. In addition to the overarching gatekeeping of the profession, the monitor role is responsible for more detailed evaluations and feedback of performance. The scope of the evaluations is determined by the setting (e.g., campus, internship, private practice). For example, internship and campus supervisors collaborate to provide formative assessments to identify strengths, weaknesses, and target areas for immediate improvement, while summative feedback is employed to evaluate student learning, which is then analyzed to help determine academic grade or status. When gainfully employed, the evaluations potentially assist in establishing the level of job performance, site compliance, readiness for promotion, or eligibility for additional financial compensation.

Coach/Mentor

The coach/mentor role centers on a supervisee's career advancement, professional ambitions, and long-term workplace strategies. In addition, the supervisor can role-model this component of supervision. Workplace strategies address individual goals and may include team-wide objectives such as meeting performance targets, increasing team cohesion, and boosting morale. Of great importance is the mentor's ability to convey and model the use of artmaking and response art for emotional processing and as structures for encountering a deeper clinical understanding. "The use of response art in supervision provides a method to hold experiences while engaging in empathetic resonance" (Fish, 2017, p. 31).

Whether through artmaking or verbal dialogue, the mentor role aims to engage the entirety of the supervisee within the holistic context of their career. Moon (2003) writes of the mentor as "a deep resource of technical information, a participant in an intuitional political system, and a capable container for swirling emotional currents and willing companion who will honor the quest of the student" (p. 43). In this context the supervision moves beyond the current evaluative role, as the mentor shifts to the role of expert, holds a wealth of information, and addresses the larger needs of the supervisee's career and aspirations. See Vignette 2.1 for an example of a supervisor moving into the coach/mentor role to help advance a supervisee's selected career path.

Vignette 2.1 Embracing the Roles of Coach and Mentor

Daniel's Story

When I first began supervising teams, I greatly feared staff members resigning. Embarrassingly, I probably used expressions such as "Please don't ever leave" and "I don't know what I'd do if you left" as ways to convey personal value. These expressions also reflected my fears. In my mismanagement of my fears I often fell prey to thoughts of personal rejection and notions of inadequacy, and was resistant to change that threatened the status quo.

My restricted approach blocked most opportunities for staff to broach their personal motivation and commitment to long-term career goals in supervision. It was not until I began to embrace the coach/mentor role that I was able to expand my supervisory skill set to include fulfillment and exit strategies. From this more inclusive lens, supervision is utilized to address the essentials each supervisee requires to be fulfilled and challenged in their current position, to champion methods to achieve the next step or stage, and hold an overarching awareness of long-term career goals.

So much unnecessary stress was alleviated, for my teams and myself, once I was able to embrace and, more importantly, nurture the natural flow of my team members. The lesson learned was to prepare individuals for advancement, not for stagnation. For example, midway in my career, a doctoral-level social worker reported to me as a clinical team leader. He supervised a team of clinicians, including art therapists, and had a deep passion for research, writing, and health informatics. After a few years of working in a clinical context of providing direct service and supervision, he was able to easily navigate to a new position within the agency where he experienced higher job satisfaction and could focus on other interests that directly benefited the clinical team from which he transitioned. Likewise, his hands-on clinical work enriched the work in his new position.

Therapist

As highlighted and considered more thoroughly in Table 1.1, supervision is not therapy and is focused on improved job performance as opposed to enhancing a sense of personal well-being. A strict boundary must be maintained to protect the supervisory relationship from morphing into a dual relationship of supervisor/therapist. A supervisor maintains focus on supervisee professional development, client care, and therapeutic outcomes. A supervisor does not actively provide mental health treatment to the supervisee. Understanding these role differences allows for structure and freedom within the defined space.

Nonetheless, the therapist role may be assumed within the supervisory session to facilitate insight, express empathy, normalize anxiety, and employ experiential learning through emotional processing in direct relationship to the therapist (supervisee) and client dynamic. There is a similar approach when a supervisee engages and holds space for a client to emotionally process, and in turn, the supervisor offers and assists the supervisee to emotionally process their reactions to the client (O'Donovan et al., 2011). Wilson et al. (1984) recognized the supervisor's role as one to identify personal struggles that impede clinical work, but clarified that a supervisee's essential self-examination needs to be clearly separate from personal therapy. When the supervisor holds a therapeutic-like space, this can model empathy, provide emotional support through reassurance and encouragement, allow the supervisee to self-disclose, and may provide guidance for future clinical interventions.

Collegial Peer

Like the therapist role, a supervisor acting in the collegial peer role needs to closely monitor the potential for blurred boundaries disrupting the established hierarchy. Normally defined by equal or shared power, the collegial peer role can be minimal, yet pivotal, in a supervisory relationship that combines elements of friendship, shares some intimate communication, and embraces mutual emotional support and feedback. Among the benefits of the role is the opportunity to: deepen the supervisory relationship by promotion of trust, invite more work-related self-disclosures, and create an opportunity to gain a better understanding of each other as individuals. On the problematic side, if this role becomes too influential, it may inhibit a supervisor's ability to maintain fairness among the team, maintain accountability, and properly prepare performance evaluations.

Consultant

The consultant role restores the focus back to the client, while simultaneously aiming to invite and fulfill supervisee needs during jointly structured supervision sessions. To benefit clients, the consultant role encourages the supervisee to brainstorm strategies and interventions, explore case conceptualization, and plan alternative interventions to address client problems, motivations, and behaviors. To advance the supervisee's ability to meet client needs, a joint agenda is shaped and space is created to explore areas for the supervisee's growth and apply theoretical concepts to intervention development specific to particular client circumstances (Pearson, 2006). A mutual agenda helps to prevent supervisors from pursuing their own agenda and sustain focus on supervisee development. If the advisor is specifically in the role of consultant and not in a direct supervisory position, the supervisee is under no obligation to follow the supervisor's guidance.

Supervision Interventions

Commonly practiced supervisor interventions for psychotherapists include case conceptualization and presentation, teaching, stimulus questions, reflective instigation, providing feedback, and modeling discussion. We have adapted some of them below for use in art therapy supervision. Keep in mind that not all interventions are necessarily utilized in each supervision session and can be drawn on as needed depending on the supervisory needs.

Case Conceptualization/Presentation

A case presentation is an oral or written presentation that contains virtually all elements occurring within case conceptualization, and expresses all the elements of the case, including the conceptual reasoning and justification, to an audience. Depending on the audience, the case presentation may need to contain more or less information regarding the setting and level of confidentiality required. In art therapy graduate training, case presentations are a common, core factor in campus-based supervision. Case conceptualization or formulation is used to better understand and organize client information, and to "hypothesis[e] about the causes, precipitants, and maintaining influences of a person's psychological, interpersonal, and behavioral problems" and is especially useful "when that information contains contradictions or inconsistencies in behavior, emotion, and thought content" (Eells, 2007, p. 4). Case conceptualization is not a single act, but originates at intake and is maintained throughout treatment. Art therapists often have the additional visual elements and artmaking processes to consider. The supervisor guides the supervisee through this framework to interpret client observations within psychological concepts and art therapy theory, in order to guide treatment and monitor progress.

A supervisor is often able to establish the tenor and strategy for those attending a case presentation, such as students in a classroom setting. The attendees have a pivotal role in deepening the educational experience by posing language-sensitive questions. For example, asking, "How were the art materials used?" is invitingly open-ended and may elicit a more perceptive and observant response than "What art materials were used?" Case presentations are described more in Chapter 10, *Group Supervision*, and a guide to case presentations is found in Appendix B.

Teaching

As a supervisory intervention, instruction allows the supervisor to teach around a host of pertinent topics. Moon (2003) describes this a "cooperative process through which the supervisor helps the supervisee use the educational structure to gain the best possible learning experience" and dually fulfills the wish for a connection with a supervisor "who knows the answers" (p. 42). This cooperative relationship and supervisory expertise dovetails nicely with Laurie Wilson describing one pivotal supervisory "role" as simply, yet profoundly, "teaching students how to ask questions" (Wilson et al., 1984, p. 100). This ability to hold the expertise while stimulating the necessity to ask thoughtful and reflective questions applies not only to students, but also professionals, as well as previous academic study and ongoing professional development. Certain instruction will be universal, though some will be supervisee-, setting-, theory-, and population-specific. Teaching topics may include diagnosis, treatment planning, art-based interventions, record-keeping and art storage, and ethical/legal matters.

Mindfulness-Based Supervision

Studies indicate intentionally incorporating mindfulness practices in supervision, through instruction and exercises, appears to advance a supervisee's ability to relate therapeutically with more genuineness, attentiveness, acceptance, responsiveness, compassion, and empathy (Campbell & Christopher, 2012; Daniel, Borders, & Willse, 2015; Sharp & Rhinehart, 2018), "while lessening defensiveness and reactivity" (Sharp & Rhinehart, 2018, p. 67). Intentionality, as described by Sturm, Presbury, and Echterling (2012), is a prerequisite for forming "a truly mindful dynamic" (p. 225) that moves beyond the inherent relational aspect of a supervisory alliance. They clarify it is crucial to accurately honor "mindfulness as a core quality or a way of being"

(Sturm et al., 2012, p. 225) rather than simply a technique. When integrated as a way of being, this form of discipline generates an exceptional "quality of unconditional presence" that allows one to stay receptive and present during a disturbing and emotional supervisory or client session (Franklin, Farrelly-Hansen, Marek, Swan-Foster, & Wallingford, 2000, p. 103).

When fostered aptly, mindfulness provides supervisees a framework to lower nervousness, potential pressures, performance anxiety, or trepidations that may reduce developmentally expected functionality. Supervisors with a more mindful approach "form stronger supervisory relationships and achieve greater depth in their supervision sessions" (Daniel et al., 2015, p. 222). As art therapists and art therapists in training, the artmaking process and the art studio provide an unrivaled space to practice mindfulness and offer "a sanctuary for self- learning, support, and partnership" (Franklin et al., 2000, p. 105). The shelter and inherent challenge of the studio extends an invitation to shift focus from outcome and result to "embrace the process of making, of wakeful participation and relationship" (Franklin et al., 2000, p. 105). As shared in Daniel's story (see Vignette 2.2), this is often a difficult transition for those who have completed rigorous, critique-driven art training focused on technique and the final art product.

Vignette 2.2 Grappling with Mindfulness

Daniel's Story

Before studying to be an art therapist, I earned a Bachelor of Fine Arts degree and utilized commercial art and illustration techniques. Needless to say, these skills were respected in my seven-year advertising career but did not transfer well to art therapy. In one course taught by Edith Kramer, the class was asked to display our artwork. Edith roamed the room with great interest and paused in front of my work – three versions of the same person's face displaying different emotions (see Figure 2.2). After a moment of silence, she asked, "Whose is this?" I silently beamed as I acknowledged my work. As she turned her back to walk away, coolly saying, "You worked in advertising. I'm not sure you got out in time." Her words cut like a knife because they were factual. My art, though well executed, was more appropriate for an advertising sketch than an art therapy assignment. Years of undergraduate critiques and advertising expectations continued to dictate my relationship with artmaking – valuing product over process. I was still mechanically producing art, not learning, and not authentically engaging with the artmaking process. Although I did not have the mindfulness vocabulary at the time, her comments challenged and encouraged me to be more mindful, more present, and honest in my art. Over time, with intention and training, I continue to work on my contemplative practice. As an art therapy educator and supervisor, I invite supervisees to approach artmaking mindfully, which may require a conscious and acknowledged disengagement from the expectations of a traditional art school critique.

Figure 2.2 Daniel Blausey (1992), Untitled drawing assignment in graduate school [charcoal and oil pastel on gray paper].

Mindfulness is centered in present-moment attention, non-judgment, and flexibility (Franklin et al., 2000; Hall-Renn, 2007; Kabat-Zinn, 2012) and often appears overtly simple and simultaneously perplexing. Attitudinal foundations for mindfulness, a framework by Kabat-Zinn's (2012), shares 16 fundamentals with the most basic being non-judging, patience, beginner's mind, trust, non-striving, acceptance, and letting go (p. 123). Assisting a supervisee to recognize their primary attitudes of mindfulness offers further means to assimilate "moment-to-moment mindfulness into client sessions" (Sharp & Rhinehart, 2018, p. 71).

Attending to Conflicts and Counterproductive Events in Supervision

If handled with thoughtfulness and awareness, conflicts and seemingly counterproductive events in supervision can provide moments for critical insight and deepening the relationship. Conflicts can also heighten the prospect of being understood by increasing the quality of communication.

However, if ignored or handled ineffectively, supervisees may identify conflicts "as hindering, unhelpful, or harmful in relation to their growth as therapists" (Gray, Ladany, Walker, & Ancis, 2001, p. 371). In fact, counterproductive events may decrease supervision satisfaction without "the presence of a strong, positive working alliance" (Cheon et al., 2009, p. 62). In their qualitative analysis, Gray et al. (2001) found counterproductive events usually bore a negative outcome on the supervisory process. They learned that a majority of the supervisees felt "uncomfortable, unsafe, or upset in response to the counterproductive events, but they also deferred to the supervisors' authority, became hypervigilant, nondisclosed, and withdrawn in supervision" (p. 381).

Regrettably, some supervisors or supervision settings may not be equipped with the critical proficiencies needed to appropriately tackle conflict and may avoid or even bungle the interaction (Nelson, Barnes, Evans, & Triggiano, 2008, p. 173). Becoming comfortable with and even embracing conflict in order to work towards resolution is essential. Grant, Schofield, and Crawford (2012) identified several direct and indirect strategies from recent studies for addressing conflict in supervision. We build upon their findings as a list of potential interventions and approaches that are both direct (see Box 2.1) and indirect in nature (see Box 2.2).

Box 2.1 Direct Strategies for Addressing Conflict

- Acknowledge and own, with humbleness, any missteps, shortcomings, or mistakes when made as a supervisor (Grant et al., 2012).
- Seek supervision on supervision, consult with colleagues, and "self-coach" (Grant et al., 2012) through planning out conflicts mentally (Nelson et al., 2008, p. 179).
- Attune to supervisee's needs, contextualizing conflicts both developmentally and organizationally (Grant et al., 2012) and look for win/win situations.
- Design and apply art-based interventions to facilitate discussion and broach difficult topics.
- Utilize immediacy, by addressing the here and now of the supervisory relationship to demonstrate the impact of behavior (Grant et al., 2012). Hill and Gupta (2018) propose the appropriate use of immediacy in supervision so that "feelings will be expressed and accepted, problems in the supervisory relationship will be resolved, the supervisory relationship will be enhanced, and supervisees will transfer their learning to their conduct of therapy with their clients" (p. 294).

- Directly address, validate, and normalize the conflict or counter-productive event as inherent while reinforcing supervisee strengths (Grant et al., 2012).
- Implementing "a more interpersonally sensitive supervisory approach may facilitate the repair of ruptured alliances" (Gray et al., 2001, p. 381). Purposely confront tentatively or directly based on the needs of the supervisee.
- Interpret parallel processes between therapeutic, supervisory, interpersonal, and other analogous behaviors to gain a broader understanding and reduce conflict (Grant et al., 2012).
- If needed, become more directive, refer to personal therapy, refuse or terminate supervision, and take action for unethical and unprofessional behavior (Grant et al., 2012). Do not go into this endeavor alone! Professionals should partner with Human Resources and students should reach out to their contact on campus.

Box 2.2 Indirect Interventions and Strategies for Addressing Conflict

- Set boundaries and expectations, provide routine feedback, and understand the limits of supervision.
- Model and facilitate the reflective process (Grant et al., 2012), model mutual respect, and support an atmosphere of mutual trust that allows trainees to feel safe (Gray et al., 2001, p. 381).
- Listen, remain patient and transparent (Grant et al., 2012), reduce advice-giving, and be intentional in the use of other therapy skills in supervision.
- Question, remain mindful, monitor (Grant et al., 2012), and clearly communicate.
- Hold general discussions about a topic before addressing specifics, particularly if they are about a supervisor's mannerisms or ways of working (Grant et al., 2012).
- "Prepare … for dealing with interpersonal conflict" (Nelson et al., 2008, p. 179) and practice giving feedback in advance.

Values Conflict

There will be times when a supervisor feels that the personal values of a supervisee do not reflect or align with expectations and requirements regarding professional values and ethics. The supervisor will still need to help the supervisee navigate their clinical work. Hathaway (2014) suggests that it may be more productive to "explore value-congruent ways to be clinically helpful to the client" as an alternative to potentially solidifying religious division and provoking a supervisee to dig in defensively "by attempting to attenuate their faith" (2014, p. 100). In other words, exploring values may be more effective than attempting to realign or correct values. Below are some recommended approaches for supervisors looking to assist supervisees who hold different value systems:

- Model introspection and self-exploration within the supervisory relationship and disclose real life struggles (Cohen-Filipic & Flores, 2014, p. 306) while demonstrating "full respect and benevolent navigation of all of the diversity areas involved: trainee, trainer, and client" (Hathaway, 2014, p. 101).
- Recognize and acknowledge the vulnerability of students when they disclose deeply held beliefs that may be uncommon in the training environment (Cohen-Filipic & Flores, 2014, p. 306).
- To foster trust required for a strong supervisory alliance, recognize the "critical influence of power and evaluation on supervisory relationships" and "initiate discussions about power and evaluation early on in supervision" (Nelson et al., 2008, p. 180).
- Increase comfort discussing religious and cultural values and deeply held beliefs they may find surprising or upsetting (Cohen-Filipic & Flores, 2014, p. 306).
- Avoid conflicts and maintain a collaborative effort regarding supervisees' personal values by communicating clear expectations for professional competence. This includes defining acceptable outcomes for each stage that are reinforced in an "integrated developmental and competency-based supervision approach" (Cohen-Filipic & Flores, 2014, p. 307). Within this dialogue, exercise transparency to clearly identify and agree about goals and roles in supervision to reduce role conflict (Nelson et al., 2008).
- Practice an individual approach, as some supervisees with value conflicts may require more time, space, and more supervision to resolve these concerns (Cohen-Filipic & Flores, 2014, p. 307). "The goal is to help the student achieve a value-congruent way to competently navigate such conflicts" (Hathaway, 2014, p. 100).
- Document the supervisee's "inability or unwillingness to attain competencies as well as the steps taken to facilitate the trainee's attainment of competence" (APA, 2013, p. 1).
- "Base any determination to require remediation or recommend dismissal on prudent, consistent, and fair adherence to established program and institutional policies" (APA, 2013, p. 1).

Takeaways

- To build a mutually supportive supervisory alliance, supervisors must be committed to perfecting a sensitive balance of gaining skills and competencies, honing applicable personal qualities, and refining the ability to implement timely and appropriate supervisory interventions.
- Social locations of the supervisor and the supervisee define and impact the inherent supervisory power dynamic, requiring the supervisor to fully understand their own social location in respect to privilege and oppression as a starting point.
- An art therapy supervisor must be accountable to the AATA's aspirational *Ethical Principles for Art Therapists* (2013) and the ATCB's consequential *Code of Ethics, Conduct, and Disciplinary Procedures*, as well as having awareness of and accountability to relevant jurisdictional laws and regulations.
- A rightful cornerstone of a truly empowering supervisory relationship is the ability to provide accurate, reliable, and knowledgeable performance feedback in a judicious and direct manner, within a standardized format and at established intervals.

Practice Prompts

Routine Methods and Tools for Assessing Performance and Competency

Reflect through quick, spontaneous, five-minute art and writing responses to your most routine methods and tools for assessing performance and competency. The practice prompt below uses clinical notes as the routine method; however, you could substitute this for a different method, such as process recording, audio recording, annual review, etc.

Read over your supervisee's clinical notes from the past week. Respond creatively, considering the aspects of where you feel your supervisee was clear as well as the areas where you feel they could improve.

- Does the artwork provide any new or additional insight into your supervisee?
- Consider if you will you share your artwork or findings with your supervisee.

Identifying Difficult Feedback

As a supervisor, identify which type of feedback is more difficult for you to provide: (a) feedback related to a supervisee's personal characteristics, (b) feedback associated to the supervisory relationship, or (c) feedback concerning your supervisee's clinical work?

- Create two pieces of artwork exploring the most challenging type of feedback. First, from your perspective as supervisor, and second, from the perspective of the supervisee.
- Compare and contrast the artmaking and art through response writing.

Providing Difficult Feedback

To enhance the actual delivery and assimilation of difficult feedback, practice art-based methods or other techniques with your supervisor.

- Practice providing difficult feedback through role-playing, empty-chair work, or other interactive methods.
- Clarify the experience through response writing to increase the ability to listen for and analyze feedback. Discuss with your supervisor.

References

AATA. (2013). Ethical principles for art therapists. Retrieved from https://artther apy.org/wp-ontent/uploads/2017/06/Ethical-Principles-for-Art-Therapists.pdf

Angus, L., & Kagan, F. (2007). Empathic relational bonds and personal agency in psychotherapy: Implications for psychotherapy supervision, practice, and research. *Psychotherapy: Theory, Research, Practice, Training, 44*(4), 371–377. doi:http://dx.doi.org/10.1037/0033-3204.44.4.371

APA. (2013). Preparing professional psychologists to serve a diverse public: Addressing conflicts between professional competence and trainee beliefs. Retrieved from www.apa.org/pi/lgbt/resources/policy/diversity-preparation.pdf

APA. (2014). Guidelines for clinical supervision in health service psychology. Retrieved from http://apa.org/about/policy/guidelines-supervision.pdf

Arczynski, A. V., & Morrow, S. L. (2017). The complexities of power in feminist multicultural psychotherapy supervision. *Journal of Counseling Psychology, 64* (2), 192–205. doi:http://dx.doi.org/10.1037/cou0000179

ATCB. (2018). Code of ethics, conduct and disciplinary procedures. Retrieved from: www.atcb.org/resource/pdf/ATCB-Code-of-Ethics-Conduct-DisciplinaryProce dures.pdf

Barrett, M. S., & Barber, J. P. (2005). A developmental approach to the supervision of therapists in training. *Journal of Contemporary Psychotherapy, 35*(2), 169–183. doi:10.1007/s10879-005-2698-8

Beinart, H. (2014). Building and sustaining the supervisory relationship. In C. E. Watkins, Jr. & D. L. Milne (Eds.), *The Wiley international handbook of clinical supervision* (pp. 257–281). Chichester, UK: John Wiley & Sons. http://dx. doi.org/10.1002/9781118846360.ch11

Borders, L. D., Glosoff, H. L., Welfare, L. E., Hays, D. G., DeKruyf, L., Fernando, D. M., & Page, B. (2014). Best practices in clinical supervision: Evolution of a counseling specialty. *The Clinical Supervisor, 33*(1), 26–44. doi:10.1080/07325223.2014.905225

Campbell, J., & Christopher, J. (2012). Teaching mindfulness to create effective counselors. *Journal of Mental Health Counseling, 34*(3), 213–226.

Cheon, H. S., Blumer, M. L. C., Shih, A. T., Murphy, M. J., & Sato, M. (2009). The influence of supervisor and supervisee matching, role conflict, and supervisory relationship on supervisee satisfaction. *Contemporary Family Therapy, 31*, 52–67.

Cohen-Filipic, J., & Flores, L. Y. (2014). Best practices in providing effective supervision to students with values conflicts. *Psychology of Sexual Orientation and Gender Diversity, 1*(4), 302–309.

Cook, R. M., McKibben, W. B., & Wind, S. A. (2018). Supervisee perception of power in clinical supervision: The Power Dynamics in Supervision Scale. *Training and Education in Professional Psychology, 12*(3), 188.

Cummings, J. A., Ballantyne, E. C., & Scallion, L. M. (2015). Essential processes for cognitive behavioral clinical supervision: Agenda setting, problem-solving, and formative feedback. *Psychotherapy, 52*, 158–163. doi:http://dx.doi.org/10.1037/a0038712

Curtis, D. F., Elkins, S. R., Duran, P., & Venta, A. C. (2016). Promoting a climate of reflective practice and clinician self-efficacy in vertical supervision. *Training and Education in Professional Psychology, 10*(3), 133.

Daniel, L., Borders, L. D., & Willse, J. (2015). The role of supervisors' and supervisees' mindfulness in clinical supervision. *Counselor Education and Supervision, 54*(3), 221–232.

Eells, T. D. (2007). History and current status of psychotherapy case formulation. In *Handbook of psychotherapy case formulation* (2[nd]ed., pp. 3–32). New York, NY: Guilford Publications.

Epstein, R. M., & Hundert, E. M. (2002). Defining and assessing professional competence. *Journal of the American Medical Association, 287*(2), 226–235. doi:10.1001/jama.287.2.226

Falender, C. A. (2014). Clinical supervision in a competency-based era. *South African Journal of Psychology, 44*(1), 6–17.

Farber, B. A., & Doolin, E. M. (2011). Positive regard. *Psychotherapy, 48*(1), 58–64. doi:http://dx.doi.org/10.1037/a0022141

Fish, B. J. (2012). Response art: The art of the art therapist. *Art Therapy: Journal of the American Art Therapy Association, 29*(3), 138–143. doi:10.1080/07421656.2012.701594

Fish, B. J. (2017). *Art-based supervision: Cultivating therapeutic insight through imagery.* New York, NY: Routledge.

Franklin, M., Farrelly-Hansen, M., Marek, B., Swan-Foster, N., & Wallingford, S. (2000). Transpersonal art therapy education. *Art Therapy, 17*(2), 101–110.

Freeman, E. M. (1985). The Importance of Feedback in Clinical Supervision. *The Clinical Supervisor, 3*(1), 5–26. doi:10.1300/J001v03n01_02

Gaete, J., & Ness, O. (2015). Supervision: From prescribed roles to preferred positionings. *The Clinical Supervisor, 34*(1), 57–77. doi:10.1080/07325223.2015.1006068

Grant, J., Schofield, M. J., & Crawford, S. (2012). Managing difficulties in supervision: Supervisors' perspectives. *Journal of Counseling Psychology, 59*, 528–541. doi:http://dx.doi.org/10.1037/a0030000

Gray, L. A., Ladany, N., Walker, J. A., & Ancis, J. R. (2001). Psychotherapy trainees' experience of counterproductive events in supervision. *Journal of Counseling Psychology, 48*, 371–383. doi:10.1037/0022-0167.48.4.371

Hall-Renn, K. E. (2007). Mindful journeys: Embracing the present with non-judgmental awareness. *Journal of Creativity in Mental Health, 2*(2), 3–16.

Hathaway, W. L. (2014). Trainer beliefs, multiculturalism, and the common good. *Psychology of Sexual Orientation and Gender Diversity, 1*(2), 98–101.

Hess, A. K. (2008). Psychotherapy supervision: A conceptual review. In A. K. Hess, K. D. Hess, & T. H. Hess (Eds.), *Psychotherapy supervision: Theory, research, and practice* (2nd ed., pp. 3–22). Hoboken, NJ: Wiley.

Hess, A. K. (1980). Training models and the nature of psychotherapy supervision. In A. K. Hess (Ed.), *Psychotherapy supervision: Theory, research, and practice* (pp. 15–25). New York, NY: Wiley.

Hernandez-Wolfe, Ph, & McDowell, T. (2014). Cultural equity and humility: A framework for bridging complex identities in supervision. In T. C. Todd & C. L. Storm (Eds.), *The complete systemic supervisor: Context, philosophy and pragmatics* (2nd ed., pp. 43–61). Hoboken, NJ: John Wiley & Sons.

Hill, C. E., & Gupta, S. (2018). The use of immediacy in supervisory relationships. In O. Tishby & H. Wiseman (Eds.), *Developing the therapeutic relationship: Integrating case studies, research, and practice* (pp. 289–314). Washington, DC: American Psychological Association.

Inman, A. G., Hutman, H., Pendse, A., Devdas, L., Luu, L., & Ellis, M. V. (2014). Current trends concerning supervisors, supervisees, and clients in clinical supervision. In C. Edward Watkins, Jr. & D. L. Milne (Eds.), *The Wiley international handbook of clinical supervision* (pp. 61–102). Chichester, UK: John Wiley & Sons.

Kabat-Zinn, J. (2012). *Mindfulness for beginners: Reclaiming the present moment – and your life.* Boulder, CO: Sounds True.

Kadushin, A., & Harkness, D. (2014). *Supervision in social work.* New York, NY: Columbia University Press.

Karcher, O. P. (2017). Sociopolitical oppression, trauma, and healing: Moving toward a social justice art therapy framework. *Art Therapy, 34*(3), 123–128.

Kirschenbaum, H., & Jourdan, A. (2005). The current status of Carl Rogers and the person-centered approach. *Psychotherapy: Theory, Research, Practice, Training, 42*(1), 37.

Lanyado, M. (2016). Transforming despair to hope in the treatment of extreme trauma: A view from the supervisor's chair. *Journal of Child Psychotherapy, 42*(2), 107–121. doi:10.1080/0075417X.2016.1191198

Mann, S. T., & Merced, M. (2018). Preparing for entry-level practice in supervision. *Professional Psychology: Research and Practice, 49*(1), 98–106.

McNamee, C. M., & McWey, L. M. (2004). Using bilateral art to facilitate clinical supervision. *The Arts in Psychotherapy, 31*(4), 229–243. doi:doi:10.1016/j.aip.2004.06.007

Miller, A. (2012). Inspired by El Duende: One-canvas process painting in art therapy supervision. *Art Therapy: Journal of the American Art Therapy Association, 29*(4), 166–173. doi:10.1080/07421656.2013.730024

Milne, D., & Watkins, C. E. (2014). Defining and understanding clinical supervision: A functional approach. In C. Edward Watkins, Jr. & D. L. Milne (Eds.), *The Wiley international handbook of clinical supervision* (pp. 3–19). Chichester, UK: John Wiley & Sons.

Moon, B. L. (2003). *Essentials of art therapy education and practice.* Springfield, IL: Charles C. Thomas.

Nelson, M. L., Barnes, K. L., Evans, A. L., & Triggiano, P. J. (2008). Working with conflict in clinical supervision: Wise supervisors' perspectives. *Journal of Counseling Psychology, 55*(2), 172.

O'Donovan, A., Halford, W. K., & Walters, B. (2011). Towards best practice supervision of clinical psychology trainees. *Australian Psychologist, 46*(2), 101–112. doi:https://doi.org/10.1111/j.1742-9544.2011.00033.x

Pearson, Q. M. (2006). Psychotherapy-driven supervision: Integrating counseling theories into role-based supervision. *Journal of Mental Health Counseling, 28*, 241–252.

Purswell, K. E., & Stulmaker, H. L. (2015). Expressive arts in supervision: Choosing developmentally appropriate interventions. *International Journal of Play Therapy, 24*(2), 103–117. doi:http://dx.doi.org/10.1037/a0039134

Robbins, A. (2007). The art of supervision. In J. Schaverien & C. Case (Eds.), *Supervision of art psychotherapy: A theoretical and practical handbook* (pp. 153–166). New York, NY: Routledge.

Rogers, C. (1977). *Carl Rogers on personal power: Inner strength and its revolutionary impact*. New York, NY: Delacorte Press.

Sharp, J. E., & Rhinehart, A. J. (2018). Infusing Mindfulness and Character Strengths in Supervision to Promote Beginning Supervisee Development. *Journal of Counselor Practice, 9*(1), 64–80.

Stinchfield, T. A., Hill, N. R., & Kleist, D. M. (2007). The reflective model of triadic supervision: Defining an emerging modality. *Counselor Education and Supervision, 46*(3), 172–183.

Sturm, D. C., Presbury, J., & Echterling, L. G. (2012). The elements: A model of mindful supervision. *Journal of Creativity in Mental Health, 7*(3), 222–232.

Sweitzer, H. F., & King, M. A. (2018). *The successful internship: Personal, professional, and civic development in experiential learning* (5 ed.). Boston, MA: Cengage.

Vec, T., Vec, T. R., & Žorga, S. (2014). Understanding how supervision works and what it can achieve. In C. Edward Watkins, Jr. & D. L. Milne (Eds.), *The Wiley international handbook of clinical supervision* (pp. 103–127). Chichester, UK: John Wiley & Sons.

Watkins, C. E., Jr. (2017). Convergence in psychotherapy supervision: A common factors, common processes, common practices perspective. *Journal of Psychotherapy Integration, 27*(2), 140–152.

Watkins, C. E., & Wang, D. C. (2014). On the education of clinical supervisors. In C. Edward Watkins, Jr. & D. L. Milne (Eds.), *The Wiley international handbook of clinical supervision* (pp. 177–203). Chichester, UK: John Wiley & Sons.

Wilson, L., Riley, S., & Wadeson, H. (1984). Art therapy supervision. *Art Therapy: Journal of the American Art Therapy Association, 1*(3), 100–105. doi:10.1080/07421656.1984.10758761

Yalom, I. D., & Leszcz, M. (2005). *The theory and practice of group psychotherapy* (5th ed.). New York, NY: Basic Books.

Ybrandt, H., Sundin, E. C., & Capone, G. (2016). Trainee therapists' views on the alliance in psychotherapy and supervision: a longitudinal study. *British Journal of Guidance & Counselling, 44*(5), 530–539.

3   What Supervisees Need to Know about Supervision

Introduction

Art therapists are supervised throughout their careers. Hopefully, this is highly desirable to the supervisee and received as a form of "life-long learning and development" (Vec, Vec, & Žorga, 2014, p. 103) allowing the content and subsequent gains of supervision to evolve as needs change over time. The advantages of a solid, supportive supervisory relationship are diverse, and include the potential for ongoing mentorship, increasing clinical competency, space to routinely reframe mistakes as opportunities, a chance to reduce burnout, and the ability to provide professional stability during high-stress periods and moments of self-doubt. Embracing a largely open, curious, and positive mindset around supervision is critical, and may limit damage if a difficult supervisory relationship or rupture occurs. To best engage supervision, it is vital to understand the roles and corresponding responsibilities of engaging in a strong and productive supervisory relationship (Borders et al., 2014; Sweitzer & King, 2018).

In this chapter, we explore best practices for supervision by naming ideal supervisee qualities, suggesting actionable items for engaging in supervision, and sharing how supervision differs during stages of your career. We have modified and built upon Sweitzer and King's (2018) *who, what, where, when, why,* and *how* of supervision and Delano's (2001) 13 guidelines to create a framework for art therapy supervision. Our intent for this chapter is to inform students, new professionals, and even more seasoned supervisees how to distinguish and hold best practices as a supervisee. The skills we address in this chapter are beneficial throughout any supervisory relationship.

How to Best Receive Supervision

Passively attending to supervision is not sufficient. As a supervisee, it is imperative to actively receive and engage supervision with the same eagerness, approachability, and accountability as a client session. Within the supervisory dynamic, a supervisee is encouraged to activate their power and embrace a professional capacity for self-reflection. It is essential for a supervisee to generate strength, competence, and a vulnerable openness in order to further articulate their needs, well-intentioned mistakes, unintended oversights, unmet expectations, and self-reflections. Rønnestad and Skovholt (2003) identify the aptitude for self-reflection as the most important characteristic for professional growth.

Sarnat's (2010) definition of self-reflective competence is germane to all: self-reflection "requires a highly developed capacity to bear, observe, think about, and make psychotherapeutic use of one's own emotional, bodily, and fantasy experiences when in interaction with a client" (p. 23). Communication of these experiences and recognition of competence, as a supervisee, is often complicated by reactions of false bravado, unwarranted embarrassment, and gratuitous apology. Thus, developing a capacity for self-reflection is necessary for identifying areas of competence, coaxing out vulnerabilities, and linking influences, and avoiding inadvertent counterproductive actions such as creating a power struggle, awkwardness, or simply acquiescing in order to please. In these moments, rather than projecting an image of perfection or being regarded as unduly agreeable, self-reflection helps maintain focus on becoming a better supervisee.

Ideal Supervisee Qualities

The supervisory relationship benefits greatly when supervisees possess an authentic interest in and desire for the supervisory process. Although many supervisees experience some level of apprehension, it is incredibly helpful when a supervisee chooses to be present, dependable, and vulnerable, and actively participate, despite any anxieties they may have. When this mindset is paired with personal enthusiasm and eagerness rather than the threat of judgment, it is easier to remain motivated and take the initiative in learning. This focused approach allows for flexibility within the interpersonal relationship, the theoretical approach, and the clinical application. Ideal supervisee qualities include:

- Showing interest and desire;
- Being present and dependable;
- Exhibiting openness and authenticity;
- Compatibility;
- Being vulnerable through self-disclosure with minimal defensiveness;
- Engaging with introspection, psychological mindfulness, and interpersonal curiosity; and
- Attending to personal dynamics.

Interest and Desire

A genuine interest, enthusiasm, and desire for supervision (Berger & Buchholz, 1993; Watkins, 2017) is demonstrated first and foremost by arriving on time, being prepared to learn, and paying careful attention to the supervisory process. Bring questions to supervision, artwork created by your clients, artwork you created in response to your clients, articles of interest, and anything else that shows your interest and desire to learn. In Vignette 3.1, Daniel suggests some additional ways in which he could have been more engaged in supervision.

Vignette 3.1 Showing Genuine Interest

Daniel's Story

Looking back, I realize that early on in my graduate training I did not know how to receive supervision, attend supervision with an appropriate interest, or express a genuine desire in the supervisory relationship. Adding to the dynamic was an inexperienced supervisor who often appeared disinterested, and, in hindsight, was potentially experiencing burnout. Although initially anxiety-provoking, supervision became less worrisome as I quickly realized the spotlight could be shifted away from me. Since I had no expectations of supervision, and my supervisor most likely had little or no training in supervision, she steered my shortened supervision time towards expressing her disappointment over site limitations, feelings of powerlessness with unmotivated clients, and a litany of other issues unrelated to progressing my clinical knowledge or creating critical dialogue reflecting on my experience. Sadly, I eagerly supported this shift in focus away from me. I experienced immediate relief when my vulnerabilities and shortcomings were not going to be reviewed, highlighted, or confronted.

Further complicating my situation was the intimidation I felt as an inexperienced student in an unfamiliar city. Late in the academic term, as I listened to classmates speak of their supervisory relationships, I realized the consequences of not receiving the supervision I deserved. I shared my concerns with my educational setting and requested a new site with a strong supervisor for the following semester.

In retrospect, I was unaware of how my privilege as a white man may have impacted the supervisory relationship with a woman who was younger than I was. Her supervisory power may have been moderated by social location. Had I put aside my fears of being exposed and demonstrated an interest and desire in my own supervision, there is a chance I could have learned more about the population I was working with, while also helping an art therapy colleague become a better supervisor. These actions could have been quite simple, such as formulating population-related questions, requesting or researching articles on the population, and preparing an agenda for supervision. A more direct intervention on my part may have included discussions on the purpose of supervision and setting boundaries that brought the focus of supervision back to my learning and self-reflection.

Present and Dependable

Arriving on time, as expected, ready to learn and share observations and clinical interactions, are aspects of being present and dependable. Consistently arriving late to supervision can make it seem like you are prioritizing other tasks or demonstrates carelessness, lack of awareness, or simply an attempt to dodge supervision. Likewise, being on time and engaging in small talk may be helpful in establishing surface rapport, but may also serve as a less obvious or unconscious distraction if it leads to dancing around the agenda. For example, an evasive supervisee can easily sidetrack a harried supervisor by shifting the focus elsewhere, such as to the staff chatter buzzing around the organization, or a recent episode of a must-watch television series.

When a supervisee engages with being present and dependable, the depth of the dynamic with a skillful supervisor is ready to be enhanced. Likewise, a supervisee that remains present and maintains focus may help reign in a meandering supervisor. "Emotions may occur outside of awareness or drive behavior before one clearly acknowledges them" when one is less mindfully aware (Brown & Ryan, 2003, p. 823). Being present starts with being on time, but the significance here is on the profounder meaning of being fully present in the moment with attention given to the layers of learning, apposite self-disclosure, and deepening of the therapist identity. "For example, rumination, absorption in the past, or fantasies and anxieties about the future can pull one away from what is taking place in the present" (Brown & Ryan, 2003, p. 823).

Openness and Authenticity

Openness and authenticity can minimize defensiveness and pave the way to share and discuss errors, identify opportunities for growth, and reveal a realistic level of functioning. "To promote openness and to reinforce best practices, ethnic background, age, sexual orientation, and other diversity aspects pertinent to the supervisor and the supervisee should be discussed as it relates to the supervision and the work with clients" (Sue & Sue, 2007, p. 277). More importantly, the supervisee can share any preconceptions, expectations, hopes, worries, and fears. "Openness about these matters eases the level of anxiety; assists in identifying the most salient areas of focus; and provides a framework for future evaluative and/or problem solving discussions" (Berger & Buchholz, 1993, p. 87).

In other words, openness can be simply defined as allowing oneself to be genuinely witnessed. Authenticity is a form of sincerity, without pretense, that is faithful to a supervisee's individuality, spirit, and integrity. As a supervisee, it is important to be seen from all perspectives and not merely a crafted, well-manicured lens. Openness allows for the lessons hidden within mistakes to be revealed, evaluated, and assimilated. Embraced missteps can be leveraged through supervision for a deeper level of understanding and accountability. This openness is all within the context of a training therapist and requires established, yet flexible, boundaries between the personal and professional.

Compatibility

A well-suited supervisory match allows the supervisee "to feel accepted at their own level and know their capacity to grow and learn from mistakes is a factor being assessed by supervisors" (Wilson, Riley, & Wadeson, 1984, p. 101). Investing in the supervisory relationship can reap long-term benefits since supervisors can hold indeterminate power and influence depending on future reference needs. For instance, it is common practice to request a recommendation for a job search, doctoral application, accreditation, or licensure application from a former supervisor many years after the supervision has taken place.

Stripped to its simplest form, attentive supervisors "strive to embrace, empower, and emancipate the therapeutic potential of the supervisees with whom we have the privilege to work" (Watkins, 2012, p. 193). This approach is called strength finding, and is based on an inherent confidence in the therapeutic promise of each supervisee. This approach works to galvanize the therapist identity and decision-making. Similarly, a supervisee strives to believe "in the supervisory expertise of the supervisor and embraces the supervision being delivered" (Watkins, 2017, p. 204). This compatible combination of attentive supervisor and supervisee contributes to the ability to appropriately receive supervision.

Self-disclosure and Minimal Defensiveness

Supervisees can actively minimize defensiveness by assuming an approach steeped in professionally appropriate self-disclosure, a willingness to grow, risk-taking, and being receptive to feedback. When struggling with specific cases, appropriate self-disclosure by the supervisee is critical, especially when the supervisor relies on self-reports (Kreider, 2014, p. 260). If not encouraged, the lack of supervisee self-disclosure may manifest as defensiveness within the supervisory relationship and interfere in the accuracy of self-reporting on sessions, clients, or the supervisory relationship.

Introspection, Psychological Mindedness, and Interpersonal Curiosity

Introspection, psychological mindedness, and interpersonal curiosity are three critical factors that assist in fostering reflection (Berger & Buchholz, 1993). Introspection allows for personal thoughts, emotions, and sensations to be self-examined and contemplated as they relate to therapeutic interchanges. For example, this may lead to identifying implicit biases, unresolved family dynamics, a potential savior complex, or underlying physiological reactions that are unconsciously influencing supervisory and client interactions. Psychological mindedness and interpersonal curiosity are similar to introspection but often expand from the personal – the therapist's self-awareness – to client motives and intentions. Litman and Pezzo (2007) define curiosity as an inherent desire to "stimulate interest or relieve uncertainty" (p. 1448) through gaining new information. Interpersonal curiosity is the internal impetus to pursue material concerning people. Psychological mindedness in therapy entails an "interest in and ability to extract and make sense of psychological information (thoughts, feelings and behaviours) from a situation," and through the very nature of therapist's role and training "demand[s] therapists think about motives, distortions and inner experiences of others" (Rai, Punia, Choudhury, & Mathew, 2015, p. 130).

"Further, clinical supervisors use self-reflections related to learner interactions to appraise thoughts, emotions, and behavior, and how each affects the learner's experience in supervision" (Curtis, Elkins, Duran, & Venta, 2016, p. 134). Supervision is a place to cultivate countertransference and clinical interactions and interventions. Through a theoretical perspective, supervision integrates psychological mindedness, introspection, and interpersonal curiosity. Without this cultivation, supervisees will have limited personal insight, no matter how strong their intellect or how conscientious they are, and may find it difficult to gauge "the interpersonal dynamics within therapy and use that information to develop appropriate strategies" (Barrett & Barber, 2005, p. 172).

To gain personal insight, it is critical to understand the differences between supervision and therapy by establishing boundaries for self-examination. This allows the supervisee to fully realize the focus and create clear limits for the supervisory relationship, which precludes addressing personal problems and mental health issues (Case, 2007; Wilson et al., 1984). Maintaining mental health through psychotherapy and other self-care measures is important. Wood contends the "quality of containment" provided to clients is directly related to the psychological health of the therapist (2007, p. 190). This considered approach allows the supervisee to fully differentiate and actively participate in both supervision and personal therapy.

Personal Dynamics

Introspection, psychological mindedness, and interpersonal curiosity fuel the supervisee's ability to identify and address the potential of their unique personal dynamics to sway the supervisory and therapeutic processes. Consciousness and comprehension of this sway better prepares supervisees to appreciate and engage cultural influences. Supervisees who demonstrate responsiveness to the "ways in which their own culture affects them … respect the diversity of values espoused by other cultures" (Corey, 2013, p. 20) and are better equipped for self-reflection and disclosure in supervision.

One vital area is racial self-understanding, which is the prerequisite for cultural competence and cultural humility. Supervisees

> need to be challenged to explore their own racial identities and their feelings about other racial groups. This is equally true for understanding how microaggressions, especially those of the therapist, influence the therapeutic process. Understanding your social location brings to the surface possible prejudices and biases that inform racial microaggressions.
>
> (Sue et al., 2007, p. 283)

Sue et al. (2007) identified nine categories of microaggressions with clear themes that can be effective for supervisees' self-reflection of their work: "alien in one's own land, ascription of intelligence, color blindness, criminality/assumption of criminal status, denial of individual racism, myth of meritocracy, pathologizing cultural values/communication styles, second-class status, and environmental invalidation" (p. 275). The willingness to identify, investigate, and own microaggressions demonstrates respect, empathy, and appreciation for individual differences. These explorations can be utilized in supervision to begin accepting responsibility for the consequences of related behavior. Supervision, ideally, is a place that affords the potential to "ponder and free-associate" (Wood, 2007, p. 185) when the "supervisor offers a non-judgmental holding relationship," granting space to hold expressions such as guilt, desolation, and embarrassment (Robbins, 2007, p. 154). The topics of race, ethnicity, and socio-cultural differences as they relate to supervision are covered more thoroughly in Part 3.

Receiving Supervision

We firmly believe supervisees must not wait for a supervisee to become a better supervisor. There are many ways that a supervisee can support their supervisors. With the understanding that supervision is a relationship, we provide some actionable items for supervisees to best take ownership of supervision. This includes a self-assessment to determine the kind of learner you are, what you want to get out of supervision, and how this relates to the supervision style of your supervisor.

We have modified Sweitzer and King's (2018) categories of the supervisor, the supervision itself, and the location, and Delano's (2001) 13 guidelines to effectively own your supervision to create a framework for art therapy supervision for art therapy supervisees.

The Supervisor(s)

The logistics of identifying your supervisor(s), the time, and the place are basic but essential in establishing some of the who and where of supervision.

- Identify your supervisor-of-record and their education and credentials. Compile and store this information in an easily retrievable manner for licensure, registration, and certifications in the future. If contact information is site-specific, consider requesting additional professional and/or personal email address for your supervisor(s) in the event they leave the site.
- Identify additional staff (and their education and credentials) designated to supervise your work and request alternate contact information.
- Identify back-up supervisor(s) and how to contact them when your supervisor-of-record is not available. Have some clarity around expectations and appropriate circumstances for contacting a back-up supervisor. Do not hesitate to judiciously utilize all avenues within the accepted boundaries and supervision.
- Determine the location and time for supervisory individual or group sessions. Supervision ought to be held at regularly scheduled times to permit ample transition and prep time. Verify if meetings will be face-to-face, or will some meetings take place remotely in a Health Insurance Portability and Accountability Act (HIPAA)-compliant manner (e.g., doxy.me software). See Part 4, *Locations, Places, and Spaces: Supervision Formats*, for more detailed information on individual, group, and distance supervision.
- Research your supervisor. A supervisee can learn more about their supervisor through research on LinkedIn or other professional social media platforms, as well as articles they have authored, a published bio or CV, and presentations. Limit social media exploration to professional accounts.
- Maintain a delicate balance of acknowledging and periodically deferring to a supervisor's work demands and related pressures while still achieving the need for consistent, uninterrupted supervision. If a supervisor cancels or moves supervision on a regular basis, a supervisee can explore a more stable scheduled time.

The Supervision Session

Establishing expectations surrounding agendas, expectations, conflict, and other session basics helps build the foundation of a successful supervisory alliance.

- Clarify the focus and expectations for you and your supervisor during supervisory sessions. It is important to know what is included, how the agenda is set, protocols for sharing artwork, and how artmaking will be incorporated. If artmaking is not the norm, investigate whether they are open to artmaking.
- A mutually-agreed-upon agenda can help drive and maintain focus in supervision by demonstrating investment in learning and building trust with a supervisor. For transparency, the agenda should be provided a minimum of 24 hours in advance. Delano (2001) suggests a shared model, essentially allowing a third of the agenda to be driven by the supervisee, a third by the supervisor, and the last third to allow for space for where the conversation goes. Artmaking can easily fit into one of these thirds; if unrelated to the rest of the agenda, artmaking can potentially be a fourth element.
- Supervision is an opportunity for growth and should not be a threat or therapy. Nonetheless, you have permission to grow personally in supervision. Reframing supervision, from merely being a monitoring device, and thus a potential threat, to a mindset of opportunity, is essential and quite liberating.
- Request the assessment methods applied to determine progress in each situation. Students may be evaluated through campus-based methods (e.g., midterm and end-of-term evaluations) and professionals through employer-assigned standards (e.g., probationary period, yearly evaluations). If not provided, a new hire can request a blank evaluation form, rating rubric, and the intended review timeline within the first few weeks of starting. The evaluation feedback allows a supervisee to appropriately understand level of functioning in respect to expectations. Most employers have structured evaluation timelines for new employees and annual reviews thereafter. Even if not requested by a supervisor, it is helpful to independently complete the evaluation document as a supervisee to see how the results align. If weekly supervision sessions are being utilized properly there should be no surprises, only confirmations of what is being conveyed and discussed in supervision.
- Thoroughly take advantage of the review process if you receive an unexpectedly difficult review. When the review is shared, limit interruptions, engage with active listening, set aside defensiveness, write notes, and save your comments until the supervisor finishes. Stay objective, allow time for reflection, and consider a candid, two-way

feedback approach during the meeting. However, the focus must remain on the supervisee; this is not a time to note a supervisor's flaws or interpersonal dynamics. Schedule a separate meeting to discuss these types of issues. This is a time to explore the ways the supervisee is seen by the supervisor. Make art in any manner helpful to the process. This may be in preparation for the meeting or after to explore material churned up from the evaluation on a deeper level. If artmaking is a routine part of supervisory sessions, there may be a way to incorporate art during the evaluation meeting.

- Delano (2001) encourages an openness to seek supervision anytime and from anyone. This approach is not crafted to circumvent or minimize routine supervision and is ideally undertaken with a supervisor's guidance. Embrace all interactions as an opportunity to be taught, observe, and have a deeper understanding of the therapeutic process. Initiate dialogue with colleagues who have specific areas of expertise, attended a recent training, or have a differing therapeutic approach.

- According to Delano (2001), supervisors "have an obligation to assess how a supervisee best learns and then attempt to teach that way" (p. 63). Likewise, it is important for a supervisee to take a step back and acknowledge a supervisor's strength in teaching and leverage that style for maximum learning. Determining whether a supervisor excels at meticulous theoretical explanations or at direct practice may be prescriptive in establishing the best approach to an agenda topic.

- Whether in group or individual supervision, fully participating by engaging in verbal and non-verbal forms of participation, contributing by sharing pertinent observations, asking needed questions, and encouraging others helps to temper the temptation to hide and not take risks.

- Understand the structure of supervision and how it fits with your style of learning. Some supervisors emphasize a more didactic method while others are more experiential and conversational. Regardless of your supervisor's style, determine how to maximize the experience to attain your learning goals through your learning style. Determine how artmaking may be incorporated within the structure of supervision to enhance your learning style.

- Identify the formal ways in which you are being supervised. Determine whether it will be individual supervision, group supervision, team meetings or some combination, and whether the format will include experientials. Clarify the intent of your role in each supervisory setting.

- Determine informal methods for obtaining supervision. This may include spontaneous check-ins between formal supervision sessions, beginning- or end-of-shift updates, or after group debriefings.

Managing Up

This is an empowering approach where you cultivate skills to better manage the supervisory relationship by braving the traditional top-down management flow. This entails stepping up, even in a relationship that is working well, to shift dynamics in a manner that best positions the supervision for success. In many ways, managing up is a way of identifying blind spots and barriers in the supervisory relationship, and maneuvering to reduce impact by providing clarification for supervisee requisites and expectations. Ways to manage up include creating an agenda, refocusing a wandering supervision session, or simply requiring uninterrupted and private time for supervision.

Delano (2001, p. 62) says, "The most direct and efficient way to get information is to ask questions." Ideally, the invitation and expectation to ask engaging, direct, and rapport-building questions is encouraged and embraced. This form of active participation is not lightly disguised flattery or pleasant passive aggression. Questions should range from client- and site-specific questions, to population-generated questions, to questions about the field at large. See Box 3.1 for a scenario where an intern's responses reflect different levels of reaction and inquiry to a co-led art therapy group.

> **Box 3.1 Consider the Following …**
>
> An art therapy intern co-leads a difficult and frenzied art therapy group with their supervisor. Pay attention to how language impacts the supervisee's perspective of themselves, their supervisor, and the group.
>
> INTERN RESPONSE #1: Cool, you were amazing in group. Are you always that good? I could never do that!
>
> INTERN RESPONSE #2: What happened in there? When Michaela began addressing the group I simply wanted to be anywhere but that room. How do you do this work?
>
> INTERN RESPONSE #3: Wow, that was an intense group. I was really feeling the tension throughout my body. I appreciated how you intervened by engaging Lee to respond to Michaela. From my perspective, that really brought Michaela more fully into the group dynamics. What prompted your decision to engage Lee at that moment?
>
> The first response by the supervisee is superficial yet flattering and self-deprecating, engaging the supervisor with a single closed

question. The second response appropriately shares the supervisee's reaction to a specific situation in the group, yet fails to ask open-ended questions to further her learning and understanding of the clinical interventions. The final response shares an appropriate emotional response, sites a particular intervention, provides an assessment of what transpired, and ends with a well-placed, open-ended question to gain stronger clinical insight of a certain interaction.

- Strike a balance by learning from multiple resources. Complement your work with your supervisor with internal and external training and conferences. Even with an experienced supervisor working within a productive dynamic, an outside perspective can provide a fresh perspective. Delano (2001) encourages a supervisee to create an image as a "thirsty learner" (p. 63). Continually learning and being exposed to new theories and approaches enhances growth and helps supervisees establish a professional identity. Attending training boosts the potential to not only learning from the instructor but also those in attendance.

- Every so often, maybe more frequently, a supervisee is perplexed and exasperated by a supervisor's decision regarding a clinical or administrative matter. Delano identifies "two magic questions": "What information do they have that I don't that will help me to understand this better?" and "What information do I have that they don't that will help them see it my way?" Understanding these situations may provide clarity on how decisions are made and reduce frustration (Delano, 2001, p. 62).

- Confrontation is frequently avoided and often executed ineffectively, magnifying the power differential within the supervisory relationship. However, a direct and constructive confrontation often lessens the likelihood of experiencing a range of uncomfortable emotions such as anger or disappointment, or potentially experiencing a rupture of trust. According to Overton and Lowry, determining whether to confront is the first decision to make when faced with conflict, and requires exploration of potential gains and risks of addressing the specific issue. If the issue is sufficiently troublesome, in a way that influences your behavior or bears on your conscience, consider addressing it. They emphasize the need to clearly delineate and distinguish "the perceived difficulty of the conversation with determination of whether it will be beneficial and appropriate to proceed" (2013, p. 261). To fruitfully present and receive constructive confrontation takes practice and preparation. Embracing constructive confrontation and conflict with a positive approach and the ability to sit with the conversation reduces the opportunity for misunderstandings, defensiveness, and hurt feelings, while promoting the likelihood of a successful confrontation resulting in the desired change. Constructive confrontation is a compelling and essential practice in the supervisory relationship.

Being a Supervisee at Different Stages in Your Career

The beautiful thing about being an art therapist is that you can never know everything. We change, our clients change, and the world changes. Our understanding of ourselves, our clients, and the world we live in also changes. Supervision enhances our clinical work by providing space and time to focus on being the best art therapists we can be to the people we work with. While all therapists begin their supervision journey while in school, supervision continues as a professional to obtain licensure and/or credentials, and beyond.

Student Intern

The intentional design of the graduate student internship affords opportunity to learn, take risks, implement coursework, and experience theory in practice. However, internships differ greatly between different placements and educational programs. Students may or may not be able to select the specific population, site, and/or supervisor. Even when students have the ability to choose, some sites have a competitive application process involving submission of a resume, references, and an interview prior to the final selection. Other sites are less formal in their internship selection process and operate on a first-come, first-given approach.

Selecting an Internship

As a supervisee, best practices start before the internship is secured. Knowing the best personal balance ought to increase the likelihood for success in the internship. If given the opportunity to interview, be curious about the supervisor's experience with art therapy, clinical approach, advanced training, and supervisory style, and the significance of the intern role from their viewpoint. The student may want to consider the following factors:

- Am I more interested in working with a specific supervisor or a specific client population?
- Am I more interested in learning from an art therapy supervisor or a non-art therapy supervisor practicing with a favored population?
- What kinds of students have been most successful and satisfied in supervision (or at this site) (Pearson, 2004)?

- What kinds of students have been least successful or satisfied (Pearson, 2004)?

Starting an Internship

At the start of an internship, a student may experience nervous anticipation and excitement that often slips into "waves of anxiety, confusion, uncertainty, vulnerability and helplessness" (Edwards, 1993, p. 214). These emotions are potentially heightened by an unfamiliar setting, a new client population, the inherent disconnect of implementing theory into practice, and the task of building rapport with a clinical supervisor. This presents a unique opportunity to delve into the clinical work as well as dynamically joining the supervisory relationship to cultivate self-efficacy. In this instance, self-efficacy "is the belief that the individual has both the confidence and competence necessary" to facilitate effective psychotherapy (Curtis et al., 2016, p. 134).

Site Supervisor

The relationship between a student and the internship site supervisor is an interconnected and dual relationship in multiple ways. First and foremost, the supervisor is liable for the oversight and provision of ethical and competent services to clients, and is thus a gatekeeper of the profession (Borders et al., 2014; Gaete & Ottar, 2015; Pearson, 2004). Secondly, the supervisor is responsible for the ongoing assessment and communication of student skill and knowledge acquisition, both within the site and to the university internship coordinator or other representatives. A supervisor's ability to observe a student may be limited; thus, a supervisor's assessments of "skills and knowledge are impacted by the student's behaviors in supervision" (Pearson, 2004, p. 362). To gain an accurate understanding of a student's functioning hinges on the ability of the supervisory relationship to move towards direct, truthful, and vulnerable communication. "Hiding mistakes and challenges makes beginning students … seem defensive or arrogant and increases the real threat to students and their supervisors by almost guaranteeing that real, versus imagined, problems will occur" (Pearson, 2004, p. 367). Thus, operating with the intent of increasing transparency lessens the urge to withhold errors and blind spots, reducing the likelihood that a student appears self-justifying or condescending.

Campus Supervisor

Although client care is of utmost importance, the relationship between the student intern and the campus supervisor centers on the application of clinical theory within the internship setting and is primarily viewed through an academic lens, as course assignments are often given and graded. This differs from the relationship with the site supervisor who places considerable attention on the dynamics and operation of the internship site as a whole, but largely hones in on the client care, clinical interactions, and countertransference of the intern.

Group supervision, provided by the campus supervisor, is the method in which art therapy students engage on-campus supervision. This format allocates time to share internship experiences with others at a similar stage of therapist development (i.e., year of fieldwork). This allows the sensations of being overwhelmed, often handled in isolation, to be normalized. Ideally, exposure to different styles, methods, and formats of supervision is included in the class format. Art-based supervision is a method often utilized for "improving case conceptualization skills, developing self-awareness, facilitating awareness of transference and countertransference, exploring the supervisory relationship, reducing stress, and improving well-being" (Deaver & Shiflett, 2011, p. 272). For more information on the different forms of supervision refer to Part 4, and for additional methods turn to Chapter 7. Although art is seemingly inherent in art therapy supervision, in our observation and experiences it is often not readily or fully engaged. However, campus supervisors are strategically positioned to establish the bond of artmaking as a structure for establishing and upholding the art therapist identity (Deaver & Shiflett, 2011; Miller, 2012; Moon & Nolan, 2019; Robb & Miller, 2017; Wadeson, 2003). For example, the art therapist identity can be reinforced when art, created in response to a session, promotes "attention to intense responses to treatment and offer a means to investigate their deeper meaning, which in turn can inform treatment and bring personal insights" (Fish, 2012, p. 138).

Student Outlook

Supervision is not a bystander exercise but rather a relational interaction. How a student attends to supervision influences the outcome. An eager, enthusiastic student demonstrating great interest and desire to learn will likely be more motivated and responsive, and take initiative to help shape the supervisory relationship. This does not necessarily mean a gregarious presence is required; rather, being fully present in a mindful, forthcoming, and purposeful manner is central. This prepares a supervisee to receive a range of feedback as many supervisees feel anxious and fear exposure, consequently viewing supervision as a place to be judged, punitively reviewed, and criticized. Bing-You and Trowbridge (2009) maintain students with "distressing reactions to feedback tend to devalue it as not useful" (p. 1330) and may avoid feedback all together as an act of self-preservation, viewing it as a personal attack. Devalued and discounted feedback does not lead to enhanced functioning. By crafting an ability to receive critical feedback, a supervisee is more likely to experience improved performance.

Over the years, countless students have been drawn to the field of art therapy because they identify as compassionate listeners imparting caring advice to family and peers. Rønnestad and Skovholt identify this period of "trying to help others to make decisions, resolve problems and improve relationships" as the Lay Helper Phase (2003, p. 10). In contrast to the start of the internship, this role feels authentic and quite natural as the lay helper who "provides strong emotional support, and gives advice based on one's own experience" often promptly recognizes the problem (Rønnestad & Skovholt, 2003, p. 10). For others entering the field of art therapy, they have personally utilized art as a tool for personal growth and survival, intuitively comprehending the healing nature of the art process. Few of these well-honed skills (e.g., advice-giving), first developed as a trusted confidant or an art for self-healing, transfer perfectly to a professional role. As a student, supervision is a place to cultivate considerations of your clinical interventions with a psychological mind-edness, contemplate your motivations with introspection, and expand your interpersonal curiosity through a theoretical perspective.

Student supervisees are encouraged to investigate their authentic artistic voice to better understand themselves as art therapists, and to "use image making to help them process the feelings evoked by difficult clinical material" (Schaverien & Case, 2007, p. 172). Stark, Frels, and Garza (2011) suggest "utilizing metaphor creates therapeutic distance, allowing for supervisees to go deeper" (p. 280). One approach, described by Miller (2012), is inspired by the artistic struggle of *el duende*. This one-canvas process painting, layered with clinical insight amid archetypal awareness "becomes a metaphoric reflection of the students' evolving selves as they learn to become art therapists" (Miller, 2012, p. 166).

New Professional

The transition from a student who is paying tuition to a financially compensated new professional drastically alters your routine campus support. Classroom and studio interactions with fellow students and professors often come to a sudden close after several intense years along a similar academic timeline. This is especially true for those who were trained within a cohort model where a healthy dependency and network of academic and emotional support has been established. Further separating factors include relocating from the geographical location of the academic setting, competition for employment, and starting as a professional at different times and environments than others in the cohort.

New professionals are typically hired into existing teams. The team may include additional art therapists or mental health professionals, and potentially staff from other disciplines. In some cases, the hiring manager may be the direct supervisor. Either way, acclimating strategies are an important topic within the early supervision meetings since entering a well-established team requires sensitivity and engagement skills. Insulating initial connections to team members with similar job titles and education limits learning and understanding of the site. Building a working relationship with the direct supervisor and the entire team is of utmost importance to ease the transition. Therefore, we encourage interdisciplinary interactions and purposeful relationship-building.

An intern may be hired and transition to a staff position after completing a successful internship at their field placement. In this situation, the new professional builds upon the gains made during internship; though the supervisory dynamic will adjust as the employee supervision changes focus to a different set of responsibilities. Although clinical growth continues as a central element, a shift from educational outcomes to agency deliverables often occurs, which may increase the administrative aspect of supervision. "Administrative supervision is primarily concerned with the supervisee's functioning as an employee, evaluation of supervisee work practices, and the clinical programs of the organization within which the supervisor and supervisee operate" (Kreider, 2014, p. 258). New professionals, and even more seasoned art therapists, may consider moving to a new locale. See Box 3.2 for tips to consider.

Box 3.2 Tips for Relocating New Professionals

If relocating to a new job in a different area, be sure to connect with local art therapists, creative arts therapists, and/or psychotherapists to build community. Obtaining a local supervisor and not opting for a long-distance relationship with a former supervisor or professor could also aid in learning more about a new locale. Social media, such as LinkedIn; local art therapy chapters; and area educational institutions are potential spaces to network.

Experienced Professional

A challenging client, unfamiliar clinical issues, and the ethical responsibility to continue providing the highest level of care are just a few of the reasons why an art therapist with extensive experience may engage in additional supervision through peer consultation, group supervision, and contracted individual supervision. As noted by Yasmine's supervisee, "It feels exciting to be in a place where I am receiving supervision by choice, not to meet the requirements of governing agencies" (B. Asch, personal communication, September 5, 2019). We further describe the benefits and differences between seeking out an individual art therapy supervisor in

Chapter 9, *Individual and Dyad Supervision*, and a non-art therapy supervisor in Chapter 7, *Disciplinary Differences: When Your Supervisor Is Not an Art Therapist.*

Experienced art therapists who engage in direct client work over the pursuit of supervisory or management positions will likely, in time, report to a professionally and chronologically younger supervisor. Although not inherently problematic, it can be a point of tension if the power dynamic is not managed in a thoughtful, beneficial manner. As a supervisee, it is important to remain fully engaged in the supervisory relationship by honoring the role, allowing the supervisor to hold space for clinical reflection, administrative details, and the potential for growth. Directly acknowledging the differing career stages may eliminate any unfounded assumptions and unintended consequences that could be lingering in unspoken expectations.

A Learning Curve: "How Do I Learn All of This?!"

This chapter might be a bit daunting – it is full of ideals. Let us reassure you, as a supervisee you will not always do the right thing; mistakes will be made, and learning may feel slow. Wisdom by trial and error, making blunders, and floundering at times are unequivocally part of the process to gain competence and confidence. Just as an art therapist works to strengthen their skill set through practice and ongoing education, a supervisee continues in their journey for aptitude.

Takeaways

- Determining your motivation for supervision, as well as clearly understanding the roles and corresponding responsibilities, demonstrates receptiveness to take part in a productive supervisory relationship.
- Effectively owning your supervision is less complex when integrating our adaption of Delano's 13 guidelines.
- Identification and self-disclosure of learning styles in supervision increases openness, authenticity, and communication in supervision.
- The articulations of needs, well-intentioned mistakes, unintended oversights, and unmet expectations, as well as self-reflections, are critical to a supervisee's success in supervision.
- A challenging client, unfamiliar clinical issues, or the ethical responsibility to continue providing the highest level of care are several reasons to seek additional supervision through peer consultation, group supervision, and contracted individual supervision.
- Incorporating a willingness to identify, investigate, and own microaggressions allows an art therapist to accept responsibility for their

consequences as well as demonstrating respect, empathy, and appreciation for individual differences.

• Managing up is an empowering approach that braves the traditional top-down management flow without unnecessary confrontation.

Practice Prompts

Creating a Triptych of Supervisee Qualities

Utilizing art materials of your choice, create a triptych with the following prompts to further explore individual supervisee qualities:

• On the first panel recognize three qualities of an ideal supervisee that you presently embody.
• On the second panel acknowledge three qualities an ideal supervisee you are currently working towards attaining.
• On the final panel integrate the six qualities.
• Silently view the triptych and create a one-page witness-response writing.

Mapping Supervision Experiences

Create a roadmap or genogram of your (clinical and nonclinical) supervision history including roadblocks and relational history. Consider factors such as type of supervision (i.e., individual, group, consultation, etc.), supervisor's professional identity (i.e., art therapist, other mental health provider), supervisor's personal identities (i.e., race, gender, age, sexual orientation, ability status, etc.), and if the supervisor was by choice or if it was supervision that was required (i.e., school-based supervision where the supervisor was assigned, workplace supervision, etc.).

• If creating a roadmap, how did you manage roadblocks? What path did you take?
• If creating a genogram, what colors and shapes are you using to represent your supervisors?

See Color Plates 3 and 4 for examples.

Confronting Fears

Create a found object sculpture of your fears surrounding supervision.

• From the *voice* of the sculpture, write a one-page response.
• Review the sculpture and share your findings in supervision.

References

Barrett, M. S., & Barber, J. P. (2005). A developmental approach to the supervision of therapists in training. *Journal of Contemporary Psychotherapy, 35*(2), 169–183. doi:10.1007/s10879-005-2698-8

Berger, S. S., & Buchholz, S. E. (1993). On becoming a supervisee: Preparation for learning in a supervisory relationship. *Psychotherapy, 30*(1), 86–92.

Bing-You, R. G., & Trowbridge, R. L. (2009). Why medical educators may be failing at feedback. *JAMA, 302*(12), 1330–1331. doi:10.1001/jama.2009.1393

Borders, L. D., Glosoff, H. L., Welfare, L. E., Hays, D. G., DeKruyf, L., Fernando, D. M., & Page, B. (2014). Best practices in clinical supervision: Evolution of a counseling specialty. *The Clinical Supervisor, 33*(1), 26–44. doi:10.1080/07325223.2014.905225

Brown, K. W., & Ryan, R. M. (2003). The benefits of being present: mindfulness and its role. *Psychological Well-Being Journal of Personality and Social Psychology, 84*(4), 822–848.

Case, C. (2007). Review of literature on art therapy supervision. In J. Schaverien & C. Case (Eds.), *Supervision of art therapy: A theoretical and practical handbook* (pp. 11–27). London, UK: Routledge.

Corey, G. (2013). *Theory and practice of counseling and psychotherapy.* Belmont, CA: Brooks/Cole.

Curtis, D. F., Elkins, S. R., Duran, P., & Venta, A. C. (2016). Promoting a climate of reflective practice and clinician self-efficacy in vertical supervision. *Training and Education in Professional Psychology, 10*(3), 133.

Deaver, S. P., & Shiflett, C. (2011). Art-based supervision techniques. *The Clinical Supervisor, 30*(2), 257–276. doi:10.1080/07325223.2011.619456

Delano, F. (2001). If I could supervise my supervisor: A model for child and youth care workers to own their own supervision. *Journal of Child and Youth Care, 15* (2), 51–64.

Edwards, D. (1993). Learning about feelings: The role of supervision in art therapy training. *The Arts in Psychotherapy, 20*(3), 213–222.

Fish, B. J. (2012). Response art: The art of the art therapist. *Art Therapy: Journal of the American Art Therapy Association, 29*(3), 138–143. doi:10.1080/07421656.2012.701594

Gaete, J., & Ottar, N. (2015). Supervision: From prescribed roles to preferred positionings. *The Clinical Supervisor, 34*(1), 57–77. doi:10.1080/07325223.2015.1006068

Kreider, H. D. (2014). Administrative and clinical supervision: The impact of dual roles on supervisee disclosure in counseling supervision. *The Clinical Supervisor, 33*(2), 256–268. doi:10.1080/07325223.2014.992292

Litman, J. A., & Pezzo, M. V. (2007). Dimensionality of interpersonal curiosity. *Personality and Individual Differences, 43*(6), 1448–1459.

Miller, A. (2012). Inspired by El Duende: One-canvas process painting in art therapy supervision. *Art Therapy: Journal of the American Art Therapy Association, 29*(4), 166–173. doi:10.1080/07421656.2013.730024

Moon, B. L., & Nolan, E. G. (2019). *Ethical issues in art therapy* (4th ed.). Springfield, IL: Charles C Thomas.

Overton, A. R., & Lowry, A. C. (2013). Conflict management: Difficult conversations with difficult people. *Clinics in colon and rectal surgery, 26* (04), 259–264.

Pearson, Q. M. (2004). Getting the most out of clinical supervision: Strategies for mental health. *Journal of Mental Health Counseling, 26*(4), 361–373.

Rai, S., Punia, V., Choudhury, S., & Mathew, K. J. (2015). Psychological mindedness: An overview. *Indian Journal of Positive Psychology, 6*(1), 127.

Robb, M., & Miller, A. (2017). Supervisee art-based disclosure in El Duende process painting. *Art Therapy, 34*(4), 192–200.

Robbins, A. (2007). The art of supervision. In J. Schaverien & C. Case (Eds.), *Supervision of art psychotherapy: A theoretical and practical handbook* (pp. 153–166). New York, NY: Routledge.

Rønnestad, M. H., & Skovholt, T. M. (2003). The journey of the counselor and therapist: Research findings and perspectives on professional development. *Journal of career development, 30*(1), 5–44.

Sarnat, J. (2010). Key competencies of the psychodynamic psychotherapist and how to teach them in supervision. *Psychotherapy: Theory, Research, Practice, Training, 47*(1), 20.

Schaverien, J., & Case, C. (Eds.). (2007). Supervision of art psychotherapy: A theoretical and practical handbook. New York, NY: Routledge.

Stark, M. D., Frels, R. K., & Garza, Y. (2011). The use of sandtray in solution-focused supervision. *The Clinical Supervisor, 30*(2), 277–290.

Sue, D., & Sue, D. M. (2007). *Foundations of counseling and psychotherapy: Evidence-based practices for a diverse society.* Hoboken, NJ: John Wiley & Sons.

Sue, D. W., Capodilupo, C. M., Torino, G. C., Bucceri, J. M., Holder, A., Nadal, K. L., & Esquilin, M. (2007). Racial microaggressions in everyday life: Implications for clinical practice. *American Psychologist, 62*(4), 271.

Sweitzer, H. F., & King, M. A. (2018). *The successful internship: Personal, professional, and civic development in experiential learning* (5 ed.). Boston, MA: Cengage.

Vec, T., Vec, T. R., & Žorga, S. (2014). Understanding how supervision works and what it can achieve. In C. Edward Watkins, Jr. & D. L. Milne (Eds.), *The Wiley international handbook of clinical supervision* (pp. 103–127). Chichester, UK: John Wiley & Sons.

Wadeson, H. (2003). Making art for professional processing. *Art Therapy, 20*(4), 208–218.

Watkins, C. E. (2012). Psychotherapy supervision in the new millennium: Competency-based, evidence-based, particularized, and energized. *Journal of Contemporary Psychotherapy, 42*(3), 193–203.

Watkins, C. E., Jr. (2017). Convergence in psychotherapy supervision: A common factors, common processes, common practices perspective. *Journal of Psychotherapy Integration, 27*(2), 140–152.

Watkins, C. E., Jr (2017). How does psychotherapy supervision work? Contributions of connection, conception, allegiance, alignment, and action. *Journal of Psychotherapy Integration, 27*(2), 201–217.

Wilson, L., Riley, S., & Wadeson, H. (1984). Art therapy supervision. *Art Therapy: Journal of the American Art Therapy Association, 1*(3), 100–105. doi:10.1080/07421656.1984.10758761

Wood, C. (2007). Agency and attention. In J. Schaverien & C. Case (Eds.), *Supervision of art therapy: A theoretical and practical handbook* (pp. 185–199). London, UK: Routledge.

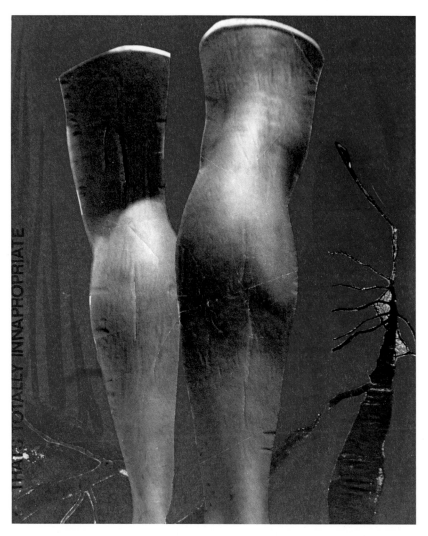

Plate 1 Yasmine J. Awais (1999), Untitled response art to internship (THAT'S TOTALLY INAPPROPRIATE) [magazine collage with vinyl lettering]

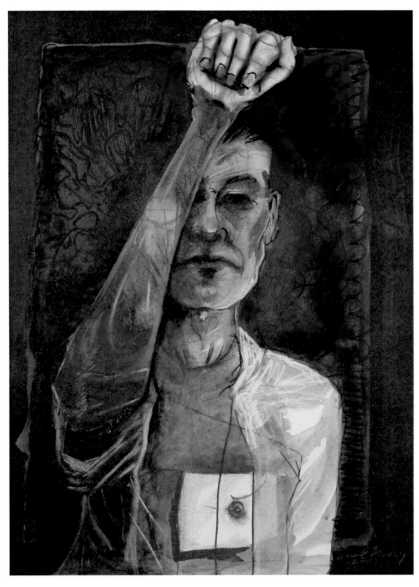

Plate 2 Daniel Blausey (2011), *Up in Arms* [acrylic, oil pastel, chalk pastel, charcoal, and pencil]

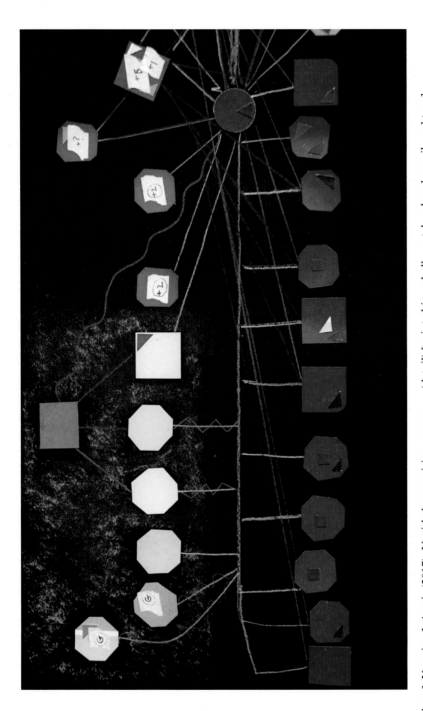

Plate 3 Yasmine J. Awais (2017), Untitled supervision genogram (detail) [paint chips, chalk pastel, colored pencil, and tape]

Plate 4 Daniel Blausey (2019), *Genogram 2019* [scratchboard foil, glue, and cardboard]

Part 2

The Business and Administrative Sides to Supervision

The nuts and bolts of supervision are often overlooked. Most therapists are drawn to the field because of aspects of the work such as supporting growth and learning. As therapists, we may not be as comfortable with the business and administrative aspects of supervision. Yet, we have probably used administrative supervision to our benefit – when we wanted to avoid the challenges of educative and supportive roles. However, many therapists often consider administrative aspects of the job as less important than clinical aspects.

In this part, we promote the administrative aspects of supervision as *necessary* for the role of the supervisor and encourage clinicians to be purposeful in their administrative supervisory roles. This area is often not addressed in supervision texts and tends to be *a learn as you go* endeavor. The business and administrative sides to supervision, in particular, tend to be missed when learning about supervision on the fly. Therapists learning to be supervisors by observation may not see these parts of the process, since they are often conducted outside of the supervision space.

This part contains two chapters:

- Navigating Professional Identity: Credentials, Representation, and Relationships; and
- Confidentiality and Informed Consent.

Over the years, we have had heavily administrative supervision roles in our careers, yet much of what we learned as administrative supervisors has been informed by our roles as clinical supervisors. To bolster our skillset, we both participated in training on administrative supervision – Daniel attended agency-specific supervision training for managers at his former sites and Yasmine attended an institute for middle managers in non-profit agencies. In order to offer concrete tools for your supervisory roles, we describe and provide sample consent forms and supervision contracts for readers to build upon. While our training and experiences are specific to the non-profit sector, we believe this chapter will be useful to those in other settings.

4 Navigating Professional Identity

Credentials, Representation, and Relationships

Introduction

What credentials are available, obtainable, and most rewarding to pursue can incur a thought-provoking and tense decision-making process. Art therapists inherently hold multiple identities (e.g., therapist, artist, art educator) concerned with both artmaking (the art part) and the practice of psychotherapy (the therapy part). Holding a dual degree (art therapy and counseling) or an additional mental health graduate degree (e.g., doctorate in psychology) further complicates the reality of multiple professional identities when considering credentials, representing one's self, and maintaining professional relationships. Navigating this choice requires a hard look at continued state residency versus likelihood of relocation, portability of licensure, expense, and commitment to the field of art therapy. To make an informed decision, one must understand the distinctions between the qualifications of national credentialing and state licensing. This is particularly challenging for art therapists as not all states have a distinct art therapy license, resulting in practice without the title of *art therapist*. Furthermore, sustaining multiple professional identities may require a supervisee to engage with several supervisors. Early-career art therapists, as well as other mental health professionals supervising art therapists, can draw on this chapter to better understand the complexities therapists face as they work to achieve professional goals through licensure and other credentials.

Developing a professional identity, which involves achieving and maintaining licensure and various credentials, involves various administrative aspects of supervision. This process may include credentials to supervise, and other kinds of paperwork (i.e., documenting supervision encounters, supervision contracts). When considering your own professional identity and deciding which credentials to strive for or maintain, therapists should consider: professional and ethical concerns (including understanding, identifying, and the managing of dual relationships), realizing our scope of practice, and appreciating the differences between supervision and similar relationships such as therapy and mentorship.

Administrative aspects of supervision may not be as appealing to some art therapists, since our training tends to focus on supporting (through the therapeutic relationship) and educating (through psychoeducation). As such, navigating professional identity, which involves many administrative components, may not come as naturally. Whether you are a supervisee looking for help navigating your career, or a supervisor looking to provide support around career navigation, you will need to incorporate these administrative aspects into the supervisory relationship. In this chapter, we cover the art therapists' scope of practice and art-therapy-specific credentialing, explore licensure considerations, describe supervision credentials and how to track continuing education hours, and define the purpose and features of a supervision disclosure statement.

Scope of Practice for Art Therapists

As articulated by the Art Therapy Credentials Board (ATCB), "Art therapists must not provide services other than art therapy unless certified or licensed to provide such other services" (2018c, p. 3). We use the scope-of-practice definition of art therapy as written by the American Art Therapy Association (AATA):

> an integrative mental health and human services profession that enriches the lives of individuals, families, and communities through active art-making, creative process, applied psychological theory, and human experience within a psychotherapeutic relationship ... Art Therapy is used to improve cognitive and sensory-motor functions, foster self-esteem and self-awareness, cultivate emotional resilience, promote insight, enhance social skills, reduce and resolve conflicts and distress, and advance societal and ecological change.
> (AATA, 2017, Concise Definition of Art Therapy, paras 1 and 2)

The ATCB Standards of Conduct are contained within the larger, complete *Code of Ethics, Conduct, and Disciplinary Procedures* document (ATCB, 2018c). The Standards of Conduct relate to the specific practice of art therapy, including how art therapists represent themselves and their services, documentation and communication, maintaining boundaries between personal and professional relationships (i.e., dual relationships), and how the art therapy itself is conducted (e.g., charting, confidentiality, termination). Readers should understand that state licensing boards have their own scope of practice particular to each license. If you hold a license or are pursuing a license that qualifies you to practice, please refer to your specific scope-of-practice document as issued by your state licensing board.

The Practice of Art Therapy

In order to supervise art therapists, one must understand what an art therapist actually practices. This is true for supervisors who are art therapists and those who are coming from different clinical fields and disciplines. According to the ATCB (2019), "Art therapy uses art media, the creative process and the resulting artwork as a therapeutic and healing process" (para. 1). Services can be conducted in a variety of ways (e.g., individual, group, family, couples, and with communities) and held in multiple settings (e.g., private practice, medical hospitals, psychiatric hospitals, schools, prisons, non-profit organizations, group homes, veteran associations, domestic violence shelters). Art therapy is provided to address diagnosed mental health issues (e.g., depression, anxiety, post-traumatic stress disorder) and issues related to psychosocial matters, such as coping with a long-term illness, divorce, or other life event. At times, aspects of art therapy may appear similar to art education, as teaching artistic skills may occur in session. Indeed, art therapists are trained in art and many identify as artists and art educators. While art therapy has roots in art education (see Chapter 1, *What Is Art Therapy Supervision? Reasons and Expectations* for more), art therapy is a distinct field of study "grounded in the knowledge of human development, psychological theories and counseling techniques" (ATCB, 2019, para. 5). Another key difference between art therapy and art education is the art therapists' responsibility for documentation and communication, attending to dual relationships, and representing themselves accurately.

Professional Meets Personal: Navigating Relationships

Dual relationships, or having overlap between a personal and professional relationship, are a justifiable concern for supervisors, just as they are for therapists. However, we are often told to simply avoid dual relationships (see Fish, 2017) rather than being taught how to navigate them with secure boundaries. Since supervisors are also therapists, there are various considerations and strategies for navigating these relationships in order to avoid misunderstandings. For example, an art therapist is unable to enter a therapeutic relationship with a current student or supervisee since this crosses an ethical boundary. However, can an art therapist supervise a former student? How can one maintain a professional relationship, particularly when the field is small or when practicing in an area where the number of art therapists is limited? On a personal level, everyday points of connection between a supervisor and a supervisee may involve attending the same religious institution, participating in the same community organizations, having children enrolled in the same school or afterschool activities, receiving invitations to mutual friends' events, actively following the same social media feeds or dating apps, and even frequenting the same local gym, salon, or coffee shop. At the professional level, intersections include: undertaking volunteer assignments or board work for the local chapter of the AATA, attending and presenting at regional and national conferences, and vying for the same job openings and clients, as well as the potential for compelled service provision to friends and family (e.g., school-based or inpatient). In locations outside of supervision, the supervisee may hold more organizational standing or cultural privilege and power than the supervisor, necessitating a shifting power dynamic. Some communities, whether rural or in the midst of the largest metropolitan areas, do not afford the advantage of a straight-out, no-dual-relationship declaration. Nor is it necessarily the ideal. Planning and communication is key to navigating a dual relationship.

We suggest utilizing supervision disclosure statements, discussed in detail later in this chapter, at the start of the supervisory relationship to minimize misunderstandings. For example, will you and your supervisee or supervisor connect on social media? If you are already networked, will that change? Will personal phone numbers be exchanged? How quickly will texts or emails be answered? How will romantic or sexual feelings be addressed? Maintaining professional relationships is considered valuable, yet determining what is "professional" may depend on context and location. See Yasmine's story, Vignette 4.1, which illustrates the importance of a supervision contract when supervising former students. If living or practicing in an area with fewer art therapists or practice specializations, it may be common or best practice for a supervisee to refer potential clients to their supervisor, whereas in other situations an art therapist may not make such a referral.

Vignette 4.1 Supervising Former Students

Yasmine's Story

When a current student is seeking supervision post-graduation, or a former student reaches out with an interest in obtaining supervision from me, I am humbled and honored. I believe supervision is at the cornerstone of a clinician's training and understand this individual has the choice to seek out other previous professors or supervisors for their ongoing training post-graduation. Former students may seek my services as a supervisor because they valued our work together with me as their supervisor or professor. Similar to contracted supervision with professionals, my work as an on-campus group supervisor occurs off-site where the work is not directly monitored. Yet, there are distinctions between supervising a former student and a professional.

After thanking the student for considering me as their supervisor, I provide them with my supervision contract. This immediately distinguishes the difference between required, school-based supervision and contracted professional supervision. We also explicitly discuss the differences, including the payment schedule, benefits, and disadvantages of off-site supervision.

I always recommend that new professionals negotiate for supervision when they are offered their first job, especially if they are not being provided on-site supervision that meets all of their licensing and credentialing needs. Students are often hesitant to negotiate anything as they are often very concerned about just getting a job! I frame the ask as a way for students to advocate for themselves as professionals. New professionals can explain how the site will benefit from obtaining proper supervision, including staying current with clinical trends and obtaining licensure and/or credentials. I rank the order of asks as follows:

1 Ask for the employer to pay the supervisor directly for supervision.
2 Ask for reimbursement for all supervision hours.
3 Ask for half of supervision hours to reimbursed (rationale: both parties, the employer and the supervisee, benefit).
4 If no financial compensation can be provided, ask for one hour of work "off" to obtain supervision, which may mean leaving work one hour early or arriving to work one hour later, one day a week. This hour off should not be counted against their vacations, paid time off, etc.

Representation: Identifying Strengths and Limitations

How does an art therapist represent themselves to the public with clarity and correctness? Does the approach differ for an art therapy supervisor? For art therapists, the degree to practice is at the master's level, and while art therapy may be considered a specialized form of psychotherapy, art therapists are still considered generalists. Similar to other mental health professions, specializations, which may become strengths and areas of expertise, occur after years of practice or with additional training. It is important to recognize experience with a specific population does not necessarily equate to clinical expertise. This is especially true early on in a supervisory practice. For instance, recent grads and new professionals may gain instrumental experience or attend advanced training for skill enhancement with a particular population; nevertheless, they have not yet attained expertise. Limitations and weaknesses may be more difficult to identify, especially for new practitioners, because identifying blind spots is considered an advanced skill (Barrett & Barber, 2005; Harris, 2017). Harris states that one developmental goal of an Intermediate therapist is to "increase personal and professional awareness", while one goal of an experienced therapist is to "increase awareness of countertransference" (2017, p. 89).

Art therapists should represent themselves and their services accurately at all times – on the web, in print, and verbally when applying for jobs; in advertisements and within resumes, curricula vitae, and contracts. Accuracy is determined not only by professional truthfulness (e.g., credentials, supervisory philosophies) but also by terms established by national credentialing bodies and state regulations (e.g., licensure, title protection). For the art therapy supervisor, accurate representation allows for supervisees to understand the theoretical orientation of the supervisor, and the supervisor's training and credentials.

A supervisee may opt to pursue supervision with a supervisor based on their clinical expertise with a specific population or theoretical approach, or simply for the supervisor's expertise in supervision. In the latter, the supervisory skillset is sought and centers on the supervisory relationship as the overarching teaching tool, which differs from a supervisor-as-population-based-expert approach. Clearly and concisely representing your supervisory philosophy and approach is an invaluable resource for art therapists seeking supervision. While no supervisor is an expert in all aspects of therapy, a supervisee should be able to make an informed decision about their supervisor.

Art-Therapy-Specific Credentials

In Chapter 1 we describe maintenance of credentials as part of the administrative aspect of supervision. More specifically, the application is largely administrative (i.e., tracking clinical supervision and client-contact hours, gathering transcripts, obtaining recommendations, etc.). While participating in continuing educational experiences that improve theoretical understanding and clinical practice skills are educational in nature, the tracking of these continuing education credits (CECs) or continuing educational units (CEUs) is an administrative task (see Box 4.1).

Box 4.1 Tracking Your Hours

There are many ways to track the clinical hours needed to obtain licensure and credentialing, along with continuing educational hours for licensure or credentialing maintenance. Depending on the license or credential one is applying for, you may have to track different details. For example, is the clinical work psychotherapy or psychoeducational? Was the work conducted in an individual, family, or group therapy format? Distinguish between direct, face-to-face clinical hours and hours spent on paperwork, etc. Similarly, for the tracking of supervision hours, note who is supervising you and what license(s) and credential(s) they hold. Identify if the supervisory hours were obtained in an individual or group setting, face-to-face (live and in-person) or long-distance (e.g., online or telephonically). The methods we describe to track your hours are calendars, apps, and electronic spreadsheets.

Calendars

Using a paper calendar in conjunction with an electronic calendar may be the most straightforward method to track hours. We recommend using both a paper and electronic version in case one gets lost. Because there are so many details to track, we suggest keeping these separate from personal-use calendars, dedicating specific paper and electronic calendars to tracking professional hours and other details.

Apps

Yasmine has had supervisees use apps that track supervision hours, such as PsyKey (www.psykey.com/). Using an app may be beneficial for those who are uncomfortable with creating their own electronic spreadsheets or forgetful about writing things down. Supervisees that have used such apps have noted many benefits – they are easy to use, offer different licenses per state, and allow for printing of reports. Furthermore, supervisees noted that using an app made it easier to remember to record clinical and supervisory activities, since the app allows for reminders to be set. Furthermore, use of the app can be incorporated into supervision – one can log in the hours at the start or end of every session. Even if the phone or device is lost, the chance of the information itself being lost is slim, as the app developer stores the information. The downside is that one must pay for the app and not all details for every state license or credential are guaranteed.

Electronic Spreadsheets

Yasmine tracks her ongoing continuing education for licenses in two states and two art therapy credentials using an Excel spreadsheet. Her columns include the pertinent information of the activity attended or conducted:

- Year;
- Month/day;
- Presenter (including self);
- Hours;
- Topic (particularly important as some topics are required, such as ethics);
- Title; and
- Location.

Four additional columns identify the licenses and credentials being tracked. These are labeled with the name and the dates of the tracking period. When an activity meets the requirements of the license or credential, then the corresponding hour goes into that column. See Figure 4.1 as an example for tracking professional continuing education hours.

As a reminder, the ATCB grants national credentials to protect the public and profession of art therapy by ensuring art therapists have earned the qualifications and experience necessary to obtain ATCB credentials. The information on ATCB credentials (i.e., ATR, ATR-P, ATR-BC, and ATCS) that follows is based upon ATCB published requirements at the time of this writing. We encourage readers to review the most up-to-date applications and handbooks to ensure they are complying with current standards.

Registration

The entry-level credential for art therapists granted by the ATCB is registration, known as the ATR. Requirements for the ATR include obtaining hours of supervised, clinical art therapy experiences. For those who have graduated from an AATA-approved or Commission on Accreditation of Allied Health Education Programs (CAAHEP)-accredited program, a minimum of 1,000 direct art therapy client-contact hours are required; for those who did not graduate from an approved or accredited program, an additional 500 hours are needed, equaling 1,500 hours of direct art therapy client-contact hours. The applicant must also have corresponding supervision of their clinical work: either 100 hours or 150 hours (respectively for approved/accredited or non-approved/accredited graduates). At least half of these hours must be provided by an ATR-BC or ATCS (see below). The following may provide the remaining half of the supervision hours:

a fully licensed or credentialed practitioner with a master's degree or higher in art therapy or a related mental health field and whose

HOURS	TOPIC	TITLE	LOCATION	ATCB 7/1/13 - 6/31/18	LCAT (NY) 1/1/14 - 12/31/17	LPC (PA) 3/1/15 - 2/28/17	ATCS 7/1/13 - 6/31/18
7	Anti-Racist Training	Anti-Racist Training for Behavioral Health Services Providers	Organization Name	7	7	7	
1.5	Feminism	What Does Feminism Have to do With Art Therapy? Envisioning New Paradigms of Care	Conference Name	1.5	1.5	1.5	
1	Supervision	Art-based Supervision: Supported by Response Art and Technology at Home and Abroad	Conference Name	1	1	1	1
1	Ethics	IPE Competencies: Values and Ethics	School/University Name	1	1	1	
1.5	Ethics	Ethics and Technology	School/University Name	1.5	1.5		
2	Diversity	Therapy of the Oppressed: Clinical Care in the Age of Injustice	School/University Name	2	2		
1	Suicide Prevention	Suicide Prevention Protocols For Juvenile Justice Youth	[website of online course]	1		1	
3	Child Abuse	Recognizing and Reporting Child Abuse	[website of online course]			3	
1.5	LGBTQ	An Evening on Gender Diversity	School/University Name	1.5	1.5		
			CURRENT CREDITS	15.5	15.5	14.5	1
			CREDIT GOAL	90	36	30	10
			CREDITS NEEDED	74.5	20.5	15.5	9

Figure 4.1 Example of tracking continuing education hours using an electronic spreadsheet.

license/credential is for independent practice. Automatically acceptable related fields are counseling, marriage and family therapy, social
work, psychology, addictions counseling, psychiatric nursing, and
psychiatry. Other related mental health fields are considered on
a case-by-case basis.

(ATCB, 2018d, p. 3)

For graduates of an AATA-approved or CAAHEP-accredited master's
program employed as full-time art therapists, achieving the ATR takes
new professionals approximately one to two years.

PROVISIONAL REGISTRATION

The ATCB introduced an optional provisional credential called the ATR-P.
This informs the public the individual graduated from a master's program,
is undergoing supervision, and is currently accruing hours for the ATR.
Art therapists must have secured both a place to practice and a supervisor
in order to apply for the ATR-P.

Board Certification

In addition to meeting the clinical practice requirements of registration,
art therapists who are board-certified (indicated as ATR-BC) have also
passed the ATCB Examination (ATCBE). At the time of this writing, the
computer-based test is provided during four windows of time in the
United States. An art therapist is eligible to take the ATCBE after they
obtain their ATR credentials. However, art therapists who are applying
for licensure in states that consider the ATCBE as a qualifying licensure
exam can take the ATCBE prior to holding the ATR. The exam is
multiple-choice, with questions in seven knowledge areas (ATCB, 2018a):

- Theoretical approaches;
- Intake and evaluation;
- Assessment and evaluation instruments;
- Diagnosis and populations;
- Art therapy environment;
- Professional practice and ethics; and
- Clinical skills and application.

Since every program emphasizes various aspects of art therapy, we recommend studying in groups composed of individuals who attended different
programs. This way, supplementary reading materials, approaches, and
other resources can be shared.

Supervision

The ATCS, Art Therapy Certified Supervisor, is a specialist credential only board-certified and registered art therapists (ATR-BCs) are qualified to hold. According to the ATCB, "Working with an ATCS ensures that current art therapy students and early-career practitioners receive the best art therapy clinical supervision available" (2018b). As of this writing, art therapists seeking national ATCB credentials are not required to have a supervisor with ATCS credentials. However, considering the trends in related professions, it would not be surprising if this becomes the norm in the future.

There are two pathways to obtain an ATCS at the time of this writing – experience and education. For the educational based requirements, a minimum of 35 continuing educational credits in the area of clinical supervision, including the supervision of art therapists, or three semester hours of graduate course work, is required (ATCB, 2018b). Similar to the clinical designation of ATR, where the applicant must have supervised clinical experience, an ATCS must have supervised supervisory experience. The supervision of supervision can involve seeking a supervisor to discuss the ATCS applicant supervising students in the academic setting or clinicians in the professional setting. Alternatively, this experience of supervision of supervision can be replaced with other national or state supervision credentials, such as the ACS, which is described in more detail below.

Licensure Considerations

Evaluating one's scope of practice beyond art therapy is necessary, since art therapists often work with multiple titles due to their place of work or state of practice. Holding a license, particularly one that is not art-therapy-specific, may entail a different scope of practice. For example, in California an art therapist may have a scope of practice that includes family therapy, where in Pennsylvania this same art therapist may have a scope of practice that does not include family therapy but includes general counseling. In New York, the same art therapist's scope of practice may also encompass music, dance, and drama therapy. However, if this professional chooses to obtain a mental health counseling license instead of a creative arts therapy license, the scope of practice widens in some areas (i.e., the mental health counseling) but eliminates others (i.e., creative arts therapy practice, including art therapy). When determining your individual scope of practice, consider:

- The discipline or field of practice in which you received your degree;
- Your license;
- Your state-determined title protection and other restrictions; and
- Expertise gained through extensive clinical and supervised experience, along with additional training, certifications, or time in the field.

As this book is specific to supervision and art therapy, art therapists whose scope of practice encompasses additional disciplines (e.g., expressive therapy, social work, etc.) or specialties (e.g., Dialectical Behavior Therapy, Cognitive Behavioral Therapy) should refer to additional resources, including supervision specific to that practice.

Supervision Credentials

The scope of practice for art therapy supervisors falls under the scope of practice for art therapists in general (see ATCB, 2018b). However, we find it valuable to distinctly understand the scope of practice for supervisors, particularly for new clinicians. While in training, supervisors or supervisees may be assigned without much or any say. Outside of required supervision for master's training programs, art therapists tend to supervise early-career professionals seeking entry-level credentials and more seasoned clinicians seeking advanced credentials. Supervision-specific credentials require the supervisor to be clear on their scope of practice, including their specialties or expertise and theoretical framework.

Supervision credentials indicate the credential holder has obtained specific requirements, such as training and skills specific to supervision, in addition to the typical clinical training of the master's degree and licensure or other certification. As described earlier, the ATCS is offered by the ATCB (2018b) and at the time of this writing is not a requirement for supervision. We understand art therapists may hold credentials outside of art therapy, and readers interested in learning about other supervision credentials should seek out information in other resources.

As many states offer counseling licensure for art therapists, those clinicians may also be interested in the Approved Clinical Supervisor (ACS), a national credential granted by the Center for Credentialing and Education (2016). There are several states using the ACS "as a supervision credential of choice", meaning that in order to supervise an individual applying for licensure, their clinical experience must be supervised by an individual who holds an ACS or, in the case of New Jersey, has taken a three-credit course on supervision at the graduate level (State of New Jersey, 2017). There are two options to meet the specific supervision requirements needed to apply for the ACS. Either three graduate-level training credits from a Council for Accreditation of Counseling and Related Educational Programs (CACREP)-accredited program or 45 credits of approved continuing education. Art therapists may consider obtaining an ACS in conjunction with the art-therapy-specific ATCS, particularly if they are licensed as counselors or if they live in a state that prefers or requires the ACS to supervise licensure applicants.

Regarding additional related professions of potential overlap and interest, Approved Supervisor status is available for marriage and family therapists (American Association of Marriage and Family Therapy,

2018) and the Registered Play Therapist-Supervisor (RPT-S) is offered by the Association for Play Therapy (2016). In some states, a supervisor credential is required in order to provided supervision for those clinicians seeking licensure. Some fields require professionals to seek supervision exclusively from designated supervisors (in the case of play therapists), and others require specific status to supervise students (such as the SIFI [Seminar Training in Field Instruction] to supervise social work students). Some states require those applying for licensure to be supervised by only credentialed supervisors.

As you can see, this makes for a complicated system! Remember, qualifications change. We highly suggest that readers interested in supervision credentials, either to become an authorized supervisor or to receive supervision from such an individual, check their various authorizing bodies first and not rely solely on the information provided in this chapter. The information provided here is offered to readers in order to show that there is not merely one supervision credential, and there are many factors to consider when looking for a supervisor. All of the supervision credentials named in this chapter require supervision of supervision. In other words, if you are interested in becoming a credentialed supervisor, you must have been supervised on how you are supervising or training other individuals (such as professionals or students) by a supervisor who is trained in clinical supervision. The ATCS and ACS also require a professional disclosure statement.

Supervision Disclosure Statement

A disclosure statement describes brief but pertinent details outlining the qualifications, approach, and expectations of the supervisory relationship. The disclosure statement is designed and written for, reviewed with, and provided to, your supervisees. This section touches upon the required supervision disclosure statements of the ATCS.

Important features of the ATCS disclosure statement include an opportunity to express understanding of the multilayered functions of clinical supervision while providing the supervisee with "instructions about ATCB's complaint procedures and how a supervisee with concerns may file a complaint with ATCB and any other relevant licensure board or credentialing body" (ATCB, 2018b, p. 1). The disclosure statement, as of this writing, must also include (ATCB, 2018b):

- Your name;
- Supervisor's name (if applicable);
- Business or employer's name, address, telephone number, and email address;
- Description of formal training and education, including highest relevant degree and educational institution;

- Description of relevant art therapy credentials;
- Description of all professional affiliations, memberships, licensing, and certifications, including credential number and issuing state or organization;
- Affirmation of past and present adherence to the ATCB *Code of Ethics, Conduct, and Disciplinary Procedures*;
- Areas of competence and services provided;
- Philosophical/theoretical approach to supervision;
- Description of relevant academic training or professional experience in demonstrating competency in clinical supervision;
- Fees for supervision (must state specific fee or fee range). If there is no fee, this must be stated; and
- Instructions regarding how a supervisee should address any dissatisfaction with the supervision process, including how to file a complaint with ATCB, Inc., and the ATCB's address, telephone number, and email address.

Takeaways

- Art therapists often have multiple identities that are made more complex by navigating licenses and credentials. Remember, these two identity markers are different! Licensure is overseen by state bodies while credentials are conferred by organizations, which are not bounded by location. For example, even though the ATCB is a body in the United States, art therapists outside of the United States can hold this credential and it may be recognized. However, licensure in the United States is only recognized by the state that has issued it.
- Recognizing what dual relationships are and how to mitigate them is more valuable than simply stating that they should be avoided. Utilizing a supervision disclosure statement can help mitigate dual relationships with a supervisee and supervisor.

Practice Prompts

What Makes You Unique?

Creating a disclosure statement can be difficult. Why should a supervisee seek out your supervision services? Theoretical orientation or supervision philosophy and areas of competence or expertise are examples of what may distinguish one supervisor from another.

- We have created a worksheet (Appendix C) to help you to identify your strengths and supervisory style. Complete this worksheet prior to the actual writing of your supervision disclosure statement.

Creating Your Disclosure Statement

Review the disclosure statement requirements for the ATCS, ACS, or other accrediting body from which you are pursuing supervision credentialing. Start to create your own disclosure statement using the template we have provided (Appendix D). Be sure to include the strengths and unique offerings you have identified by completing the activity above. Once you have created your first draft, review with your supervisor.

References

AATA. (2017). What is art therapy? Retrieved from www.arttherapy.org/upload/whatisarttherapy.pdf

American Association of Marriage and Family Therapy. (2018). Responsibilities and guidelines for AAMFT Approved Supervisors and supervisor candidates. Retrieved from www.aamft.org/iMIS15/AAMFT/Content/supervision/Responsibilities.aspx

American Association of Play Therapy. (2016). Play therapy credentials. Retrieved from www.a4pt.org/page/CredentialsHomepage

Art Therapy Credentials Board (ATCB). (2018a). Art therapy credentials board examination (ATCBE). Retrieved from www.atcb.org/resource/pdf/ATCB_Prep_Guide.pdf

Art Therapy Credentials Board (ATCB). (2018b). Art therapy certified supervisor (ATCS) 2018 application handbook. Retrieved from: www.atcb.org/resource/pdf/ATCS_ApplicationHandbook.pdf

Art Therapy Credentials Board (ATCB). (2018c). Code of ethics, conduct and disciplinary procedures. Retrieved from: www.atcb.org/resource/pdf/ATCB-Code-of-Ethics-Conduct-DisciplinaryProcedures.pdf

Art Therapy Credentials Board (ATCB). (2018d). Registered art therapist (ATR): 2018 application handbook. Retrieved from www.atcb.org/New_Applicants/Apply_ATR

Art Therapy Credentials Board (ATCB). (2019). What is Art Therapy? Retrieved from: www.atcb.org/Public/WhatIsArtTherapy

Barrett, M. S., & Barber, J. P. (2005). A developmental approach to the supervision of therapists in training. *Journal of Contemporary Psychotherapy, 35*(2), 169–183. doi:10.1007/s10879-005-2698-8

Center for Credentialing and Education. (2016). Approved clinical supervisor (ACS). Retrieved from www.cce-global.org/Credentialing/ACS

Fish, B. J. (2017). *Art-based supervision: Cultivating therapeutic insight through imagery.* New York, NY: Routledge.

Harris, S. (2017). Systemic dual-developmental supervision: An approach for psychotherapy practitioners and supervisors. *The Family Journal, 25*(1), 84–90.

State of New Jersey. (2017). New Jersey Division of Consumer Affairs: Professional counselor examiners committee frequently asked questions. Retrieved from www.njconsumeraffairs.gov/pc/Pages/FAQ.aspx

5 Confidentiality and Informed Consent

Karen Myers and Daniel Blausey

Disclaimer

This chapter is not meant to provide specific legal advice. For specific legal advice based on one's locality, consultation with an attorney is recommended.

Introduction

Just as confidentiality and informed consent are fundamental concepts between therapist and client, the supervisory relationship has similar obligations. "Clients have the right to know [that] the art therapist is receiving supervision and that their relationships with the art therapist may be subject to discussion in supervision sessions" (Moon, 2006, p. 32). Not only do clients have the right to know, in many states they are required by law to know their therapist is receiving supervision, particularly if they are working with new professionals seeking licensure. Clients also have a right to fully understand what supervision means, so it is important to provide all clients with a clear, concise statement of confidentiality as it applies to their sessions.

It is imperative to address barriers related to language or literacy difficulties when discussing confidentiality and informed consent with both students and clients. There are times when the supervisor, supervisee, and the client (or guardian) may each have a different primary language or cultural expectation of privacy. Adequately and sensitively addressing any language or literacy obstacles honors a client's rights and allows information to be clearly shared "about who is on their health care team and the nature of the services they may be offered" (Hodgson, Mendenhall, & Lamson, 2013, p. 35), along with other pertinent information related to their care.

Before consenting to participate, a supervisee, like their client, has a right to understand and agree to the boundaries of the supervisory relationship even if they have no power to define the legal factors (Thomas, 2007, p. 22). In this chapter, confidentiality essentials will be covered along with ability to consent, written consent, social media, and artwork, among other confidentiality-related topics. We will define confidentiality and informed consent, outline what consent can clarify, and review related topics from the Art Therapy Credentials Board's (ATCB) *Code of Ethics, Conduct, and Disciplinary Procedures.* The final section will address documentation and communication, and will include the Health Insurance Portability Accounting Act (HIPAA), the Family Education Rights and Privacy Act (FERPA), technology, storage, and other pertinent matters.

Confidentiality at Its Core: The Basics

At its core, confidentiality demands art therapists and other legally obligated healthcare professionals refrain from disclosing inferred or client-communicated information without the client's consent. Once understood, confidentiality may allow a deepening of trust and development of safety within the therapeutic alliance. It honors a client's right of self-determination in what information they choose to share based on the parameters of confidentiality.

Many clients begin art therapy without thoroughly understanding what personal disclosures will be kept in confidence, whether offered verbally, communicated in the creative process, or potentially revealed in the artwork. Essentially, they may be unaware of their rights and lack any understanding of the supervisory requirements of their therapist. The same lack of comprehending confidentiality may be true for a supervisee, so it is vital supervisors ensure supervisees understand how to speak about confidentiality with their clients. As a supervisor, it is essential to be well versed in and educate supervisees on the essentials of confidentiality and how this can serve the client within the therapeutic alliance and the supervisory relationship.

Let us start with basics: confidentiality is critical in the initial engagement phase of a therapeutic relationship to build trust, honor a client's right of privacy, and advance a client's self-determination. Therefore, a client deserves to be informed and a therapist is obligated *right from the start* of the therapeutic relationship to discuss confidentiality. Educating a client is often just one step, since most art therapists function as a part of a larger team or in conjunction with outside providers. Whether working within a private practice, small non-profit, school setting, or larger institution, systems to secure and enforce confidentiality need to be designed and implemented. This requires commitment and awareness at multiple levels of accountability to reduce violations. Hodgson et al. (2013) provided an overview of confidentiality in an integrated primary care setting that easily applies to other environments, large or small:

> Hallway conversations, shared record systems, uncertainty about how to engage those who come to the appointment with a patient, and

poorly built clinics (e.g., inadequate space, thin walls, lack of waiting room seating) all give way to possibilities for a breach in confidentiality within and by integrated primary care teams. According to HIPAA's Privacy Rule (45 CFR 164.506; U.S. Department of Health & Human Services, 1996), confidentiality functions as a foundation of federal protection for personal health information, carefully balanced to avoid creating unnecessary barriers to the delivery of quality health care.

(p. 28)

Basically, unless a patient gives authorization, or there is a compulsory legal reason, every bit of information concerning patient care must continue to be private (Hodgson et al., 2013, p. 32).

Although clarifying to a client when an art therapist needs to break confidentiality is important, Hodgson et al. (2013) clearly reminds us confidentiality concerns are more complex (e.g., multiple providers, minors, state laws) and do not rest solely within the session. Nevertheless, we will begin by reviewing how to approach confidentiality in session. The actual dialogue is based on each site's confidentiality policy that must adhere to the ATCB Code of Ethics, HIPAA, and state and local confidentiality laws. Utilizing a confidentiality form, in addition to discussing confidentiality verbally, is often recommended. The confidentiality form is ideally provided as a written document in the client's primary language and reviewed verbally for clarification at the beginning of a session or during intake.

When discussing confidentiality with supervisees, it is important to be explicit on what confidentiality means and when there are exceptions in treatment and in supervision. Always encourage supervisees to consider the following:

- Use and define the word "confidentiality" in a verbal statement so it is clear and understandable to the client.
- Review the confidentiality definition (in the client's primary language) before a signature is required.
- Name the exception of serious imminent danger to self or others. This includes mandatory reporting of potential harm to vulnerable populations like children, older adults, and people with cognitive disabilities.
- Discuss the exception of "Duty to warn", which is the requirement that all health professionals, including art therapists, act preemptively if they consider or have direct knowledge that a client is in danger of harming a specific person or persons. Duty to warn case law varies from state to state in terms of what is required and which relationships are privileged. The 1976 Tarasoff case is the early "duty to warn" decision that subsequent case law often cites.

- Explain confidentiality is no longer applicable if one is subpoenaed or required by a court. However, information provided should be limited to what is absolutely necessary; i.e., if a court needs to know about a client's attendance at sessions then attendance records are all that should be disclosed, not the substantive case notes about those sessions, unless that is also required/subpoenaed. It is extremely important to seek relevant legal consultation if you receive a subpoena.
- As a supervisor, you may share information about supervision sessions with your supervisor(s) and/or colleague(s) within the site who are also bound by confidentiality.
- When applicable, explain that cases are discussed in contracted, off-site supervision. This would include external individual and group supervision or a peer consultation group.

There are situations where a client may request confidential information be shared with others. For example, a client may need to provide confirmation they are seeing a therapist for probation, parole, employee assistant program, child visitation rights, etc. In these cases, written consent must be obtained. Typically, these agreements are good for a maximum of one year from the signed date unless the client revokes consent. This consent can be revoked at any time. There is an exception when the client is court-mandated and the art therapist is required to disclose certain information without consent. Confirm through written and verbal review that the client understands this exception from the outset of treatment and especially prior to releasing information. The consent form should include:

- Signature;
- Date;
- Specific details about what information will be shared;
- Details of who the information will be shared with; and
- The purpose of the sharing of information. For general purposes, we often use the phrase "for continuity of care".

Minors and Others Unable to Consent

The age from when an individual can provide informed consent varies state by state with ethical and legal requirements that control informed consent but invariably impact confidentiality as well. Adherence discussions between supervisors and supervisees are critical to ensure everyone is operating from the same compliance intent. Speaking specifically of LGBTQ youth, Solomon, Heck, Reed, and Smith (2017) stressed the importance of understanding how jurisdictional regulations influence whether consenting caregivers are entitled to treatment information, or if the confidential information can be withheld if a minor client is likely to be harmed by the disclosure. Navigating these decisions should start in supervision, and may require legal consultation in some situations. Special consideration may be given, for example, in deciding whether to disclose an adolescent's LGBTQ identity with parents or legal guardians who are homophobic and unaccepting (Solomon et al., 2017).

Morality Issues

An art therapist must be willing to critically self-examine, in supervision, those moments when there is an urge to breach confidentiality over "morality" issues when one of the above exceptions does not apply. For example, what does an art therapist do when a client discloses committing a crime, but the crime does not endanger the patient or others? Some other examples to consider:

• A client discloses current drug use or sales. Are you considering reporting this to the police?
• Do you withhold marital infidelity from a client's spouse?
• Do you maintain confidentiality of the sexual attraction explorations of an LGBTQ adolescent client from a parent or guardian?

Clearly an art therapist's or their supervisor's individual moralistic views are not a rational basis for breaking confidentiality. However, the client's actions may still warrant an in-session therapeutic intervention and discussion from a judgment-free viewpoint. The decision to pursue a particular topic in session ought to be thoroughly discussed in supervision and be spurred by client need, not the therapist's morality.

Inadvertent Disclosures

Be very careful to avoid inadvertent disclosure. Even when redacting a client's name, enough information can often be gathered from facts to make assumptions about an identity, so a client's demographics and circumstances need to be *significantly* changed if used for discussion/case studies, including during group supervision sessions. Avoid having any conversations about clients in public spaces, including staff meeting areas, elevators, stairwells, etc. Files and paperwork, whether hard copy or electronic, also require careful oversight. Inadvertent disclosures can happen if one physically takes paperwork home. Imagine being in a car accident or having your backpack stolen and having confidential files discovered. Or, when working on an electronic file in a coffee shop, someone sitting next to you sees client information on your screen.

State- and Location-Specific

Some requirements related to confidentiality and disclosure of information are workplace-specific while others are state-specific, so it is important to know what applies in your particular location. Art therapist–client privilege is often determined by state case law and can be quite murky to navigate. New interpretations may set new precedents, so it is important to consult with a legal professional who is keeping up with these types of changes.

Social Media

The magnitude of social media impact cannot be understated. Social media "carries a sense of both permanence and impermanence: permanence in that users leave behind evidence of the sites they have visited and impermanence due to the speed at which current information supersedes previous data" (Boddy & Dominelli, 2017, p. 180). Social media can be a constructive and valuable forum – for professional exposure, to publicize art therapy services, to promote art therapy and educate others about it, to destigmatize mental health treatment, etc. However, personal social media accounts can be readily viewed and there are many considerations to make when using social media. "Without judicious consideration, social media use by psychotherapists can lead to inadvertent self-disclosures … that risk damaging the therapeutic alliance, interfering with therapeutic processes, and placing both the client and clinician at risk" (Baier, 2019, p. 341). Social workers Boddy and Dominelli (2017) identified the challenge "to use the benefits and opportunities that social media enables, without causing harm and reflect critically on their incorporation into everyday practice" (p. 174).

Posting client or supervisee quotes, pictures, videos, or other artwork to social media, even to platforms designed to disappear quickly (e.g., Snapchat), is hardly ever advisable or acceptable. There may be times when a client art show is being advertised and all appropriate consents have been obtained where this is ethically reasonable; however, it is impossible to "take back" this information. For example, if an individual revokes their consent, a digital footprint is left, even if the post is deleted. One way to protect the identity of clients and supervisees and the nature of the work is by using cropped photos of the art.

Additionally, many social media platforms include a "friending" or "following" component that adds to the complexity of social media and to the potential of unintentionally breaking confidentiality. The ATCB (2018) has a strict social media code for credential holders, stating that professional and personal profiles must be kept separate and no confidential information can be posted (p. 11). Furthermore, "art therapists shall not engage in any relationship, including through social media, with current or former clients, students, interns, trainees, supervisees, employees, or colleagues that is exploitative by its nature or effect" (ATCB, 2018, p. 8).

To recap, an understanding of confidentiality is important for many reasons. Most importantly: the role confidentiality plays in building relationship with a client, the related legal ramifications, and the considerable ethical concerns. Thus, it is always important to end the confidentiality statement/explanation by asking the client if they have any questions or concerns about confidentiality. Do not make assumptions! It is better for a client to hear it more than once than to not hear it at all.

Informed Consent

This section defines and reviews informed consent between client and therapist in the context of supervision, supervisor, and supervisee, and explores additional suggestions for the professional disclosure statement to increase understanding of the supervisory relationship. Informed consent, regardless of your theoretical approach, is a respectful and indispensable legal and ethical obligation that happens before the art therapy assessment or treatment begins (Corey, 2013; Knapp, VandeCreek, & Fingerhut, 2017). This is also true within the supervisory relationship.

It is essential for supervisors to educate supervisees on how to best implement and monitor informed consent to empower clients. Hodgson et al. (2013) define informed consent as the "process of bidirectional communication between a patient and provider that results in the patient's authorization or agreement to undergo a specific medical or mental health intervention(s)" (p. 30). Besides agreeing to participate in art therapy services, informed consent can clarify:

- General art therapy/counseling goals;
- The credentials and experience of the art therapist, including whether one is in training;
- Fees and compensation, if appropriate;
- The role and responsibilities of the art therapist;
- The function and ownership of art and artistic expression in therapy;
- The role and responsibilities of the client in therapy;
- The benefits and risks of therapy;
- Services provided and related legal and ethical boundaries; and
- How the client's case may be discussed outside of therapy – e.g., individual or group supervision, peer consultation, team meetings.

In addition, the communication exchange to establish informed consent empowers autonomous engagement and trust-building with the client "when they have the legal or cognitive capacity to do so" (Knapp et al., 2017, p. 88). Supervisors must understand and convey to supervisors the legal nuances to consent for treatment. As with confidentiality, the age of consent for obtaining art therapy services differs state by state with exceptions allowing minors to "give legal consent for treatment under certain circumstances, such as during an emergency or if they are legally emancipated" (Knapp et al., 2017, p. 88). When this is not the case, informed consent must be secured from a legal guardian before medical or mental health services commence (Williamson et al., 2017, p. 201). Likewise, some adults are not psychologically or medically able to consent for treatment and their "guardianship or decision-making powers for health care" are granted to an assigned, capable adult (Knapp et al., 2017, p. 88). In such cases informed consent is required from the responsible individual, not the adult client.

Whether it is a minor or an adult who has had their powers for health care granted to another adult, the legal guardian needs to be available to consent. Unavailability can be problematic and develop into a treatment barrier prior to the beginning of treatment if consent is difficult to obtain due to work schedules or other pressing family obligations (Williamson et al., 2017). Supervisors can support the development and implementation of population-specific and culturally respectful strategies to gain consent. Socioeconomic status and cultural influences such as caregiver roles can hamper obtaining informed consent. For example, families who depend on "kinship care (extended family or relative)" often rely on family members and friends who lack legal guardianship to manage a child's medical care and mental health needs (Williamson et al., 2017, p. 200).

Professional Disclosure Statement

Informed consent between supervisor and supervisee is not required per se, but a state or another governing body may set specific requirements. However, as discussed in Chapter 4, the ATCB requires the implementation of a professional disclosure statement in the application for the ATCS certification. The professional disclosure statement formalizes informed consent between the supervisor and the supervisee. Preparing the informed consent allows the supervisor to clearly articulate precisely what they expect of supervisees (Thomas, 2007). In addition to the required elements of the ATCB's professional disclosure statement for supervision covered in Chapter 4, we include additional steps to take when completing a supervisory disclosure/informed consent document:

- Explain that the supervisor must report unethical behavior by a supervisee to a licensing board or boards governing professional behavior;
- Define the supervisory alliance and clarify supervision to be provided;
- Clearly define the relevancy of accumulated supervision hours towards expected application – registration, licensure, increased clinical knowledge, etc.;

- Agree on means to evaluate the supervisee and the supervisor;
- Review ownership, storage, and use of art made in supervision;
- Include documentation and record-maintenance expectations;
- List emergencies contingencies, especially when a supervisor is not available; and
- Describe circumstances to end the supervisory alliance or refer to an additional/different supervisor.

Ethical Standards and Standards of Conduct

As mentioned throughout this book, art therapy supervisors must be familiar with and fulfill the ATCB *Code of Ethics, Conduct, and Disciplinary Procedures* (ATCB, 2018), which contain ethical standards (see Box 5.1) and standards of conduct (see Box 5.2) relating directly to a supervisor's responsibility to a supervisee or student regarding confidentiality and informed consent. We briefly highlight these standards and encourage all supervisors and supervisees to further familiarize themselves with the complete document.

Box 5.1 General Ethical Standards

The art therapy supervisor ensures the student/supervisee will:

- Inform clients of their professional status, and the name and contact information of the supervisor; and
- Obtain informed consent from clients to share client artwork or reproductions in supervision.

Art therapy supervisors shall provide supervisees with:

- A professional disclosure statement affirming the supervisor's adherence to the Code of Ethics, Conduct, and Disciplinary Procedures; and
- Instructions to address dissatisfaction with the supervision process.

Box 5.2 Standards of Conduct

Use and Reproduction of Client Art Expression and Therapy Sessions

The supervisor ensures the student/supervisee will:

- Obtain consent "before photographing the client's art expressions, making video or audio recordings, otherwise duplicating, or permitting third-party observation of art therapy sessions" (ACTB, 2018);
- Obtain written, informed consent before displaying the client's art; and
- Obtain signed consent for specific use of the client's art or information from sessions and treatment.

Electronic Means

The supervisor ensures student/supervisee will:

- "[I]nform clients of the benefits, risks, and limitations of using information technology applications in the therapeutic process and in business/billing procedures"; and
- "[Utilize encryption standards within Internet communications and/or take such precautions to reasonably ensure the confidentiality of information transmitted" (ACTB, 2018).

Artwork Release

Supervisors can alleviate much of the stress associated with artwork consent by recognizing that the artwork release – which asks clients if, when, and how their artwork can be released – empowers a client or supervisee to determine how their artwork can be used. While some sites have artwork release or consent forms, others do not. The supervisor is responsible for ensuring a release exists and is incorporated into practice, and that the supervisee is trained on implementation. Often times, trainees, new art therapists, or inexperienced supervisees are afraid of asking – unsure what words to use or how to explain the purpose of the consent form. Sometimes it is the fear of rejection, knowing a client or supervisee may refuse to provide consent. The perceived rejection ought to be reframed as simply a person's preference and not a personal attack. Implementing artwork release or consent forms protects client or supervisee privacy and clinical interactions. It ensures ethical treatment, regardless of where the work is being done. We are addressing this topic since it is often overlooked in supervision, and many supervisees are unsure of how to create an artwork release or approach a client about signing one.

We recommend that before art therapy sessions begin, art therapy clients be provided with an artwork release form. Often clients and supervisees wonder what will happen with the artwork they create in session. This form helps curtail any fears and clearly outlines the rights and privileges of the artist. An artwork release form empowers the client to make an informed decision on how their artwork or any reproductions may be used by the art therapist. This includes options such as:

- Consent to artwork being utilized for either exhibition, publication in a professional journal, presentation at professional conferences, or educational purposes.
- If consent is given, expressly identify whether the client wishes to remain anonymous or be identified.
- Deny consent for artwork to be utilized for all purposes.

Additionally, it is important to note the art may be discussed with a clinical supervisor, fellow clinical supervisees, and in consultation with other mental health professionals. Of course, site-specific jurisdiction requirements always prevail. A client can change their decision at any time, but clients must always be aware they cannot reverse any previously permitted use of the art. Since pleasing the therapist may be in play during the intake process, as a rule we often encourage clients to choose to keep their artwork private and decide at a later date if they would like to grant permission. We recommend initiating the discussion of artwork consent in the beginning of therapy rather than the middle or end, so clients do not feel they made anything particularly notable (good or bad!) in session worth "showing". For those who need to create their own form, see Appendix E for a sample artwork release form. If working for a site, be sure to have your on-site supervisor or administrator check the form to ensure compliance with all policies and procedures.

Documentation and Communication

What makes art therapy distinct from counseling and other forms of psychotherapy is the visual art used in the process of therapy, oftentimes resulting in an art product. As such, the artwork is part of the therapy and therefore must be documented and treated like written notes. This means both written notes in charts and the artwork are to be kept secure and accessible only by individuals who are part of the treatment team. This boundary needs to be held fast and confidentiality must be honored. However, "keeping mental and medical providers, records, and treatments separate propagates the stigmatization and fragmentation of care common to mental health and substance abuse issues" (Hodgson et al., 2013, p. 28). To reduce mental health stigmatization, concerted efforts need to be made while following the documentation protocol based on the site's requirements. Art therapists are also required to confidentially record the work they perform, and supervisors are required to ensure their supervisees are cognizant of this and comply.

Health Insurance Portability Accounting Act

Documentation protocols must comply with federal privacy laws, specifically HIPAA, for clients seeking mental health services. The purpose of HIPAA is to protect an individual's health information while permitting the exchange of needed health information, and encourage "high quality health care and protect the public's health and wellbeing" and "[strike] a balance that permits important uses of information, while protecting the privacy of people who seek care and healing" (U.S. Department of Health and Human Services, 2003, p. 1). Even though HIPAA promotes the sharing of health information, minimal disclosure is an explicit and central principle to be adhered to. The U.S. Department of Health and Human Services (n.d.) describes HIPAA in the following way:

> The HIPAA Security Rule establishes national standards to protect individuals' electronic personal health information that is created, received, used, or maintained by a covered entity. The Security Rule requires appropriate administrative, physical and technical safeguards to ensure the confidentiality, integrity, and security of electronic protected health information.
>
> (para. 1)

Family Education Rights and Privacy Act

For supervisors working with art therapy students, FERPA applies as well. FERPA is

> a federal law that affords parents the right to have access to their children's education records, the right to seek to have the records amended, and the right to have some control over the disclosure of personally identifiable information from the education records.
> (U.S. Department of Education, n.d., para. 1)

Once an individual turns 18 years of age or enrolls in a postsecondary institution, the parents are no longer entitled to their child's FERPA rights, as the rights transfer to the student. FERPA covers supervisees currently matriculated in a postsecondary institution and determines confidentiality of student records.

Documentation

Regardless of the format, all client information, including artwork, reproductions of the artwork, case records, etc., must be secure. Secure storage can be locked filing cabinets, locked offices, and password-protected computers and websites. Supervisors must instruct supervisees in these practices and verify all security measures are adhered to.

Documentation is often done in a chart dedicated to the client. Charts can be a paper file or electronic. In hospitals and other locations where multiple services or people work with the same client, the chart may be accessed and read by multiple providers. Documentation of the art therapy session can take narrative form, or it can be more structured. In either case, the art therapist writes the significant points of what occurred in session.

Artwork

If you have unlimited storage space, original artworks can be kept in locked cabinets or rooms, similar to how paper charts are stored. However, this is not the case for many art therapists, especially when working with three-dimensional materials, which take up significantly more space than works on paper that can be stored in flat files or portfolios. Furthermore, art therapists may work with individuals or groups to create an installation, an environmental or site-specific piece, or even a mural on an outdoor wall – none of these are possible to store in the traditional sense of the word. When art is created in a group setting, whether with supervisees or clients, ownership should be addressed (Deaver & Shiflett, 2011).

In the case where original artworks cannot be stored, the art therapist can photograph the artwork. Since digital photography is now widely available, artworks can easily be photographed, and then either printed to be put in a physical paper chart, stored electronically in the client's electronic file, or otherwise stored in an encrypted manner. In the case of electronic art documentation, it is important to note the size and materials of the works created. Also consider photographing artworks from multiple angles and include detailed (i.e., close-up) shots to ensure that nuances such as materials, pressure, etc., are recorded.

Technology

Smart phones, laptop computers, USB flash drives, notebook computers, and digital cameras have adeptly transformed how we store and transfer protected client data. However, technology can complicate confidentiality – electronic case records must be carefully secured. Supervisors are tasked with guiding supervisees on best practices for maximizing confidentiality and minimizing risk. Encryption is one critical method that restricts the reading of a message solely to the sender and the intended recipient. Encryption protects the data from being viewed when inadvertent acts of disclosure, such as accidently sending a file to the wrong email address, or calculated threats such as robbery and theft, occur.

Takeaways

- Confidentiality and informed consent within the supervisory relationship are as equally important as confidentiality between the art therapist and the client.
- Confidentiality is pivotal to trust-building in the initial stages of the art therapy alliance, and should not be viewed as a barrier. This process of defining and clarifying what confidentiality entails allows for the affirmation of legal boundaries, including responsibility for verbal and written disclosures by an art therapist, as well the use and purpose of client art created in session.
- Confidentiality and informed consent can be modeled within the supervisory relationship; it is a topic that should be routinely monitored in supervision.
- Embracing confidentiality and informed consent reframes the obligation of an art therapist to maintain a legally responsible role that protects the client from harm to himself or herself or others, and limits unwanted and unnecessary disclosures.
- In all situations, the art therapist must adhere to the most applicable jurisdiction, depending on licensure, certification, credentials, and code of ethics.

Practice Prompts

At some point you will most likely be required to break client confidentiality as a mandated reporter. In preparation, review your state's mandated reporter guide, such as the *Summary Guide for Mandated Reporters in New York State* (https://ocfs.ny.gov/main/publications/Pub1159.pdf). This will provide guidance when required to report suspect child abuse, maltreatment, or another potential offense from your professional capacity. For example, if an elementary student shares suicidal ideation with a plan (i.e., walking into traffic, access to a gun) this is a mandated reporting situation.

Breaking Confidentiality with Composure

Create a storyboard or comic strip layout of you compassionately breaking confidentiality, such as the duty to warn, in a manner that could potentially build trust.

- Recognize the way a warranted breaking of confidentiality is truly in service of the client and the therapeutic alliance.
- Role-play with supervisor using your storyboard as a rough script. Switch roles for maximum understanding.

Moral Interference

During a supervision group, use art to depict three instances where your personal moral impulses or beliefs may urge you to inappropriately break confidence in a professional setting.

- For example, a young adolescent suggests they are engaging in sexual activity and you are considering disclosing this to the parents or caregivers.
- Share art and discuss it with fellow supervisees.

Confidentiality: A Barrier or Opportunity?

In supervision, recall a specific client experience where you and/or the client perceived of and engaged confidentiality as an obstacle to the therapeutic alliance.

- Free write, without censorship, about this incident for three minutes. If you and/or the client experienced confidentiality as an obstacle, was this eventually overcome? If not, what did you learn from the experience? Share and discuss your findings with your supervisor.
- In a free-writing format, write about a specific client experience where you and/or the client engaged confidentiality as a springboard to build trust. Share with your supervisor for more in-depth discussion.

Additional Resources

- The Complexities of Client Confidentiality – www.socialworktoday.com/news/eoe_0216.shtml
- The Limits of Confidentiality – www.socialworktoday.com/news/eoe_041402.shtml
- Essential Law in Social Work Ethics – www.socialworktoday.com/news/eoe_101813.shtml
- Social Worker Duty to Warn vs. Confidentiality – https://work.chron.com/social-worker-duty-warn-vs-confidentiality-8895.html
- Confidentiality and the Duty to Warn: Ethical and Legal Implications for the Therapeutic Relationship – www.socialworker.com/feature-articles/ethics-articles/Confidentiality_&_the_Duty_to_Warn:_Ethical_ and_Legal_Implications_for_the_Therapeutic_Relationship/

References

ATCB. (2018). Code of ethics, conduct and disciplinary procedures. Retrieved from www.atcb.org/resource/pdf/ATCB-Code-of-Ethics-Conduct-DisciplinaryProcedures.pdf

Baier, A. L. (2019). The ethical implications of social media: Issues and recommendations for clinical practice. *Ethics & Behavior, 29*(5), 341–351.

Boddy, J., & Dominelli, L. (2017). Social media and social work: The challenges of a new ethical space. *Australian Social Work, 70*(2), 172–184.

Corey, G. (2013). *Theory and practice of counseling and psychotherapy.* Belmont, CA: Brooks/Cole.

Deaver, S. P., & Shiflett, C. (2011). Art-based supervision techniques. *The Clinical Supervisor, 30*(2), 257–276. doi:10.1080/07325223.2011.619456

Hodgson, J., Mendenhall, T., & Lamson, A. (2013). Patient and provider relationships: Consent, confidentiality, and managing mistakes in integrated primary care settings. *Families, Systems, & Health, 31*(1), 28.

Knapp, S. J., VandeCreek, L. D., & Fingerhut, R. (2017). *Practical ethics for psychologists: A positive approach* (3rd ed.). Washington, DC: American Psychological Association.

Moon, B. L. (2006). *Ethical issues in art therapy* (2nd ed.). Springfield, IL: Charles C Thomas.

Solomon, D. T., Heck, N., Reed, O. M., & Smith, D. W. (2017). Conducting culturally competent intake interviews with LGBTQ youth. *Psychology of Sexual Orientation and Gender Diversity, 4*(4), 403.

Thomas, J. T. (2007). Informed consent through contracting for supervision: Minimizing risks, enhancing benefits. *Professional Psychology: Research and Practice, 38*(3), 221–231.

U.S. Department of Education. (n.d.). Protecting Student Privacy: What is FERPA? Retrieved from https://studentprivacy.ed.gov/faq/what-ferpa

U.S. Department of Health and Human Services. (2003). OCR privacy brief: Summary of the HIPAA privacy rule. Washington, DC: Office for Civil Rights, HIPAA Compliance Assistance. Retrieved from www.hhs.gov/sites/default/files/privacysummary.pdf

U.S. Department of Health and Human Services. (n.d.). The security rule. Retrieved from www.hhs.gov/hipaa/for-professionals/security/index.html

Williamson, A. A., Raglin Bignall, W. J., Swift, L. E., Hung, A. H., Power, T. J., Robins, P. M., & Mautone, J. A. (2017). Ethical and legal issues in integrated care settings: Case examples from pediatric primary care. *Clinical Practice in Pediatric Psychology, 5*(2), 196.

Part 3

Embracing and Working with Differences

Working with difference is the cornerstone of this book. Difference influences how we navigate our roles as clinicians, supervisors, educators, and our personal lives. This part acknowledges the importance of naming differences, particularly race, ethnicity, and other socio-cultural factors. The different perspectives of the supervisor, supervisee, and the client are also important to take into account. The title of this part includes *work* – an intentional word choice. Naming differences and attending to their influences on the therapeutic and supervisory alliances is work – often hard work.

One reason we chose to co-author this book is we have very different lived experiences, and a long history of not only naming but also working with the differences between us. Maintaining a commitment to acknowledge and work through blind spots and differing perspectives has, at times, been easy, and at other points it has been quite uncomfortable. It is difficult, rewarding work. Fortunately, since 1999 we have navigated the many changes of our professional relationship and personal friendship to create a rich history of navigating difference. Our intent is to utilize our own intersectionalities of race, gender, sexuality, age, and other points of difference to strengthen the content and focus of the book.

While this book as a whole embraces and centers diversity and difference, this distinct part is dedicated to this work because we firmly believe it warrants additional attention. This part contains three chapters:

- Racial, Ethnic, and Socio-cultural Differences: Supervisor, Supervisee, and Client;
- Disciplinary Differences: When Your Supervisor Is Not an Art Therapist; and
- Disciplinary Differences: When Your Supervisee Is Not an Art Therapist.

To help you explore this work, and illustrate these crucial topics, we highlight vignettes from former supervisees and supervisors, arts-based supervision interventions, and practice prompts. This part is heavily influenced by Feminist Multicultural Supervision, which recognizes the necessity of acknowledging differences and attending to power dynamics.

6 Racial, Ethnic, and Socio-cultural Differences across Supervisor, Supervisee, and Client

Introduction

Our identities and social location impact the clinical work we engage in with clients and supervisee alike. Within the supervisory relationship, cultural issues tend to focus on the therapist–client dyad. We want to highlight other aspects of the triadic supervisor–supervisee–client relationship, including the supervisor–supervisee and supervisor–client dyads, and systemic differences between supervisee–agency and supervisee–community. To frame our approaches to this work in supervision, we review how feminist and critical race theories can help ground the supervisor and supervisee to have conversations surrounding power and difference.

Cross-cultural supervision is described in terms of what is visible (e.g., race and gender) and aspects that are often more hidden (e.g., sexual orientation, religion, ability). Culturally aware supervision has been explicitly discussed in the supervision literature (see Hardy & Bobes, 2016); we expand on how supervisors in art therapy can further this endeavor. Studies of effective and ineffective cross-cultural clinical supervision incidents (see Wong, Wong, & Ishiyama, 2013) are appraised and applied to the art therapy supervision relationship. An emphasis on encouraging the supervisor and the supervisee to intentionally "introduce cultural issues into the supervisory relationship" is also made (Hird, Cavalieri, Dulko, Felice, & Ho., 2001, p. 116). To help with this undertaking, we propose helpful ways of broaching difference (Day-Vines et al., 2007; Hays, 2016) and tips on how to encourage dialogue if a supervisor or supervisee is not ready to talk about such differences.

We also provide case examples to illustrate the importance of recognizing and discussing cultural differences, and how broaching them in supervision can promote meaningful clinical work. We value the supervisory relationship as a place to enhance the supervisee's ability to navigate differences within the therapeutic alliance, whether between the supervisor–supervisee, supervisee (therapist)–client, or supervisor–client. We "think and talk openly about our different backgrounds and experiences within a multi ethnic, mixed racial, global frame, [to decrease the likelihood that] white, Eurocentric, middle class, heterosexual assumptions and stereotypes will continue within supervision settings where we practice" (Dudley, 2013, p. 493).

Every therapeutic relationship contains multiple intersecting diversities. It is of the utmost importance to delve into these intersections within the supervisory relationship. Of particular importance to the field of art therapy is that the majority of art therapy students, who identify as white and female, reportedly work with clients of racial or ethnic minorities (Awais & Yali, 2015). Acknowledging and bridging the multiple dimensions can be pivotal in determining outcomes of therapy and influence client-centered age and culturally appropriate goals and interventions. Therapists must integrate the bearing of their personal culture, privilege, and professional experience within the therapeutic context. Strategies, such as practicing mindfulness, are promoted to help therapists hold an awareness of their various identities and impact in the therapeutic relationship to better serve clients with similar or differing identities.

Therapists also have an ethical responsibility to maintain a safe practice for clients and themselves. Remember, we live in the same climate as our clients. However, we may be impacted differently. During these challenging times, in which we witness instances of racism, mass shootings, sexism, and terrorism on a frequent basis, counselors and therapists are required to serve persons of all backgrounds. Yet hate bills are being passed that allow therapists to refuse to see clients based on "sincerely held principles" (Talwar, 2017, p. 102), which does not promote working constructively across differences. Addressing political and social issues in session, how to work with clients who have views that are prejudiced, and how to work with clients who are different from us, racially or culturally, will be discussed. This chapter also provides tools to address difficult issues.

Defining Culture, Acknowledging Differences and Similarities

The first step to working across cultures (and, we would argue, also working *within* cultures) in supervision is to understand power, privilege, and social identity. In *Racism in the United States: Implications for the Helping Professions*, Miller and Garran describe agent status identities (i.e., areas of more social power and privilege) and target status identities (i.e., those which have less social power and privilege) (2017). While this chapter does not go into multicultural therapy/counseling techniques in depth, we name a few models that can guide a clinician's work and be discussed in supervision. Racial identity development models impact supervisors, supervisees/clinicians and clients. Each model considers the social location of the therapist. In other words, the therapist is not a neutral, raceless, genderless blank slate but an individual who is impacted by the environment and other persons. Ideally, the supervisor and supervisee/clinician understand their own identity *before* working with clients. These models are useful in thinking about ourselves as supervisors, our supervisees as therapists, and the clients that engage in art therapy.

Pamela Hays's ADDRESSING framework is a concrete tool for individuals who are just starting to incorporate addressing issues of diversity and difference in supervision. She highlights and raises awareness to the fact that race, ethnicity, and culture are often conflated in ways that perpetuate hegemonic practices (Hays, 1996). ADDRESSING is an acronym that specifies aspects of identities:

- **A**ge and generational differences;
- **D**evelopmental or other **D**isability;
- **R**eligion and spiritual orientation;
- **E**thnic and racial identity;
- **S**ocioeconomic status;
- **S**exual orientation;
- **I**ndigenous heritage;
- **N**ational origin; and
- **G**ender.

Hays reminds us power and privilege are contextual and what constitutes power in one cultural context may be of target status in another. For example, in the current climate in the United States, identifying as Muslim is not privileged – however, in Saudi Arabia it is. See Vignette 6.1 for Yasmine's story of how differences are perceived by location.

Vignette 6.1 How Differences are Perceived

Yasmine's Story

My experience as an expat in Japan and Saudi Arabia, layered on top of my experience growing up first-generation in an immigrant household in the United States, has allowed me to have different perspectives on how power and privilege are perceived. Growing up in an upper-middle-class suburb, I had access to high-achieving public education in a mostly white neighborhood. Simultaneously, I (and my family) were always the ones who were "different" in regard to race and culture, not fitting in. In Japan, I was valued because of my American-accented English, yet simultaneously questioned as I did not "look" American. I lived in a Brazilian enclave, which resulted in being addressed in Portuguese. Being perceived as Brazilian in my neighborhood implied that I worked in a factory and most likely was less educated than an American expat.

Moving to Saudi Arabia, I was perceived differently again. Wearing a name badge at work, I was perceived as Saudi and addressed in Arabic on account of my name and physical features. Because of my mixed religious background, I was seen by some as Muslim, and by others as not Muslim enough. As Saudi Arabia also has a history of importing its work force, I was simultaneously seen as privileged by Pakistanis – who tend to be employed as laborers – and Filipinx who were employed as nurses. I was often reminded how "lucky" I was to be FilAm (Filipinx American). Furthermore, in Saudi Arabia, expats are paid not only by their degree and position title, but also according to which passport they hold. Holding a blue American passport gave me access and privilege my colleagues did not have.

The five-stage Racial/Cultural Identity Development model (R/CID) is widely used, and fully explained in *Counseling the Culturally Diverse* (Sue, Sue, Neville, & Smith, 2019). R/CID is useful in supervision as a framework in understanding a person's stage of identity development, particularly for persons of color. A summary of R/CID's stages is:

1. Conformity: focus is on assimilating to the dominant white culture.
2. Dissonance: Sense of conflict develops when one realizes that one cannot escape one's culture.
3. Resistance and Immersion: increased pride of one's own culture and rejecting of the dominant white culture. Actively seeking out more information about one's culture, increased anger at the dominant society and culture.
4. Introspection: discomfort in rigidly held views (i.e., my culture is good and the dominant culture is bad). Attempting to develop an integrated identity.
5. Integrative Awareness:

   The person begins to perceive [themselves] as an autonomous individual who is unique (individual level of identity), a member of [their] own racial-cultural group (group level of identity), a member of larger society, and a member of the human race (universal level of identity).
   (Sue et al., 2019, p. 245)

Janet Helms' White Racial Identity Development (WRID) is a six-stage model that looks at white identity development in relation to Black persons (1984):

1. Contact: the moment when a person notices there are people of other races. People may choose to "withdraw", or not have contact with others, or "approach" and befriend Blacks (p. 156).
2. Disintegration: the acknowledgement of whiteness.
3. Reintegration: when a white individual becomes hostile towards Blacks and more positive towards whites.
4. Pseudo-independent: "intellectual acceptance and curiosity", including cross-racial interactions (p. 156).
5. Autonomy: white individuals are accepting of racial differences, in addition to being intellectually knowledgeable.

Aponte's Person of the Therapist model (POTT) specifically looks at the therapist themselves, and how their social location impacts work with clients, regardless of model or type of therapy being utilized (Aponte & Kissil, 2016). POTT has been adapted for the supervisory relationship, with the primary goal of better clinical outcomes, not therapist growth (although that is welcomed) (Aponte & Carlsen, 2009). Aponte and Carlsen developed a group supervision instrument containing 12 questions the supervisee completes for every case attended. There is also a post-supervisory questionnaire containing four questions, which is completed after the supervisory session. Similar to POTT, equal weight is given to considering the client and supervisee's social location. Since the supervision instrument is "model-neutral", the art therapist can adapt the instrument to include artworks the client creates and the subjective responses to materials, subject matter, and quality of the artwork. In essence, the instrument's purpose

> is for therapists to then envision how they will use themselves in working with their client(s) at each stage of the therapy—the formulation of the issue, the reasoning about what comprises the issue with the consequent goals of the therapy, and finally the implementation of the therapeutic strategy with its corresponding technical interventions.
>
> (Aponte & Carlsen, 2009, p. 399)

Wilbur, Kuemmel, and Lackner (2019) identify "diversity factors, including disability [as a] key variable in the quality of the supervisory relationship" (p. 112). Disability is often overlooked in diversity discussions and requires thoughtful planning and implementation in the supervision process (Wilbur et al., 2019).

Tools to Address Differences

Identifying art therapy and counseling supervision strategies is essential to supporting supervisees as they navigate differences competently within the therapeutic alliance. When integrated skillfully into therapeutic practice, the verbal and arts-based interventions, along with supervisor self-disclosure, can advance the supervisor–supervisee and supervisee–client alliance in numerous ways. For example, one game-changing intervention is simply perceiving the contributing factors to bias and prejudice as a symptom of racism rather than as *the* problem. Routine interventions need to recognize basics such as mitigating the influence of privilege and addressing the bearing of values variance on the supervisory and therapeutic alliances.

Theory and Praxis

Theoretical approaches cognizant of differences are also useful in clinical relationships. A colorblind approach to therapy can lead to microaggressions (see Sue et al., 2007). Similarly, an approach that neglects to address cultural differences, particularly race, can, at best, lead to similar microaggressions, or, at worst, can be damaging (see Hardy & Bobes, 2016). Acknowledging and speaking about differences in supervision demonstrates to the supervisee the importance of bringing cultural competence and humility to the forefront of our work. In other words, by acknowledging differences between supervisee and supervisor, supervisee and client, and supervisor and client in the supervision space, art therapy that is social justice oriented can be promoted in the art therapy studio/clinical realm. The field of art therapy has been increasingly interrogative of the dominant paradigm, and is currently reflecting on more inclusive, reflective, and critical pedagogies. Practitioners are introducing intersectionality, critical race theory, and critical race feminism (CRF) into our fields and disciplines: in art therapy specifically (Talwar, 2010, 2018), and more broadly in the creative arts therapies (Mayor, 2012; Sajnani, 2012; Sajnani, Marxen, & Zarate, 2017) and psychology (Rosenthal, 2016). Some of these critiques allude to the need to pay attention to the training of practitioners (see Mayor, 2012; Rosenthal, 2016). However, supervision activities, vital to promoting these theoretical approaches in practice, are notably missing from these readings. We implore art therapists to further these critical perspectives in the supervisory relationship, to allow for the movement of these ideas back and forth into the therapeutic space.

CRITICAL RACE FEMINISM

It is out of the scope of this chapter to fully discuss the theories from disciplines outside of the psychotherapy and mental health paradigms that influence applications in approaching difference in supervision. However, as clinicians, supervisors, and supervisees, understanding social science theories provides grounding to challenge hegemonic ways of practice. One particularly useful theoretical approach that promotes discourse surrounding race and gender is CRF. As suggested in the name, CRF has roots in critical race theory and a range of feminisms. These paradigms are especially important in a context of neoliberalism, which promotes: the notion of colorblindness, the idea that all individuals are equal, and individualism and meritocracy for profit and gain. CRF also strives to counter hegemonic practices, meaning it questions the claim that those in power are in such positions due to ability, effort, or skill – not wealth, power, privilege, and systemic racism. Unlike first- and second-wave feminisms, which have been critiqued for focusing on the narratives of able-bodied white women, CRF situates itself along the lines of race, gender, class, sex, age, and ability. See Sajnani (2012) for more on CRF in the creative arts therapies.

INTERSECTIONALITY

For therapy and supervision, the relevance of intersectionality is the capacity for identities to be seen collectively; meaning, it is necessary to consider factors such as race and gender *together* and not as individual demographic factors. Intersectionality is an epistemology rooted in critical race theory and Black feminism, originating from legal studies and currently applied in a wide range of contexts (Carbado, Crenshaw, Mays, & Tomlinson, 2013). The five core themes of intersectionality have been identified by Carbado and colleagues (2013) as:

1. Being always in motion as a work in progress;
2. It has an interdisciplinary nature, including law, sociology, psychology, education, history, and political science;
3. It is global and not bounded by the United States borders;
4. It lifts up the voices of Black women and their experiences; and
5. It understands the importance of social movements.

CULTURAL HUMILITY AS PRAXIS

We put forth cultural humility as one strategy that can be adapted for supervision. While the American Art Therapy Association (AATA, 2015) promotes "multicultural and diversity competence" as an ethical principle, the notion of competency can be problematic as it implies a fixed awareness, knowledge, and skill base. While some authors suggest cultural competence is a lifelong learning process (see Sue et al., 2019), others prefer an approach referred to as *cultural humility*. Coined by Tervalon and Murray-Garcia (1998), cultural humility was originally conceptualized for the physician–patient relationship, and has made its way into psychology (Hook, Davis, Owen, Worthington, & Utsey, 2013). "Cultural humility incorporates a lifelong commitment to self-evaluation and critique, to redressing the power imbalances in the physician-patient dynamic, and to developing mutually beneficial and non-paternalistic partnerships with communities on behalf of individuals and defined populations" (Tervalon & Murray-Garcia, 1998, p. 123). While cultural competency can potentially be achieved by focusing on the "other", cultural humility is an iterative process that involves self-reflection and self-critique. This foundation is aligned with critical race practices and intersectional frameworks.

Self-reflexivity is an inherent part of cultural humility. Talwar[1] (2010) questions the "reductive paradigm of normal versus abnormal" (p. 16) promoted by art therapy due to its western psychodynamic roots. In the Commission on Accreditation of Allied Health Education Programs' (CAAHEP) *Standards and Guidelines for the Accreditation of Educational Programs in Art Therapy* (2016), cultural competence curriculum expectations are addressed in Content Area n: Cultural and Social Issues. The content area clearly anticipates students will "understand the relevance of cultural competence to strategies for working with diverse communities, understanding of privilege and oppression and reflective thinking in regards to the therapist's own attitudes and beliefs" (p. 27). With these directives, students and newer graduates may be better versed in the capacity of reflective thinking around privilege and oppression.

Hook et al. (2013) identify three implications for training therapists in cultural humility: encouraging a partnership between therapists and clients for therapists to learn about the client's worldview, even if the therapist has "expertise" in diversity matters; in addition to knowledge and skills, learning how to practice "humility"; and aligning with social justice goals. Hook et al. (2013) state these are related to training of psychologists broadly, and do not discuss how cultural humility can occur specifically in supervision. The benefit of exploring cultural humility in supervision, in addition to the classroom or field at large, is supervision often occurs more intimately and for longer periods of time. Because of these factors, being vulnerable (i.e., sharing one is not an expert) is well suited to the intimate supervision setting. This is not to say cultural humility should be relegated to supervision; however, supervision can be a safer place to practice cultural humility before taking the risk to be vulnerable with a client. This can be achieved by asking questions and through role-playing clinical experiences in supervision, rather than trying to be the expert on the culture of your supervisor or supervisee.

FEMINIST MULTICULTURAL PSYCHOTHERAPY SUPERVISION

Another application of theory is Feminist Multicultural Supervision (FMS), which focuses on power and power dynamics between the various relationships involved in treatment – supervisee/therapist–client, supervisor–supervisee, and supervisor–supervisee–client–society. Alexis Arczynski and Susan Morrow (2017) asked "how do self-identified FM psychotherapy supervisors conceptualize and practice feminist supervision that is explicitly multicultural?" (p. 193). Seven categories were identified through the analysis of the 14 participants:

1. Power is present and complex inside and outside of the supervisory relationship.
2. The histories of the supervisors influence their work, particularly their experiences of racism and oppression.
3. Trust is built by having a transparent supervisory relationship, which included purposefully disclosing how their identities and values may influence the supervisory relationship.
4. Ongoing collaboration, including times of evaluation.
5. Attention to developmental processes of supervisees, understanding that all supervisees are at different stages of learning.
6. Being "consciously aware" and "exploring how bias creeps in" (p. 200).
7. Paying attention to context and how society and culture impact clients' mental health and can also be used to impact change.

Arczynski and Morrow (2017) further explain the inherent power in supervision can be mitigated by paying attention to the following:

*   Bringing history into the supervision room;
*   Creating trust through openness and honesty;
*   Using a collaborative process;
*   Meeting shifting developmental (a)symmetries;
*   Cultivating critical reflexivity; and
*   Looking at and counterbalancing the impact of context (p. 202).

Vignette 6.2 Addressing Differences in Supervision

Emily's Story

Emily, now a licensed and board-certified professional, was once an art therapy and counseling intern at a camp for New York City (NYC) families directly impacted by HIV/AIDS, where Yasmine was her supervisor. In this vignette, Emily reflects on how her professional and personal identities crossed during her training.

The camp was hours away from the families' homes, away from public transportation so one could not leave camp without effort. This is notable since, in NYC, public transportation is a cultural norm. For the adults, the camp included daily psychosocial groups to address a variety of topics, including serostatus disclosure to family members. However, for those under 18 years of age, the camp included no therapy components and was filled with typical summer camp activities such as swimming, arts and crafts, and archery. Before camp began, Emily's internship required home visits for intakes, which included assessment for camp appropriateness.

Emily's Reflection on Discussing Differences in Supervision

I have spent the majority of my professional life working with diverse populations. With this work has come recognition of my privilege. I am a white, middle-class, young woman, in a cis-gendered heterosexual marriage. I represent the societally accepted norm of middle-class life. My work in supervision has propelled me into a deep and meaningful understanding of how my power plays out with clients. I can think back to my first two internships, when I was young and very idealistic. I wanted to help "the less fortunate" and at the same time struggled to admit to my own privilege. In supervision, I learned that any commonalities I had with a client, while valid, did not supersede my privilege and power. I spent a lot of time in supervision exploring my own bias in the context of the client's world. Just because I had been on food stamps or had been bullied or ridiculed because of my weight did not mean that I could understand the deep and vast pain of systematic and systemic racism. Supervision showed me how to look deeper at my motivations of connecting with clients: What was I searching for? Why was this kind of connection with my client was important? Would it benefit them or would it in some way validate my own struggle? I learned to stop functioning for good intentions and instead work towards a more profound understanding that would benefit my clients. Only after this internal transition did I see myself providing meaningful and authentic support to others.

Yasmine's Reflection on Supervision with Emily

Emily and I had an unusual supervisory experience. Unlike other student supervisees I have worked with, Emily and I had many types and locations of supervision. In addition to formal, sit-down supervision where we reflected on the work we did with clients as a whole, we had informal supervision between home visits. The location of supervision varied – formal supervision occurred in my home prior to camp, or in a cabin at camp. Informal supervision occurred in the car. Supervision sessions, like the home visits, were intimate. They were not in an office and involved deep reflection on race, socio-economic status, and health status – three factors which profoundly impacted the lives of the campers. I perceived Emily as a student who was observant and reflective, willing to learn and grow. I wonder if part of Emily's ability to shift from saving clients to connecting with them on a deeper level centered on the intimacy of supervision, which mirrored the intimacy of conducting assessments in the client-camper homes. Because of Emily's ability to show uncertainty and overall willingness to take on a non-traditional internship, I felt more comfortable to support, yet challenge her good intentions.

Part of our discussions in supervision involved deconstructing the term "appropriateness" – what factors are to be considered? Does a family or individual being deemed appropriate for camp benefit the camp structure (e.g., the therapist, camp counselors, medical directors, and other campers) or the camper themselves? Is medication adherence a factor? If so, is an adult authorized to make informed decisions about not taking HIV medications, but children cannot? What about using a harm-reduction model of managing drug use? Should it be expected that a 6-year-old be "homesick" at camp and cry for their grandmother or big sister, when they are in a separate cabins from their family members who are at camp? In posing these questions to Emily, she was able to shift her framework to not knowing what is right for every family, but considering each individual situation for what it was at the time.

BROACHING

As noted in Vignette 6.2, Emily engaged in broaching behavior, which "refers to a consistent and ongoing attitude of openness with a genuine commitment by the counselor to continually invite the client to explore issues of diversity" (Day-Vines et al., 2007, p. 402). In supervision, we set the expectation to openly discuss differences and similarities between the clients and the therapist, particularly regarding race and socioeconomics. The supervisee and supervisor discussed topics that clients were dealing with and how the supervisee related to those issues, such as the utilization of social services and benefits, living/visiting others in public housing, and a history of attending sleep-away camp. Hird et al. (2001) suggest race and culture be brought up early in the supervisory relationship, similar to Day-Vines and colleagues (2007) encouraging discussion of issues of difference early on clinically.

Broaching behavior requires the supervisor to commit to continuously invite the supervisee to raise issues of diversity about their relationship as well as the relationship between the supervisee and client(s), regardless of whether the supervisee is raising the issue. The onus is on the supervisor to initiate these discussions, as the supervisor holds the power in the relationship through scheduling, payment, grades, promotions, and/or other aspects. However, Hird and colleagues (2001) note that the supervisee may be more eager to bring up issues of diversity, and at times the supervisor may be hesitant due to lack of training, expertise, and comfort. The authors suggest self-disclosure as one technique for creating a bridge between supervisors and supervisees (Hird et al., 2001). For example, a supervisor can disclose to a supervisee a struggle they had when working on their own blind spots. Another suggestion is for supervisors and supervisees to attend training together as a way to model learning together. Finally, supervisors should also be in their own supervision or other consultation group when they are supervising (Hird et al., 2001). For more on holding difference in therapy and supervision, see Vignette 6.3 by Blair and Yasmine.

Vignette 6.3 Differences Between Therapist and Client

Blair's Story

Blair was engaged in off-site, professional individual supervision with Yasmine. He went to graduate school for art therapy and counseling in another state and was looking for supervision that would meet multiple needs – art therapy registration (ATR), and state licensure (LPC). Furthermore, he was seeking supervision sensitive to issues surrounding race and culture.

Reflecting on Difference

Although I (Blair) understand that it is essential to be aware of ethnic differences, race, gender, and individual beliefs as a therapist, it is rare that I bring them to light when there are clear differences. Having worked with multiple races, genders, creeds, and many people who identify as different from me, I try to control the one thing that I can, and that is myself. I make sure that I am up to speed on those differences and how they will affect what types of services I give, as it is also a major part of the Functional Family Therapy (FFT) model: matching. For example, when working with Hispanic families, it is typical that the males of the house are treated as the heads of the household or the future heads of the household. In turn, they are given more freedom, privilege, and leeway than the woman of the house. Knowing this, I do not find it imperative to make it known that I am aware of this cultural difference. However, it is imperative that I map my treatment, and how I plan to administer this treatment, around that knowledge and other knowledge that I have. In turn, my lack of verbal acknowledgement is compensated by the implementation of treatment and how each family responds.

Throughout my career, I have worked primarily with teenage girls. My first job was with teen parents who were survivors of domestic violence, and my second was in a girls' residential home. I have always been conscious of the fact that I am a male within the space of females, and will never be able to fully resonate with the women I worked with. However, in my non-work life I am surrounded by female companions and few to no males. This has made it very easy to connect with young women, not only because of the contact I have in my personal life, but because, over the years, I have learned how to successfully create boundaries with the women in my life. Due to this, when working with women it is rare that I acknowledge the fact that I am a male, or the differences within our gender dynamic. When conducting the FFT model, if there is not an apparent blocker or distraction to the connection between therapist and client, we focus on the family. It is a fast-paced model, and conversation and interaction are important to the next steps.

The flip side of this is, when working with young males, ironically I find that I have to make more of an effort to make a connection. In many cases, I enter single-parent homes where there is only the mother present. In my experience, young men feel a responsibility to be the "man" of the house, resulting in them being guarded or protective of themselves and those in the household. Additionally, growing up I never felt fully comfortable around males due to misogynistic viewpoints and typical male beliefs that I never conformed to. I see similarities between the Black clients I work with and myself, due to our upbringing and environment. I also feel more of a need to be seen as a mentor for young Black men, especially those whose fathers are not in their lives. Considering that I grew up in the same types of neighborhoods and conditions as those I serve, it is important for me to show them that they can be themselves (Black) and still be successful. Ironically, due to me being a Black male who grew up in the same city, as well as presenting as young and dressing as such, these young males instantly gravitate towards me when I disclose that information, despite the fact that I am the exception to many of the cultural norms that I mentioned. They often assume that my views on life, women, and interest are similar to theirs, and are comfortable vocalizing their views with confidence that I will agree with their sentiments. Unfortunately, due to my position as an FFT therapist, those conversations are typically irreverent to the family dynamic and are brushed over. While acknowledgement of these young men's views is needed to develop rapport, focusing on their specific views around life, women, and their interests would only be relevant if those views disrupted the homeostasis of the home or their relationships with others within the home.

In the context of economic status and ethnicity, these are things that are also consciously brushed over while working with families; ethnicity in regard to white families, and economic status when dealing with Black families. Acknowledgement is necessary for the purpose of validating the family's reality. However, in many cases those contextual values are not the true source of the family's distress. Often, when I enter the home of a Black client family, their assumption is that, due to my position, I was raised in a suburban area and come from a "well-to-do" family. This theory is quickly debunked when they realize that I not only come from the same neighborhoods and environments as them, but that I also have a history of being in the system. In FFT lingo, we call this "matching". I allow a family to gather their own assessment of me after sitting with me as opposed to trying to convince them that I am "one of them". Once a family matches with me and recognize that I am just as "Black" as they are, they disclose their past theories of me to me. These families then go from becoming apologetic about their house being messy to being completely comfortable with the look of their house assuming, that I can understand their struggle when, in reality, I did not grow up in extreme poverty nor untidy conditions. Again, I do not correct them as their assumptions create a more positive "balanced alliance", in FFT lingo, with the family, and they become more forthcoming with information.

The contrast to this scenario would be walking into the home of a white family and assuming that they naturally believe that they are superior to me. While I am aware of our cultural differences, there seems to be no urgency for cleanliness, order, or fear of judgment. However, there always feels like a tension in the room where both parties are aware that we are of different ethnicity, but no one wants to address the elephant in the room, especially considering that I constantly wear clothes and accessories that show pride in my Blackness.

During one of my sessions with a family, I was completing an intake and asked the family their ethnicity – the mother said that they were Armenian. It was stated at some point in the session that my client and another one of her children were mixed, but I did not question it and went with what the mother said to me. One of the multiethnic children make a joke and said, "Armenian lives matter." Her mother jumped in and said, "All lives matter"; there was an awkward silence, which is when I looked down at my right wrist and remembered that I was wearing my "Black Lives Matter" bracelet. We both looked at each other and said at the same time, "We don't need to go down this road" as we laughed. I choose to avoid this topic because my assessment was that the issue was a difference in opinion, not a difference in skin color. Fast-forward to this family's last session of FFT, when the family surprised me with a "farewell" cake that said, "Thank you Blair #BLM." It was a marble cake, having swirls of black-and-white cake in the inside. This family ended successfully in services and we created a strong relationship with one another by the end of services, where the mother felt comfortable enough to reference the Black Lives Matter comment from intake in a light-hearted manner. For me, it made me feel as though my assessment was accurate and that I made the right choice not to address the matter in the early stages of working together. This may not always be the case, but it was in this instance.

Yasmine's Response

Blair carefully considered whether or not he should address matters of race in the moment. As he notes, it appears there were no negative consequences of noticing within yet refraining from addressing the racial disparities between himself and the family he was working. Would this have been the same case if this family told a white therapist or Latinx therapist "all lives mattered"? We do not know what the outcome would have been had Blair addressed this in the moment, or if another therapist had. However, Blair did act by discussing this in supervision. I (Yasmine) was able to ask Blair directly why he did not verbally respond to the mother's minimizing his Blackness. In this case, it was not my role as the supervisor to conclude whether it was the right or wrong choice to not say anything to the mother. I do believe it was my role for us to imagine what it would have been like if Blair *did* say something – what was holding him back, what he imagined he could have said and what may have been the response, and how this would or would not have fit within the FFT model.

Working with Disability

Individual adaptions and considerations may be necessary to meet the specific training needs of supervisees with physical disabilities (Pearlstein & Soyster, 2019) as well as visual, hearing, mental health, intellectual, and learning disabilities. In their 2019 article focused on the supervision needs of students with disabilities, "Supervisory experiences of trainees with disabilities: The good, the bad, and the realistic", Pearlstein and Soyster identified three distinct supervision areas as "(a) navigating disability disclosure with clients, (b) responding to disability-related stigma and discrimination in professional contexts, and (c) developing an identity as a therapist that respects potential disability-related limitations and maximizes the trainee's strengths" (pp. 194–195). In "Who's on first? Supervising psychology trainees with disabilities and establishing accommodations", Wilbur et al. (2019) shared research developed to effectively inform and support supervisors by gaining insight into their "experiences, attitudes, and biases" when supervising a student with disabilities (p. 111). Based on their findings, they encouraged a disability-affirming position and offered a "disability-affirming training environment as an environment of attitudinal awareness of disability culture and identity development and taking a strengths-based stance toward disability, willingness to advocate for disability rights such as universal access, and dedication to establishing accommodations" (2019, p. 116). These two articles are a helpful place to begin to expand understanding and ability to provide supervision to students with disabilities along with introducing this topic within all supervisory relationships.

Self-disclosure

Like disability disclosure, self-disclosure is another technique to discuss differences in supervision. Different than broaching, self-disclosure is the purposeful act of sharing personal details in the clinical space. While lacking a universal agreement on whether the supervisor should disclose to the supervisee or if the therapist should disclose to the client, there is an expectation the client should share "secrets" with the therapist. Similarly, there is an expectation the supervisee share with their supervisor (Yourman, 2003). Often times, self-disclosure evokes the image of the therapist sharing aspects about themselves to a client; however, it refers to anyone involved in therapeutic relationship – the supervisor disclosing to the supervisee, the supervisee disclosing to the supervisor, and the client disclosing to the therapist (Farber, 2003). When thinking of self-disclosure in this manner – every individual in the therapeutic relationship is sharing personal information – then we can see how vital self-disclosure is in supervision.

If the expectation is for supervisees to disclose information to their supervisor (examples include transference, feelings towards their clients as well as culture differences, and even activities engaged in session), why do some supervisees withhold information? Yourman (2003) believes shame is a factor, noting the more shame a supervisee feels, the greater chance the supervisee would not disclose in supervision. While it is not clear how supervisee disclosure impacts therapy directly, it does influence the supervisory relationship (Yourman, 2003). The potential for shame is reduced when a supervisor is inviting and engaged when talking about difference.

Supervision, like therapy, is often described as relational, and self-disclosure has been found to aid the therapeutic alliance. Ladany, Walker, and Melincoff (2001) surveyed 137 supervisors who came from master and doctoral training backgrounds, supervising trainees from various backgrounds (from first practicum to pre-doctoral internship to post-training) in a variety of settings (i.e., college counseling center, school, hospital, private practice, and prison). They found supervisors believed they self-disclosed more if they used attractive (e.g., collegial) and interpersonally sensitive supervision styles (e.g., invested or therapeutic). Ladany and colleagues (2001) recommend supervisors "attempt to incorporate self-disclosure into their supervisory intervention strategies as a method to help form a working alliance with their trainees" (p. 274).

Being creative, with the supervisor and supervisee making art together, can be an act of self-disclosure – it can enhance or encourage self-disclosure. Vulnerability, making mistakes, being creative, and taking risks are all elements that can allow for increased collegial relations. Artmaking can assist with intervention, conceptualization, personalization, and the roles of the supervisor, and a supervisee can conceptualize cases more deeply, particularly when the supervisee feels stuck in treatment (Koltz, 2008)

Takeaways

- Challenge hegemonic ways of practice and acknowledge differences from a framework such as ADDRESSING, agent/target status, a theoretical model such as critical race feminism or intersectionality, and from racial identity models such as R/CID or WRID.

- Supervision strategies that can support the supervisory relationship in furthering critical perspectives in therapy and supervision are cultural humility, broaching, attending to ability, and self-disclosure.
- The onus is on the supervisor to raise issues of diversity as the power lies with the supervisor. While supervisees may have more knowledge, they hold less power structurally.
- We recognize women therapists of color and therapists of other marginalized identities hold areas of target status, and the supervisor raising these issues to the supervisee early on in the supervisory relationship models is not only permitted, but expected. Supervisors should discuss identity politics, power, and privilege in supervision and in the clinical setting.

Practice Prompts

We recommend considering these prompts early in the supervisory relationship as a way to build the groundwork for future conversations about cultural dimensions of work with clients. By addressing these issues early on, discussing differences becomes expected and is not the exception. With regular attention to differences, discussions become easier in supervision, and we hope that attention also translates to the work with clients.

Dynamic Identities

Our cultural identity shifts and changes over time. Some identities remain static (i.e., race and ethnicity), while others do not (e.g., age, ability). For the supervisee to practice self-disclosure and to learn how your supervisee identifies socially and culturally, ask them to think about their cultural identity.

- In supervision, ask your supervisee to free write for one minute by completing the sentence, "I am ..."[2] After the minute has passed, ask them to share the list with you. Discuss what identities came up in the writings, and what did not. Explore potential blind spots, which may be indicated by the missing identities. To practice supervisor self-disclosure, the supervisor can also engage in this activity and share their list with their supervisee.

Conducting a Cultural Self-Assessment Using the ADDRESSING Model[3]

In which areas do you hold power and privilege? Which areas are of minority status? Conduct a cultural self-assessment using Pamela Hays's tool. This can potentially be used as a method of self-disclosure if both the supervisor and supervisee complete their own self-assessment and are willing to share their discoveries with each other.

- The supervisor can share their self-assessment first with the supervisee, modeling appropriate sharing and risk-taking, particularly if the supervisee is hesitant.

Depicting Your Social Identity

Draw a social identity pie[4] based on Miller and Garran's (2017) framework of the self being at the center, environmental factors (e.g., geography) being on the outer edge, and personal identity factors such as race, gender, age, and social class being in-between.

- Draw your pie in any shape you like, and include smaller sections within the larger pie for your different identities. Some shapes may be larger than others. Some pieces may be missing altogether (for example, if you are agnostic, religion may not be represented in your pie). How might your pie differ if you drew it five years ago? Ten years ago? How do you think it may shift two years from now? This can be created in the individual or group supervision setting by all members as individual pies or as a group. Alternatively, this can be created privately in individual reflection journals.

Broaching Behavior in Supervision

How would you initiate a discussion about power, privilege, and difference with your supervisor if you were in the position of Emily as described in the vignette? Now try this exercise from the perspective of the supervisor – how would you broach the idea of discussing difference if Emily did not explicitly discuss her personal identities?

Notes

1 Talwar's critique was largely towards the AATA as at the time of her writing, the AATA was charged with the master's educational standards – as of 2018 the Accreditation Council for Art Therapy Education (ACATE) performs this function. The Art Therapy Credentialing Board (ATCB), which oversees credentialing of professionals, however, was not directly problematized. While art therapists must hold the AATA accountable, given that supervision and training occur post-graduation, we should also hold the ATCB, the Commission on Accreditation of Allied Health Education Programs (CAAHEP), and ACATE, along with ourselves as individual supervisors who maintain ethical standards and promote social justice, accountable as well. The CAAHEP and ACATE "cooperate" with the AATA to determine appropriate standards of

quality for educational programs training entry-level professionals at the master's level. The CAAHEP accredits programs on the recommendation of ACATE.

2 This exercise is adapted from Beverly Tatum's *Why Are All the Black Kids Sitting Together in the Cafeteria?* (2003).

3 See Exercise 3.1 in Pamela Hays's chapter "Doing your own cultural self-assessment" in *Addressing Cultural Complexities in Practice: Assessment, Diagnosis, and Therapy* (3rd ed.) (CAAHEP, 2016).

4 See Exercise 1.1 in Miller and Garran's *Racism in the United States* (2nd ed.) (Miller & Garran, 2017).

References

AATA. (2015). Art therapy multicultural and diversity competencies. Retrieved from www.arttherapy.org/upload/Multicultural/Multicultural.Diversity%20Competencies.%20Revisions%202015.pdf

Aponte, H. J., & Carlsen, J. C. (2009). An instrument for person-of-the-therapist supervision. *Journal of Marital and Family Therapy, 35*(4), 395–405. doi:10.1111/j.1752-0606.2009.00127.x

Aponte, H. J., & Kissil, K. (Eds.). (2016). *The person of the therapist training model: Mastering the use of self.* New York, NY: Routledge.

Arczynski, A. V., & Morrow, S. L. (2017). The complexities of power in feminist multicultural psychotherapy supervision. *Journal of Counseling Psychology, 64* (2), 192–205. doi:10.1037/cou0000179

Awais, Y. J., & Yali, A. M. (2015). Efforts in increasing racial and ethnic diversity in the field of art therapy. *Art Therapy, 33*(3), 112–119.

CAAHEP. (2016) Standards and Guidelines for the Accreditation of Educational Programs in Art Therapy. Retrieved from www.caahep.org/CAAHEP/media/CAAHEP-Documents/ArtTherapyStandards.pdf

Carbado, D. W., Crenshaw, K. W., Mays, V. M., & Tomlinson, B. (2013). Intersectionality: Mapping the movements of a theory. *Du Bois Review, 10*(2), 303–312. doi:10.10170S1742058X13000349

Day-Vines, N. L., Wood, S. M., Grothaus, T., Craigen, L., Holman, A., Dotson-Blake, K., & Douglass, M. J. (2007). Broaching the subjects of race, ethnicity, and culture during the counseling process. *Journal of Counseling and Development, 85* (4), 401–409.

Dudley, J. (2013). The assumption of heterosexuality in supervision. *The Arts in Psychotherapy, 40*(5), 486–494.

Farber, B. A. (2003). Self-disclosure in psychotherapy practice and supervision: An introduction. *Journal of Clinical Psychology, 59*(5), 525–528. doi:10.1002/jclp.10156

Hardy, K. V., & Bobes, T. (Eds.). (2016). *Culturally sensitive supervision and training: Diverse perspectives and practical applications.* New York, NY: Routledge.

Hays, P. A. (1996). Addressing the complexities of culture and gender in counseling. *Journal of Counseling and Development, 74*(4), 332.

Hays, P. A. (2016). *Addressing cultural complexities in practice: Assessment, diagnosis, and therapy* (3rd ed., pp. 39–60). Washington, DC: American Psychological Association.

Helms, J. E. (1984). Toward a theoretical explanation of the effects of race on counseling a Black and White Model. *The Counseling Psychologist, 12*(4), 153–165.

Hird, J. S., Cavalieri, C. E., Dulko, J. P., Felice, A. A. D., & Ho., T. A. (2001). Visions and realities: Supervisee perspectives of multicultural supervision. *Journal of Multicultural Counseling and Development, 29*, 114–130.

Hook, J. N., Davis, D. E., Owen, J., Worthington, E. L., Jr, & Utsey, S. O. (2013). Cultural humility: Measuring openness to culturally diverse clients. *Journal of Counseling Psychology, 60*(3), 353. doi:10.1037/a0032595

Koltz, R. L. (2008). Integrating creativity into supervision using Bernard's discrimination model. *Journal of Creativity in Mental Health, 3*(4), 416–427. doi:10.1080/15401380802530054

Ladany, N., Walker, J. A., & Melincoff, D. S. (2001). Supervisory style: Its relation to the supervisory working alliance and supervisor self-disclosure. *Counselor Education and Supervision, 40*(4), 263–275.

Mayor, C. (2012). Playing with race: A theoretical framework and approach for creative arts therapists. *The Arts in Psychotherapy, 39*(3), 214–219. doi:10.1016/j.aip.2011.12.008

Miller, J., & Garran, A. M. (2017). *Racism in the United States: Implications for the helping Professions* (2nd ed.). New York, NY: Springer Publishing Company.

Pearlstein, J. G., & Soyster, P. D. (2019). Supervisory experiences of trainees with disabilities: The good, the bad, and the realistic. *Training and Education in Professional Psychology, 13*(3), 194.

Rosenthal, L. (2016). Incorporating intersectionality into psychology: An opportunity to promote social justice and equity. *American Psychologist, 71*(6), 474. doi: http://dx.doi.org/10.1037/a0040323

Sajnani, N. (2012). Response/ability: Imagining a critical race feminist paradigm for the creative arts therapies. *The Arts in Psychotherapy, 39*(3), 186–191. doi:10.1016/j.aip.2011.12.009

Sajnani, N., Marxen, E., & Zarate, R. (2017). Critical perspectives in the arts therapies: Response/ability across a continuum of practice. *The Arts in Psychotherapy, 54*, 28–37. doi:http://dx.doi.org/10.1016/j.aip.2017.01.007

Sue, D. W., Capodilupo, C. M., Torino, G. C., Bucceri, J. M., Holder, A., Nadal, K. L., & Esquilin, M. (2007). Racial microaggressions in everyday life: Implications for clinical practice. *American Psychologist, 62*(4), 271.

Sue, D. W., Sue, D., Neville, H. A., & Smith, L. (2019). *Counseling the culturally diverse: Theory and practice* (8th ed.). Hoboken, NJ: John Wiley & Sons, Inc.

Talwar, S. (2010). An intersectional framework for race, class, gender, and sexuality in art therapy. *Art Therapy, 27*(1), 11–17. doi:10.1080/07421656.2010.10129567

Talwar, S. (2017). Ethics, law, and cultural competence in art therapy. *Art Therapy, 34*(3), 102–105. doi:10.1080/07421656.2017.1358026

Talwar, S. K. (Ed.). (2018). *Art therapy for social justice: Radical intersections.* New York, NY: Routledge.

Tatum, B. D. (2003). *Why are all the black kids sitting together in the cafeteria? And other conversations about race.* New York, NY: Basic Books.

Tervalon, M., & Murray-Garcia, J. (1998). Cultural humility versus cultural competence: A critical distinction in defining physician training outcomes in multicultural education. *Journal of Health Care for the Poor and Underserved, 9*(2), 117–125. doi: https://doi.org/10.1353/hpu.2010.0233

Wilbur, R. C., Kuemmel, A. M., & Lackner, R. J. (2019). Who's on first? Supervising psychology trainees with disabilities and establishing accommodations. *Training and Education in Professional Psychology, 13*(2), 111.

Wong, L. C. J., Wong, P. T. P., & Ishiyama, I. F. (2013). What helps and what hinders in cross-cultural clinical supervision: A critical incident study. *The Counseling Psychologist, 41*(1), 66–85. doi:10.1177/0011000012442652

Yourman, D. B. (2003). Trainee disclosure in psychotherapy supervision: The impact of shame. *Journal of Clinical Psychology, 59*(5), 601–609. doi:10.1002/jclp.10162

7 Disciplinary Differences

When Your Supervisor Is Not an Art Therapist

Stephanie Brooks and Yasmine J. Awais

Introduction

This chapter explores the working relationship between the art therapists and the non-art-therapist supervisor. We will discuss some of the fundamental elements of supervision and common ground between the supervisor and art therapists, and explore how different professional epistemological perspectives enrich the supervisor–supervisee and client–art therapist relationships. Examples are used throughout the chapter to illustrate supervision issues. Strategies for navigating the relationship from both the supervisor's and supervisee's perspectives are proposed, including the responsibility of the supervisee to stay up to date on art therapy literature and their area of expertise (i.e., art therapy practices).

Traditional Roles and Responsibilities of the Supervisor

When discussing art therapy supervision, there may be the assumption that both the supervisor and supervisee are art therapists. While this may be the case in the clinical graduate educational setting or in contracted supervision, an art therapist may have a supervisor from a different discipline at the workplace. The actual number of art therapists practicing is actually small in comparison to other mid-level practitioners such as social workers or counselors. And when you add the number of doctoral-level clinicians (i.e., psychologists), it is clear the chance of having an art therapist for a supervisor is even smaller. For example, an art therapist may be supervised by a psychologist in a hospital, who is supervising an entire unit of individuals from various fields such as creative arts therapists, recreation therapists, and occupational therapists. In traditional supervisory relationships, the supervisor may hold more knowledge and experience, and in classic art therapy supervision models the art therapy supervisor holds more knowledge and experience, particularly about art-therapy-specific interventions that often include materials and media, and tasks or experientials. When the supervisor is not an art therapist, the supervisee tends to hold more knowledge of these art therapy practices. If this is the case, how does one negotiate the supervisory relationship? How is the relationship cultivated when there are different theoretical experiences and languages being used?

Throughout this chapter, we discuss the importance of accountability, context, pragmatics, and relationships in supervision. Supervisors can work from a specific theoretical perspective, which may have implications on how the supervisory relationship is negotiated. For example, understanding the differences between disciplines and theories (e.g., not all psychologists are behaviorally oriented). Regardless of disciplines, supervisors typically have a preferred philosophy for conducting supervision. Theoretical approaches or models, beliefs, and values guide the philosophy. Key constructs are embedded throughout the supervisor's philosophy and provide a blueprint for supervision, which in turn guides the supervisor's relational position or stance, modalities, and perspective on the supervisee's competence. For example, a Transgenerational (TG) model of systemic supervision is organized by (a) promoting relational competence by facilitating the supervisee's ability to operate from a differentiated position with a sense of personal authority; (b) facilitating the supervisee's ability to have access to their cultural self and promote use of self and reflection; (c) addressing family-of-origin (FOO) dynamics, history, and relationships relevant to the client; and (d) intentionally creating a supervisory triangle and apprenticeship relationship as a means to coach the supervisee on how to use the self of the therapist in clinical practice (Brooks & Roberto-Forman, 2014, p. 186). Although there are methods for negotiation, for the most part the TG supervision model sets up a hierarchical relationship between the supervisor and supervisee, which can privilege supervisor knowledge.

Common Ground: Where the Art Therapists and Non-Art-Therapist Supervisor Meet

One might think the best fit between a supervisor and supervisee is when they share similar worldviews, philosophies about how change takes place in psychotherapy, and an understanding of each other's theoretical approaches. While these components can be valuable ingredients for supervision, the essential elements of effective supervision require shared goals and a supervisory relationship to support those goals (Nelson, 2014). The strength of the supervisory relationship serves as a container to explore shared values between the supervisor and supervisee, and clearly articulates each other's roles in achieving shared goals. In this context, a strong supervisory relationship provides fertile ground for the supervisee and supervisor to benefit from multiple perspectives. Conceptually, the term "multiple perspectives" calls for a conscientiousness about intersectionality, power, and relational safety in supervision (Hernández & McDowell, 2010). Achieving common ground requires intentionality to promote diversity in the broadest sense, such as appreciating and respecting the supervisee/supervisor identity, professional settings, and points of convergence and divergence between disciplines. Although it may seem counterintuitive, at the heart of achieving common ground is creating a framework for cultural equity and humility, which is self-focus vs other focus (Hernandez-Wolfe & McDowell, 2014). In the clinical context, self-focus requires the art therapist supervisee to understand their individual positionality, and how their intersecting identities influence their clinical work with a client's identities. This is in contrast to other focus, which would focus on the client's identity markers alone and not take into account the art therapist identity.

Professional ethics provide a framework for clinical and supervision decision making (Art Therapy Credentials Board [ATCB], 2018). The codes of ethics for the majority of behavioral health professions are aligned to enable us to engage in best practices and risk management. In the case of a non-art therapist supervising an art therapist, it is the supervisor's responsibility to become familiar with the various art therapy codes. Because ethical codes provide broad guidelines, the supervisor should pay extra attention to ethical reasoning and applications to specific situations (Haug & Storm, 2014). We believe that it is beneficial to the supervisory relationship and process when both supervisee and supervisor participate in this learning activity. Ethical considerations are another facet of professional identity, and a component of the intersectionality between supervisee and supervisor. To strengthen the supervisory relationship, which in turn benefits clients, we recommend that an effort is made to ethically address aspects that may be invisible or situated in the social location or therapeutic discipline of the supervisor and supervisee. Most importantly, the quality of the professional relationship is nourished by transparent communication, an invitation to creativity and innovation, and a commitment to client well-being.

Haug and Storm (2014) developed a series of questions (pp. 25–26) designed to facilitate ethical reasoning in supervision:

- How does my particular sociocultural, relational, and professional context inform me regarding what is ethically appropriate?
- What is my own as well as my supervisee's level of professional experience and confidence in dealing with the demands of the particular situation depicted?
- What resources – supervision mentoring, continuing education, legal advice, and didactic training – are available to me in order to delineate and follow an appropriate course of action?
- What might be my personal blind spots/challenges in responding to this particular situation?

- Once my supervisee and I arrive mindfully at a course of action despite lingering ambiguity, how can I model for my supervisee to let the issue rest until further information is available?
- What are the personal, professional, and spiritual resources that sustain me in my work, and how can I assist my supervisee in drawing on their own personal, professional, and spiritual resources?

These questions can be used as a learning activity, providing a framework for opening dialogue between the supervisor and supervisee. While these questions are written with the supervisor in mind, these questions can be discussed in supervision, with the supervisee sharing their thoughts, which can provide another method for co-constructing a collaborative supervisory relationship. These questions also help the supervisee to evaluate what can be gained from the non-art-therapist supervisor.

How Differences between the Supervisor and Supervisee Manifest

A "healthy respect" for each other's discipline is necessary for a positive working relationship. If this is not present, the opportunity for collaborative and mutual exchange of ideas will suffer. For example, in medically oriented facilities, the medical providers are at the top of the food chain, holding more authority, where those in behavioral health are typically viewed as adjunctive and may not receive the respect deserved. Marginalization also occurs in the behavioral health arena, where the psychiatrist is at the top, then the psychologist, then all others, with art therapists typically located closer to the bottom. When these systemic hierarchies are not acknowledged or universally accepted without question as truths, there may be an inability to develop a trusting relationship between the supervisor and supervisee. The ability for a supervisee to take risks, such as exchanging ideas, expressing feelings about a case, or being vulnerable, is compromised, particularly when the art therapist views themselves as *less than* due to the hierarchical behavioral health structure. Moreover, the relationship can also be negatively impacted if the supervisee feels their supervisor is not competent to provide guidance. For example, an art therapist supervisee may feel that a verbal therapist is out of their scope of practice and not authorized to provide guidance on any art based intervention. However, the supervisor may have insights which could provide useful clinical feedback, and support a rich supervisory relationship.

The Role of Context

As noted earlier, where supervision occurs (on- or off-site), choice (i.e., if the supervisee chooses the supervisor), and other contextual factors influence how to negotiate differences between the discipline of the supervisor and supervisee. In this section we discuss various contextual factors that influence the interdisciplinary supervision relationships. The developmental phase of the clinician significantly impacts the supervision expectations, outcomes, and structure. When a clinician of another discipline supervises an art therapist, developmental phases may be even more apparent as neither person can easily assume the educational experiences of the other. Regardless of training background, new clinicians may desire to focus on "cases" rather than their growth. Those who are already licensed or otherwise credentialed may feel supervision is unnecessary, and consider an additional meeting burdensome. Regardless of how the supervisee sees supervision, the supervisor is responsible for discerning when to focus on cases, the supervisee's growth, or both. Thus, a component of crafting a successful experience requires the supervisor to evaluate the supervisee's clinical development level. Blocher (1983) describes a developmental supervisory approach that promotes the personal and professional growth. The specific developmental phases typically fall into four levels – Introductory, Intermediate, Proficient, and Advanced therapists – each requiring the supervisor to tailor supervision to meet the supervisee's changing needs (Stoltenberg, 1981; Stoltenberg & McNeil, 2010). A comprehensive discussion regarding developmental supervision is beyond the scope of this chapter, and the reader is referred to Lambie and Blount (2016), Stoltenberg and McNeil (2010), and Young, Lambie, Hutchinson, and Thurston-Dyer (2011) for an introductory literature review. For the purpose of this chapter, we will focus on the development of the Proficient and Advanced therapists, and provide a framework for how a supervisor and supervisee might maneuver their relationship, particularly when the supervisor and supervisee are coming from different therapy frameworks. Readers can refer to Chapter 10, *Group Supervision*, where on-campus and on-site group supervision for art therapy trainees are discussed, for more on the Introductory and Intermediate developmental phases of supervision.

First, consider Proficient Therapists as new professionals who possess competent clinical decision making and self-awareness about their limitations, and Advanced Therapists as possessing solid clinical decision-making abilities as well as being more experienced clinicians, flexible and accepting of multiple perspectives and self. In general, Lambie and Blount (2016) recommend the supervisor create a supervisory environment that is supportive, collegial, reciprocal, consultative, and discussion-based. Best practices suggest the supervisor approach the supervisory relationship as a collaborative colleague which includes discussion of multiple approaches to working with clients. During these developmental stages, supervision is a peer-to-peer conversation that is consultative, supportive, and validating. Ideally, the supervisor challenges the supervisee to consider divergent views and encourages them to expand their assessment and interventions. In the end, the supervisor must maintain a position of curiosity and active listening and be attuned to slight changes in the supervisee's preferred method of working. Identification that the supervisee is straying from their standard practices may be a warning sign suggesting further supervisory inquiry and intervention.

Any stage theory (i.e., identifying therapists as Proficient vs Advanced) is not static, and clinicians move in and out of developmental levels. Consider this best case scenario: a Proficient Therapist may experience a difficult case that triggers uncertainty and uncover limitations that require a shift in the supervisory approach. This shift may include introducing best practices to expand the supervisee's competence and normalize their uncertainty. On the other hand, in a more challenging scenario, following a client's violent assault on a family member, an Advanced Therapist with years of experience may question their clinical decision making, which may prompt the supervisor to become more directive and encouraging, balancing personal and professional supervisee growth. The Advanced Therapist's questioning is fraught with a sense of failure and rupture to their professional identity, and the supervisor will need to create space and guide the supervisee's professional and personal self-examination.

On-Site Supervision

When working in a hospital or agency, there is often no choice in selecting a supervisor. While sometimes a clinician will seek out a position in a setting to work specifically under a supervisor, there is always the chance that supervision responsibilities will change (as was the case with Yasmine and Daniel; see the Preface). Often, supervision matches are organized by "unit", with units divided by patient/client type or services being sought. These matches prioritize the unit, not the match of the supervisor to the supervisee. In these situations, the mission of the agency is typically the priority for clinical supervision, and the supervisor is challenged to navigate complex roles. Role strain and blurred professional functions can interfere with the supervisor's ability to foster a positive supervisory relationship. According to Killmer and Cook (2014), when supervisors wear two hats, such as clinical and administrative roles, they are thrust in a dual relationship and must develop competence at managing authority, boundaries, power, and trust dynamics. We encourage both supervisors and supervisees to discuss how they will manage competing tasks such as performance evaluations, clinical goal setting, retention and productivity, transparency, transference and countertransference, and deconstructing hierarchy, if they want to have a chance of developing a successful supervisory relationship.

Supervision in public agencies such as hospitals or behavioral health centers is framed by healthcare credentialing organizations and third-party payors. Some insurance companies require a medical director, typically a psychiatrist, to direct the agency's therapeutic care. The medical director is typically responsible for signing treatment plans, and may be responsible for pharmacological evaluations and interventions. Although the medical director is de facto responsible for treatment, they are typically employed in a consulting or part-time position, and therefore agencies concurrently assign clinicians to a psychotherapy (clinical) supervisor to monitor productivity and ensure quality of care. How does the supervisee negotiate multiple supervisors, who may have varied approaches and values to treatment, and subsequently communicate competing messages? Although the supervisee may be capable of calling attention to this problem and facilitating resolution, we believe it is the agency's responsibility to understand the implications of their respective organizational hierarchy and power dynamics. We have found that progressive systemic thinking agencies have the foresight to address and reduce institutional and structural impediments to quality of care, by creating treatment teams and policies and procedures that minimize opportunities for mixed messages to the primary clinician. A model for organizational responsibility can be found in professional academic programs when we *intentionally* give students multiple supervisors (the buck stops with the on-site supervisor) to gain multiple perspectives to enrich learning.

Off-Site or Contracted Supervision

There are cases where the art therapist chooses to have a non-art therapy supervisor in contracted or private supervision. This situation often happens when experienced clinicians are seeking consultation for a particular case or are seeking advanced credentialing. The supervisor and supervisee may be aligned in terms of clinical approaches, but not necessarily discipline. This was the case with Stephanie and Yasmine, as described in Vignette 7.1.

Vignette 7.1 Seeking Supervision as an Advanced Practitioner

Yasmine's Story

As an Art Therapy Certified Supervisor (ATCS), I (Yasmine) wanted to ensure that I was obtaining proper supervision for my supervision of clinicians. Meanwhile, I was maintaining a small caseload of clients while acclimating to a new job and city. One of the requirements of maintaining the ATCS credential is ongoing clinical supervision education, which can include supervision from a fellow ATCS or "from a licensed or credentialed mental health professional who holds the supervisory credential in his or her field" (ATCB, 2018, p. 4). At the time I was seeking a supervisor, there were no ATCS credential holders in my geographic location.

I began to look at clinicians from other fields who held supervision credentials, and found that one of my colleagues, Dr Stephanie Brooks, was an American Association for Marriage and Family Therapy (AAMFT) Approved Supervisor. I was intrigued by her interdisciplinary clinical training – she had both a Master of Social Work and a PhD in Couples and Family Therapy. Furthermore, her clinical and research expertise included an understanding of racial and cultural issues along with supervision. At the time, I was providing clinical services to a racially diverse group of clients, while simultaneously working as a professor at a predominantly white institution, providing on-campus group supervision to mostly white and female students. I hoped that Stephanie, as a Black woman, would be sensitive to issues of race and difference, and support my growth around these topics and challenges. I have had previous experiences of being supervised by therapists outside of my discipline, primarily social workers and psychologists, with some experiences being positive and others not so rewarding. However, I never chose these former supervisors. Furthermore, this was my first experience obtaining supervision from someone who explicitly claimed their interest in the practice of supervision.

I approached Stephanie by sending her my CV in order to contextualize my work. In turn, Stephanie shared with me that she had previously supervised art therapists, as well as clinicians from various disciplines. She encouraged me to bring the artwork of my clients to session, providing me the space to share insights and to actively contribute to supervision, not simply receive it. What I appreciated about our supervision was how our supervisory relationship was collaborative – we developed our agenda together, which often included where I was "stuck", the artwork that was created, and my feelings towards the client or supervisee. As a result, we continued to collaborate on various projects after formal supervision ended, such as presenting on supervision together and the co-authorship of this chapter. Stephanie also provided instrumental feedback on the early drafts of my supervision disclosure statement.

Stephanie's Response

Without question, my (Stephanie) multiple identities and social location piqued my curiosity about Yasmine's request and informed my decision. I am a cisgender, Christian, African American woman, born and raised in a northeast city. I am an AAMFT Approved Supervisor, a licensed clinical social worker, and a licensed marriage and family therapist committed to improved outcomes for clients impacted by health disparities, and an advocate for diversity, inclusion, and social justice in academic programs and health care. I welcomed Yasmine's request and viewed it as an opportunity to support a colleague with shared values regarding social justice, and a chance to enrich my own learning about art therapy. I established myself as a therapist who works from a couple and family therapist integrative framework, anchored in the fundamental belief that every client's path to change is unique, and no one approach provides a blueprint for therapy (and supervision). Therefore, from the beginning I viewed our supervision as a collaborative relationship with the hope it would create professional growth and scholarship. My earlier experience with a dually trained art therapist and couple and family therapist also influenced my willingness to work with Yasmine. The aforementioned art therapist was an amazing child development course instructor and positively contributed to my own professional development. Prior to my university employment, I worked in both inpatient and outpatient health care settings. Although each place made contributions to my development, my early years as the clinical director of a teaching hospital outpatient behavioral health clinic required me to supervise medical students, psychiatry residents, psychology interns, and social workers. From this experience I learned the importance of creating a process for identifying and evaluating supervision outcomes, truly embracing a postmodern perspective of not knowing vs an expert position (e.g., how to not to try practicing as a psychologist). I learned the importance in supervision of not being seduced by the case, and keeping my focus on the supervisee's needs and requests.

Developing a Framework for Supervision

Having a roadmap for how an art therapy supervisee can aid in making the most out of the supervisory relationship with a non-art therapist can be useful and empowering. The following are three critical areas for developing a framework for supervision – having a clear supervisor's philosophy, utilizing supervision contracts, and privileging the expertise of the art therapist.

Supervisor's Philosophy: Collaborative vs Hierarchical

A collaborative and collegial approach to supervision has been promoted as beneficial for Advanced and Proficient therapists. Collaborative supervision is philosophically aligned with postmodernist constructs. Social constructionism is at the heart of epistemological foundation for postmodern supervisors. From this perspective, knowledge and meaning are co-constructed through social interaction conversation and consensus (Gergen, 2009). The creation of meaning and new meaning in conversation opens up other ways of knowing. Information is not privileged by the supervisor. In a collaborative relationship, the supervisor is not an expert and the task is to maintain a non-expert stance (Rober, 2002; Unger, 2006). Therefore, the collaborative supervisor develops a "not knowing" stance, and their expertise is in *how* they manage the supervisory conversation (Anderson & Goolishian, 1988; Bobele, Biever, Solórzano, & Bluntzer, 2014).

Hierarchical supervision can reinforce false notions of certain positions holding more importance than others. From our perspective, multiple perspectives enhance supervision and the potential for a therapeutic fit for clients. When the supervisor has a strong sense of their own philosophy, and shares that with their supervisee, the relationship can be positively affected. The supervisee may benefit from the supervisor demonstrating respect for art therapy as a valid clinical approach. The art therapy supervisee would also benefit from not assuming that the non-art therapy supervisor is thinking less of them. Furthermore, an art therapy supervisee will learn more from their non-art-therapy supervisor if they understand the philosophy of their non-art-therapy supervisor.

Considerations for the Supervision Contracts

As discussed in Chapter 4, *Navigating Professional Identity: Credentials, Representation, and Relationships*, having a written agreement between the supervisor and supervisee aids in the development of the supervisory relationship. In the case of differing types of clinical training, a supervision contract is even more critical, since disciplines may utilize different methods or approaches. For example, a couples or marriage and family therapist may discuss the use of genograms in their supervision contract, whereas an art therapist will most likely note the use of artmaking in supervision or sharing of client artwork. A supervisee should look for a supervision contract that outlines the supervisor's theoretical approach or philosophy to supervision. They should also pay attention to the supervisor's therapeutic discipline/field of practice, and the ethical codes.

Privileging the Art Therapist's Expertise

While the supervisor typically has more experience in the field and is the party responsible for oversight on the supervisee's clinical and/or administrative work, the supervisee is responsible for bringing their art therapy expertise to supervision. Supervision provides the opportunity for the art therapist to share what is important about the artwork, their interpretations, and questions about what they see. In this sense, the art therapist is the expert, and should not expect the supervisor to provide strategies for art therapy interventions, materials, or interpretations. However, the supervisor is in a position of being a sounding board for ideas and questions. The supervisor is encouraged to adhere to a not-knowing position which is consistent with the principles of the postmodern movement (Anderson, 2005). The postmodern perspective in supervision assumes the supervisor is not the expert or keeper of the truth on the right way to conduct therapy (Rogers & Miranda, 2016; Unger, 2006). In fact, according to Anderson (2001), supervision is based on collaborative learning or learner-directed learning. As a result of providing articles on art therapy, or simply sharing artwork, the supervisee may be educating the supervisor. The art therapist supervisee must have some agency to do this, particularly if the supervisor has never supervised an art therapist before. We encourage supervisees to be strong enough to use their voice and feel they know something, particularly in settings where they are considered adjunctive or even recreational.

Strategies for Developing a Working Relationship When Working across Disciplines

A trusting and safe environment is necessary for developing a healthy supervision relationship. Cultivating a safe environment is widely identified as a core principle in supervision, and is a key supervisor responsibility (Lee & Everett, 2004; Pratt & Lamson, 2012; Rigazio-DiGilio, 2016). Methods for achieving a productive relationship include establishing regular meetings (i.e., once a week) in a confidential location with limited distractions, and clarity around parameters of supervision, including roles and responsibilities. These are key pragmatic elements of any supervision contract. A rule of thumb is to safeguard against surprises in the anatomy or structure of the supervision process.

Supervision across disciplines and cultural diversity involve mastering similar trust building and communication skills. Hardy (2016) offers a framework for "mastering context talk" and identifies ten general skills for effective communication and engagement about diversity that are applicable to other cross-cultural relationships:

- Practicing deep listening;
- Providing skillful feedback;
- Using: "I messages";
- Attending to verbal and nonverbal communication;
- Developing refined meta-communication skills;
- Developing a communication style that imbues intimacy, intensity, congruency, transparency, and authenticity;
- Effectively using expressions of acknowledgement;
- Responding therapeutically;
- Developing proficiency in expressing thoughts and feelings and recognizing the difference between the two; and
- Allowing (emotional) space for reflection and contemplation (pp. 137–138).

Both the supervisor and supervisee should continuously discuss what they want from supervision and make no assumptions about the process. It is important for supervisors to honor the supervisee's historical contexts, experiences, and social locations, while actively seeking to understand how they influence the supervisee's epistemology.

The supervisor should be curious and inquire about the supervisee's worst and best experiences in supervision, and how those contributions shape perspective (Anderson, Schlossberg, & Rigazio-DiGilio, 2000). We encourage the supervisee to accept opportunities to provide feedback on how they can co-construct a successful supervisory relationship, and we encourage the supervisor to trust the supervisee's clinical decision making. Finding out if a non-art therapist has ever supervised the art therapy supervisee is educational and illuminating for any supervisor, especially those new to cross-disciplinary supervision. Engaging in *deep listening* about what that experience was like, what worked and what did not, can help to clarify roles, responsibilities, and expectations.

As a supervisee, find out the supervisor's experiences in supervision – has the supervisor ever supervised an art therapist before? Alternatively, has the supervisor ever supervised someone outside of their discipline? Again, what worked and what did not? We encourage both parties to be open about biases, both positive and negative. Freely discuss how they might address behavioral and communication pitfalls such micro-aggressions, cultural and emotion-based triggers, and transparency about intent. For example, we believe the supervisee is the expert on the case and it is the supervisor's job is to help the supervisee make the most informed decision with the case based on what is happening. The supervisee may need to be proactive, particularly if the supervisor has never supervised an art therapist before. This can be achieved by bringing artwork into the supervision space – show your supervisor what you are doing, and share your observations and questions about the artwork with your supervisor. Just because a supervisor does not explicitly ask you to bring in artwork does not mean that you should not. Since both the supervisor and supervisee may be unfamiliar with each other's discipline, it is important for both to ask questions and develop a shared language for supervision.

What to Do When You are Stuck with a Supervisor

Conflict is essential for authentic conversations and transformative growth. The ability for both the supervisor and supervisee to engage in honest, respectful, and meaningful discussion without blaming and shaming promotes trust, connection, and growth. However, in on-site supervision, a supervisee may feel "stuck" with a supervisor (and a supervisor may feel similarly towards a supervisee!). See Vignette 7.2 on negotiating within a strained supervisory relationship.

Vignette 7.2 Managing an Unsupportive Supervisor

Yasmine's Story

At one non-profit agency, I (Yasmine) felt unsupported by my supervisor, who came from a non-art-therapy discipline. In this instance, my supervisor wanted to learn about how I handled cases, but I felt "watched" and not supported when he wanted to observe a crisis intervention. The crisis intervention did not go well, partially because my supervisor asked probing questions of the client during a vulnerable time. Looking back, there may have been additional contributing factors. For example, I did not interrupt my supervisor's therapeutic interventions during the crisis intervention because we did not have a supportive supervisory relationship. Part of this was due to not having regular times for supervision. When we did have supervision, it was often interrupted by phone calls, or unrelated thoughts would arise and be verbalized by my supervisor. At some point later in our work together, I requested a different supervision time where my supervisor would not be as distracted. While this was implemented, and did help us have more regular supervision, the relationship continued to feel strained.

If you are in the position of having a non-art-therapy supervisor, and the relationship feels stuck or strained, you have three options: leave your position, hope your supervisor leaves their position, or stay and work through the relationship. If you choose to work through the relationship, we recommend art therapists look to find areas of strength. Look outside of your supervisory relationship – can you identify qualities or skills that your employer finds remarkable? Remember: your supervisor was hired for some reason – what was that? Furthermore, if you feel stuck with your supervisor, could it be possible that your supervisor feels similarly towards you? By identifying that there is a problem in the relationship, it may be possible to alter it.

In Yasmine's case, she read an article that changed her approach to working with the supervisor she felt stuck with. "If I Could Supervise My Supervisor" is an article by social worker Frank Delano that aims to empower supervisees to "own their own supervision" (Delano, 2001, p. 51). Please see Chapter 3, *What Supervisees Need to Know about Supervision*, which outlines Delano's suggestions in greater detail. Yasmine found this article useful as it gave her permission and specific strategies to take responsibility for her supervision.

Sometimes, when you feel stuck, words escape you and it is difficult to identify the source of the problem. The Supervision Styles Index (SSI) is a 22-question survey aimed to rate your thoughts about the supervision process (Long & Lawless, 1997). The survey includes separate forms for the supervisor and supervisee to rate specific behaviors on a five-point frequency scale from *All of the Time to Never*. Sample statements for the supervisee to rate include (p. 138):

- The supervisor admits mistakes.
- The supervisor recognizes me as a person with expertise.
- The supervisor directs the conversation.

The survey was initially designed for family therapists. However, I (Stephanie) find it to be a useful tool for assessing the supervision process.

It is tempting to *other* the supervisor as a problem. While sometimes the supervisor presents a host of challenges, systems are complex and the supervisee's experience is shaped by a number of variables. Therefore, it is critical to gain clarity around your professional development and goals, which will frame how you ask for what you need in a supervisory relationship.

Takeaways

- The paradigm of the supervisor as the one who holds all the knowledge shifts when a clinician from another discipline is supervising the art therapist supervisee. When this occurs, the supervisor is not the expert in the treatment modality.
- Strategies for the supervisor in cross-disciplinary supervision involve developing a supervision philosophy that incorporates: (1) collaborative supervision, (2) utilizing supervision contracts, and (3) privileging the art therapy expertise of the supervisee.
- Strategies for the supervisee in cross-disciplinary supervision include reframing "feeling stuck" with a supervisor, and finding areas of strength.

Practice Prompts

Influences on Art Therapy Practice and Understanding

- For supervisees: What theories, art therapists, and art therapy practices influence your clinical practice? What key article(s) would you share with your supervisor who is not an art therapist to help them understand your work?
- For supervisors: What art therapy articles or resources helped you in supervising art therapists? Share them with your supervisee and have a discussion about therapist identity, since they may be experiencing confusion, particularly if the supervisee has never had a non-art therapy supervisor before.

How are Ethics in Art Therapy Practiced?

- Have both the non-art-therapist supervisor and art therapist supervisee read the ATCB *Code of Ethics, Conduct, and Disciplinary Procedures.*
- In supervision, discuss what you learned. Supervisors: share with your supervisee the similarities and differences you found with the ATCB code of ethics and your own discipline's code(s).

Discussing Art with the Non-Art-Therapy Supervisor

A key difference between art therapists and other mental health practitioners is the creation of visual art in the therapy session. How do you discuss the art that is made in session with your non-art-therapy supervisor?

- For the art therapist supervisee: what jargon do you use, what parts of the artwork do you discuss, what do you avoid, and what assumptions do you make about the artwork? If you have not brought your client's artwork into supervision or the artwork you create alongside your client, interrogate why you have not done so, and consider bringing artwork into your next supervision session. Explain to your supervisor why you feel it would be helpful to the ongoing treatment of your client(s), and note how discussing the artwork with an objective person may provide new insights and further your own clinical development.
- For the supervisor: What do you learn from seeing the artwork created in person, rather than from only hearing about the artwork? Do you value the artwork itself or do you prefer to hear how your supervisee discusses the artwork, regardless of whether it is in the room with you?

References

Anderson, H. (2001). Postmodern collaborative and person-centered therapies: What would Carl Rogers say? *Association for Family Therapy and Systemic Practice, 23*, 339–360.

Anderson, H. (2005). Myths about "not-knowing". *Family Process, 44*, 497–504.

Anderson, H., & Goolishian, H. A. (1988). Human systems as linguistic systems: Preliminary and evolving ideas about the implications for clinical theory. *Family Process, 27*(4), 371–393.

Anderson, S. A., Schlossberg, M., & Rigazio-DiGilio, S. A. (2000). Family therapy trainees' evaluations of their best and worst supervision experiences. *Journal of Marital & Family Therapy, 26*, 79–92.

ATCB. (2018). Code of ethics, conduct and disciplinary procedures. Retrieved from www.atcb.org/resource/pdf/ATCB-Code-of-Ethics-Conduct-DisciplinaryProcedures.pdf

Blocher, D. H. (1983). Toward a cognitive developmental approach to counseling supervision. *The Counseling Psychologist, 11*, 27–34.

Bobele, M., Biever, J. L., Solórzano, B. H., & Bluntzer, L. H. (2014). Postmodern approaches to supervision. In T. C. Todd & C. L. Storm (Eds.), *The complete systemic supervisor: Context, philosophy, and pragmatics* (2nd ed., pp. 255–273). Hoboken, NJ: Wiley Blackwell.

Brooks, S., & Roberto-Forman, L. (2014). The transgenerational supervision models. In T. C. Todd & C. L. Storm (Eds.), *The complete systemic supervisor: Context, philosophy, and pragmatics* (2nd ed., pp. 186–207). Hoboken, NJ: Wiley Blackwell.

Delano, F. (2001). If I could supervise my supervisor: A model for child and youth care workers to own their own supervision. *Journal of Child and Youth Care, 15*(2), 51–64.

Gergen, K. J. (2009). *Realities and relationships: Soundings in social construction.* Cambridge, MA: Harvard University Press.

Hardy, K. V. (2016). Mastering Context Talk: Practical skills for effective engagement. In K. V. Hardy & T. Bobes (Eds.), *Culturally sensitive supervision and training: Diverse perspectives and practical applications* (pp. 136–145). New York: NY: Routledge.

Haug, I. E., & Storm, C. L. (2014). Drawing the line in ethical dilemmas in systemic supervision. In T. C. Todd & C. L. Storm (Eds.), *The complete systemic supervisor: Context, philosophy and pragmatics* (2nd ed., pp. 19–42). MA: John Wiley & Sons.

Hernández, P., & McDowell, T. (2010). Intersectionality, power, and relational safety in context: Key concepts in clinical supervision. *Training and Education in Professional Psychology, 4*(1), 29.

Hernandez-Wolfe, Ph., & McDowell, T. (2014). Cultural equity and humility: A framework for bridging complex identities in supervision. In T. C. Todd & C. L. Storm (Eds.), *The complete systemic supervisor: Context, philosophy and pragmatics* (2nd ed., pp. 43–61). Hoboken, NJ: John Wiley & Sons.

Killmer, M. J., & Cook, M. (2014). Providing systems-oriented clinical supervision in agency settings. In T. C. Todd & C. L. Storm (Eds.), *The complete systemic supervisor: Context, philosophy and pragmatics* (2nd ed., pp. 108–131). City, State: John Wiley & Sons.

Lambie, G. W., & Blount, A. J. (2016). Tailoring supervision to supervisees' developmental level. In K. Jordan (Ed.), *Couple, marriage and family therapy supervision* (pp. 71–86). New York, NY: Springer Publishing Company.

Lee, R. E., & Everett, C. (2004). *The integrative family therapy supervisor: A primer.* New York: Routledge.

Long, J., & Lawless, J. J. (1997). What is your style? The SSI. In C. L. Storm & T. C. Todd (Eds.), *The reasonably complete systemic supervisors resource guide* (pp. 134–138). Boston, MA: Allyn and Bacon.

Nelson, M. L. (2014). Using the major formats of clinical supervision. In C. E. Watkins & D. L. Milne (Eds.), *Wiley international handbook of clinical supervision* (pp. 308–328). Chichester: UK: John Wiley & Sons.

Pratt, K. J., & Lamson, A. L. (2012). Supervision in behavioral health: Implications for students, interns, and new professionals. *Journal of Behavioral Health Services & Research, 39*, 285–294.

Rigazio-DiGilio, S. (2016). MFT supervision: An overview. In K. Jordan (Ed.), *Couple, marriage, and family therapy supervision* (pp. 25–50). New York, NY: Springer Publishing.

Rober, P. (2002). Constructive hypothesizing, dialogic understanding and the therapist's inner conversation: Some ideas about knowing and not knowing in the family therapy session. *Journal of Marital and Family Therapy, 28*(4), 467–478.

Rogers, T., & Miranda, M. (2016). Training a postmodern supervisor. In K. Jordan (Ed.), *Couple, marriage, and family supervision* (pp. 235–254). New York, NY: Springer Publishing.

Stoltenberg, C. D. (1981). Approaching supervision from a developmental perspective: The counselor-complexity model. *Journal of Counseling Psychology, 28*(1), 59–65.

Stoltenberg, C. D., & McNeil, B. W. (2010). *IDM supervision: An integrative developmental model for supervision counselors and therapists* (3rd ed.). New York, NY: Routledge.

Unger, M. (2006). Practicing as a postmodern supervisor. *Journal of Marital & Family Therapy, 32*, 59–71.

Young, T. L., Lambie, G. W., Hutchinson, T., & Thurston-Dyer, J. (2011). The integration of reflectivity in developmental supervision: Implications for clinical supervisors. *The Clinical Supervisor, 30*(1), 1–18.

8   Disciplinary Differences

When Your Supervisee Is Not an Art Therapist

Introduction

This chapter concentrates on themes particular to an art therapist providing supervision to a non-art-therapist clinician. Methods for introducing arts-based supervision into the relationship will be covered, along with approaches to educate the supervisor on the supervisee's professional specialty. This chapter also includes a vignette from a non-art-therapist supervisee seeking supervision from an art therapist. Similar to Chapter 7, *Disciplinary Differences: When Your Supervisor Is Not an Art Therapist*, we explore the experience of being involved in an interdisciplinary supervision. A key difference in this type of supervisory relationship is the person holding the most power is the art therapist (supervisor).

Cross-disciplinary supervision can be on-site or contracted, and occurs in a variety of settings, such as agencies, hospitals (i.e., public-institutional settings), and private practice settings. As described in Chapter 7, there are different reasons for cross-disciplinary supervision, and a range of motives for a non-art-therapy supervisee seeking an art therapy supervisor. While it is not in the scope of practice for the art therapist who is supervising a clinician from a different discipline to formally train the supervisee in art therapy, we believe art therapists can enhance the clinical practice of the non-art-therapy supervisee without impeding on any scope-of-practice boundaries. As professionals, we also understand non-art therapists do indeed use artmaking in sessions, run art groups, or have clients that spontaneously create art in session, or bring artwork to the session. Even if the non-art-therapist supervisee does not include artmaking in their work with clients, they can benefit from arts-based interventions in the supervision process.

Furthermore, many licensing and accreditation bodies permit interdisciplinary supervision. As long as supervisors meet other minimum clinical practice requirements, they may hold a master's degree in a "related field". For example, the Pennsylvania Code (2010) explicitly describes multidisciplinary interactions:

(15) The supervisor shall encourage the supervisee to work with professionals in other disciplines as indicated by the needs of each client/patient and shall periodically observe these cooperative encounters.

(16) The supervisor shall encourage the supervisee to access multidisciplinary consultation, as necessary.

(p. 49–10)

Because art therapists may be able to supervise a clinician who is not an art therapist and still be practicing within the scope of their license, we encourage you to review your state licensing code to see who you are permitted to supervise and who you can receive supervision from. This chapter describes the art therapist as supervisor with the non-art therapist as supervisee in the workplace (e.g., hospital or agency) for both on-site supervision and in private, contracted, or off-site supervision.

From the supervisor perspective, supervising non-art therapists privately can be a stimulating and refreshing change from the required supervision of agency work or supervising graduate students on-campus. Additionally, a nice balance can occur when providing on-site supervision to a clinically diverse team. Working across disciplines can allow for understanding different clinical perspectives, new theoretical orientations, and alternative ways of providing care. Although our intent is to always learn from our supervisees, this broader view and understanding gained from supervising a non-art therapist will most likely benefit your supervisory practice as well as your work as an art therapist.

Supervising in the Workplace

As noted in previous chapters, when working for an employer, whether in a hospital, agency, or other organization, one often does not have the option of choosing a supervisor. Supervisors and supervisee assignments tend to be based on work responsibilities, availability, and department or unit. Due to the fact that supervision is required through the worksite, supervision can often be routinized, focusing on meeting programmatic requirements such as charting, ensuring productivity is being met through client-contact hours, or numbers of individuals seen during a set period of time. Focusing on clinical skills of the supervisee may be difficult in the workplace when administrative tasks loom, including deadlines, audits, paperwork requirements, and high caseload demands.

Trust may be difficult to cultivate, particularly when the supervisee does not choose their supervisor. Furthermore, if the supervisee does not see any value in being supervised by an art therapist, the supervisee or the supervisor may avoid the clinical or educational aspects of supervision. Additionally, the art therapist supervisor may feel ill-equipped to supervise a clinician outside of their field. However, Farber (2003) describes the benefits of interdisciplinary supervision: "specifically, the supervisee learns to understand the value of interdisciplinary roles and care philosophies [while obtaining exposure to] interdisciplinary communication, collaboration, and working as part of a clinical team" (p. 542). Introducing art-based interventions values the art therapy supervisor's training and embraces the difference.

Hospital-Based Supervision across Disciplines

The hierarchical and medical model structure of hospital settings does not typically allow for art therapists being the supervisors of clinical staff. Often, art therapists supervise other art therapists, creative arts therapists, or recreational staff who are considered adjunctive.

Agency-Based Supervision

We have supervised clinicians, direct service workers, and supervisors of clinicians as employees and supervising consultants of non-profit agencies. Collectively, we have supervised social workers, creative arts therapists (i.e., music, dance/movement, and drama therapists), mental health counselors, psychiatrists, bachelor's-level workers, case managers, and peer educators with extensive population-based knowledge but typically minimal formal education. One strategy we have employed in multidisciplinary supervision groups is to focus on clinical skills and peer-to-peer learning. This is something we have found to be particularly useful as facilitators and as participants. When facilitated well, multidisciplinary supervision groups encourage the sharing of cases and differing viewpoints on how to best approach the work moving forward, and how to better reflect on previous interventions through multiple expertise.

One model of interdisciplinary group supervision we have implemented is rotating the presenter. During each session, one member of the group takes a turn presenting a case, followed by a case analysis from the standpoint of the varying disciplines. We also have led supervision groups designed for the sharing of clinical techniques – instead of presenting a case, the presenter shares a clinical technique or intervention. This is particularly effective when the presenter engages their fellow supervisees as experientially active participants from the clients' perspective. For example, a social worker and a music therapist may gain incredible insight if they participate in a mock drama therapy group and process their experience as well as the intervention. The presentation can share what has worked well, a "failed" intervention that did not go as planned, or even new material or a technique for feedback.

Contracted Supervision

As explained in previous chapters, contracted supervision is different from on-site supervision in that the supervisee is seeking out a specific supervisor. Supervision may be sought for a variety of reasons, as described in Chapter 1, *What Is Art Therapy Supervision: Reasons and Expectations*. Clinicians may actively seek supervisors outside of their discipline. Engaging an off-site art therapist supervisor provides similar benefits, such as objective distance, as meeting with any other qualified supervisor, with the added expectation of art-based work. As Anna, one supervisee of Yasmine's, noted, "I felt it was essential to meet outside of the spatial bounds of the clinic, as a consistent way to check my perspectives and clinical choices with a bit of distance, perspective, and light." See Vignette 8.1 for more of Anna's thoughts and experiences with choosing an art therapy supervisor.

Vignette 8.1 Seeking an Art Therapy Supervisor

Anna's Story

Anna was seeking licensure in counseling. She approached Yasmine via email, briefly describing her educational background of having two master's degrees (one in International Relations and the second in School and Mental Health Counseling), clinical experiences, and arts-related experiences, including a BFA in in Media and Performing Arts from a well-known art school, as well as training in drama therapy. In her introductory email, she also included her resume. Anna was specifically looking for off-site supervision to support her future counseling licensure application.

Becoming a Clinician

As a counselor, I (Anna) am in a continual process of exploring, cultivating, and calibrating "grayscales". In other words, I am constantly attempting to reduce black-and-white dichotomous thinking. While I work on this with my clients, I, too, am attempting the same mutual process. I worked in a methadone clinic, and in this space, dichotomies abound. Dirty/clean, positive/negative, addict/normal: the lexicon itself perpetuates polarity. Yet, daily, with each new exception, story, and interaction, a new level of understanding occurs, and the shades within the grayscale shift and calibrate once again.

I sought out an art therapist supervisor, as I felt a need to conceptualize these grayscale shifts in real time, with a professional who also viewed the world from a perspective of color, expression, and creativity. I sought out an art therapist supervisor as I suspected they could assist in promoting the power of the *process* of becoming a clinician, even when self-doubt, disenchantment, and the daunting burnout of a high caseload might feel as though the burden of *becoming* was too overwhelming. An art therapist, I gathered, was an expert in perspective, and this expertise would be crucial in cultivating a healthier working viewpoint during these times of overwhelm.

Anna was clear in discussing her supervision goals from the start. For example, in one of the first supervision sessions, as someone with an understanding and appreciation for the creative arts therapies yet not trained as an art therapist, she expressed concern about being asked to run an "art therapy group". Discussions surrounding the differences between an art therapy group versus a group that utilizes artmaking were explored. Concerns involved being new to a job and wanting to fulfil job requirements and simultaneously not misrepresenting her qualifications or the group she was facilitating. She also noted the previous group facilitator was not an art therapist setting a precedent to disrupt. In supervision, we discussed how artmaking can be incorporated into groups to help facilitate group process. Anna also shared artworks created in groups and conversations initiated by these activities.

To best incorporate art into her groups, Anna would look to art movements and films – cotemporary, historic, architecture, craft, etc. – and link these to what was relevant to her groups. She would bring her ideas to supervision, where we would refine how to present them to her groups.

How to Find an Art Therapy Supervisor

Yasmine recalls being impressed with Anna's introductory email, which provided a well-defined introduction of her professional self. Anna also noted some of Yasmine's work in her introductory email, which Yasmine found promising, as this showed Anna completed some preparatory work in seeking out individuals whose work she appreciated, which indicated to Yasmine this may be a good fit. Clients often research potential therapists by seeking information on their theoretical orientation, experience with specific diagnosis or concerns, location, and fees. It is recommended that supervisees engage in a similar research process when looking for a supervisor.

FEES

For a new professional, the first question may be surrounding the cost of the supervision services – we appreciate supervision is another expense, especially when managing student loans and the lower salaries accompanying entry-level positions. We encourage supervisees to request their employers pay for off-site supervision during the time of hire, when negotiations are more likely to be made and honored. However, supervisees can ask for supervision fees to be paid at any time, particularly if the on-site workplace supervision does not meet licensing requirements. Or, in Anna's case, the clinic was asking her to run an arts-based group, yet there was no art therapist on-site to support her work. If your workplace is unable to pay for your supervision, ask for your time to be compensated. This may mean requesting your off-site weekly supervision session count towards your work week. Some of our supervisees leave an hour early from work or arrive an hour late once a week to compensate for their off-site supervision time. If the workplace is not paying for supervision, supervision may be considered a professional expense to note for tax-related and other accounting purposes – consult with your tax preparer or accountant to see if this is applicable to your situation.

Building the Relationship

Building the supervisory relationship takes time and effort. When working across disciplines, both participants may be more aware of differences and open to sharing their previous experiences, including educational training and previous work. In both the work and contracted supervision environments, we encourage open communication between the supervisor's and supervisee's expectations, and experiences. Relationship-building occurs over the course of the entire supervisory period, although we find the beginning phase being critical, especially with differences across disciplines.

Since the supervisor holds the power within the relationship, we place the majority of the responsibility on the supervisor to set a framework, including a dedicated and consistent time and space free from distractions. The supervisor should be eager to learn how their supervisee approaches their work and theoretical orientation. Whether or not the supervisory relationship was "forced", inquire how the supervisee feels about working with an art therapist. What can the supervisee learn from the supervisor? How can you learn more about your supervisee's field? A first step in gaining basic understanding of your supervisee's field is viewing professional association and state licensing board materials on scope of practice and ethics. Next, engage in discussions with your supervisee about their education and training. Ask specifically about the theoretical orientation(s) they employ, past experiences in supervision, and whether they engaged in cross-disciplinary supervision, and request articles they find pivotal to their work. Direct observations of clinical work are useful in seeing how another professional engages in therapy. When observation is not possible, review case or progress notes.

When the reviewing of progress notes is not possible, the reviewing of process notes can be useful. Process notes allow the supervisee to write more specifically to their practice, experience, and reflection, and can be completed informally through a journal or sketchbook, or formally. See Appendix A for a process note template.

Identifying How Differences Manifest

A solid relationship allows for supervision that is meaningful. While supervision can still occur in an unestablished relationship, the supervisee may be hesitant to speak of vulnerabilities such as transferential or countertransferential issues, difficulties in their therapeutic practice, limitations, or other instances. Differences manifest when communication is lacking, particularly if the supervisor does not understand the supervisee's discipline or field, way of working, theoretical orientation, preferred communication style, or stage of racial or cultural identity development.

Learning from Your Supervisee

When supervising across disciplines, it is crucial to allow your supervisee to step into and out of the expert role for their field. While your supervisee is in the expert role, trust – but verify – their proficiency through questions and genuine interest. At times, the supervisee may have a strong sense of what they are doing, and at other times will not have clue. Targeted yet inviting questions will help hold the space of the "not knowing" of the supervisee and supervisor by gently guiding a deeper understanding. The ability for the supervisee to flounder needs to be established and held by the supervisor. A supervisee cannot be expected to hold the expertise of their field at all times. We suggest a supervisor balance their power by consistently being in learner mode considering the supervisee's field, not just when the supervisee is in active teaching mode.

Utilizing Your Art Therapy Skills

When utilizing your art-therapy-specific skills as a supervisor, consider the educational, supportive, and administrative oversight aspects. Supervisors and supervisees may be attracted to the educational components, particularly the "how to be an art therapist". It is comforting to be an expert, and provide directives on what to do with particular clients or with certain populations. When supervising non-art therapists, providing directives could be taken out of context and exercised inappropriately. Using art therapy skills and arts-based methods can be applied for greater benefit when employed in all three supervision areas: educational, supportive, and administrative.

Educational Oversight

One critical and exciting aspect of supervising a non-art therapist is when they are actively using art materials in their clinical sessions. This is an opportunity to establish clear boundaries of how non-art therapists can properly incorporate art materials without overstepping the bounds of a properly trained art therapist. Appropriate boundaries create a freedom to empower rather than discourage or potentially shame the supervisee for the use of art materials. In many ways this approach relies on the art therapist supervisor to be clear and secure in their own art therapist identity in order to help clarify boundaries for someone else.

Other supervisees, from different disciplines, may have no interest whatsoever in incorporating art into their clinical sessions, but will readily engage in art-based supervision to enrich their clinical insights and understanding. "Making and reflecting on imagery presents valuable opportunities for reflection and communication for those working in disciplines beyond art therapy. This practice is useful for those in any field who are working to gain therapeutic insight" (Fish, 2017, p. 181). In these situations, the focus of the art is quite different – it is used in support of the educational aspects of supervision. The artmaking reinforces and deepens clinical skills, theoretical understanding, and client insight. This is not supportive, or about therapist self-care – this is directly related to client care. Topics addressed through art may include boundary-setting with clients, deepening empathy when struggling with a particular client, or exploring a theoretical concept.

Supportive Oversight

For a non-art therapist, the artmaking process can be an unexpectedly powerful tool as they are less likely to have experienced or been trained to utilize artmaking as a routine part of their clinical training. A brief, arts-based check-in for supervisees can be a simple, fairly non-threatening, and quite beneficial practice to initially embrace art in session as a supportive measure. This approach differs from educational support. The supportive oversight is very much focused on the supervisee's personal experience of the professional work. The intent is to enhance comprehension in areas such as countertransference, self-care strategies to reduce burnout, and ability for self-reflection, without veering into issues more appropriate for personal therapy. Emily Reim Ifrach recognizes the "fears or shame" some therapists my experience with verbal disclosure of compassion fatigue. She notes that offering the expressive therapies as a "non-verbal means to communicate can reduce the feelings of stress and stigma around this kind of professional sharing" (Ifrach & Miller, 2016, p. 35).

Administrative Oversight

Using arts-based methods in supervision can be more than providing directives or asking a supervisee to depict themselves with clients. To address productivity, caseloads, paperwork, and other related administrative needs, it is useful to see how all of the players are involved. This is important to explore even as an on-site supervisor, since your supervisee may have a different experience of the environment. A graphic representation of the supervisee's place of work can help identify administrative problem areas as well as areas of support and strength. For example, in your supervisee's hospital or agency, are the administrators who make decisions far away or in close physical proximity? In an agency, are the funders (who may be governmental or private) in the building at all? If you are an off-site or contracted supervisor, where is your supervisee's on-site supervisor physically positioned? Does your supervisee have their own office, or do they share an office? Does your supervisee have their own computer or desk? How is paperwork completed – electronically or manually?

To better understand how a supervisee fits within a system administratively, we can explore how organizational design and physical environment impact administrative tasks. For example, when working with one supervisee Yasmine learned not only were the administrative tasks great – a high caseload with extensive documentation requirements to be completed in paper charts – but the only accessible printer was on a different floor from the supervisee's office. Every time this supervisee had to print a progress note, which required her client's signature, she had to print the note, walk to another floor, and retrieve the paper, then return to her office for her client to sign.

Takeaways

- Art therapists may supervise practitioners from other disciplines on-site (as a requirement) or off-site (by choice, through contracted supervision). In either case, we encourage art therapists supervising across disciplines to view this as an opportunity to continue to utilize their art therapy skills.
- Arts-based supervision can be utilized, even when supervising clinicians who are not art therapists. Artmaking in supervision can allow for creativity, humility, and self-disclosure in the supervisory relationship. This can be done at the beginning of supervision as a check-in, as a response to a challenging clinical encounter, or as a way to reflect on supervision itself.
- Each mental health field has its own unique methods of training, theories, and philosophies that are drawn upon. While supervisors working across disciplines cannot be expected to know everything, learning about a supervisee's profession is vital to understanding how they approach therapy. Supervisors can educate themselves on professional specialties by reading seminal works, attending trainings, and finding additional recourses.

- The requirements on who one can supervise depend on the credential(s) and/or license(s) one holds and/or is seeking. If you are a supervisor, identify which professionals you are permitted to supervise. Supervisees, identify which professionals can supervise you. Do any requirements indicate your supervisor must be an art therapist?

Practice Prompts

Article Exchange

- Share one article with your supervisee that is important to you as an art therapist. Ask your supervisee to share an article with you from their field that is integral to their way of working.
- Discuss these articles in supervision. What insights did you gain about your supervisee from reading the article they provided and from the comments they made to the article you shared?

Exquisite Corpse

This surrealist activity allows for free association and imagination. Creating an exquisite corpse poem or drawing with your supervisee is a novel way to discuss differing perspectives from each practitioner's discipline. These prompts are adapted from the Art Institute of Chicago (n.d.):

- For individual supervision, first decide on the line structure (e.g., article + adjective + noun + verb + adjective + noun). Agree on the theme. For the purposes of interdisciplinary supervision, we suggest "the benefits of learning from an art therapist". The first person writes the first two words (i.e., article + adjective), then folds the paper to hide what was written. The second person writes the next word (i.e., noun) and folds the paper so this word is hidden. Continue this process until you get to the last part of speech, then read the poem aloud. Alternatively, each person can write two words, hiding one word and revealing the last word. In this case, show the one word previously written so the next person has a prompt to work from.
- For group supervision, fold a piece of drawing paper – one fold per group member. Decide on a general image, such as a person or animal. The first person draws the top or the head of the figure, the last person draws the feet or the base, and the other participants draw what is in-between. Similar to the poetry activity, each person "hides" what they draw by folding it over; however, for the drawing activity the person drawing makes marks just over the edge of the fold so the subsequent person can continue the mark. Unfold the drawing when the last person is finished. What image was created? When considering cross-disciplinary supervision, how does this creature embody multiple perspectives? See Figures 8.1 and 8.2, and Color Plates 5 and 6 for examples.

Figure 8.1 Supervision workshop participants (2017), Untitled response to the prompt, "The Ideal Supervisor", exquisite corpse 1 [oil pastels and markers].

Figure 8.2 Supervision workshop participants (2017), Untitled response to the prompt, "The Ideal Supervisor", exquisite corpse 3 [oil pastels and markers].

Understanding Your Off-Site Supervisee's Workplace

- Ask your supervisee(s) to draw their workplace to better understand their interpretation of the work environment. Items to include are: their workstation, the location where therapeutic services occur, break rooms, locations of managers, locations of clients, etc.
- Use this map as a way to discuss areas of strength, stress, rejuvenation, learning, and any other topic useful to learn about your supervisee's work experience.

References

The Art Institute of Chicago. (n.d.). Interpretive resource. Family activity: Surrealist Games. Retrieved from www.artic.edu/aic/resources/resource/1049

Code, P. (2010). Chapter 49. State board of social workers, marriage and family therapists and professional counselors-licensure of professional counselors code of ethical practice and standards of professional conduct. Retrieved from www.pacode.com/secure/data/049/chapter49/chap49toc.html

Farber, B. A. (2003). Self-disclosure in psychotherapy practice and supervision: An introduction. *Journal of Clinical Psychology, 59*(5), 525–528. doi:10.1002/jclp.10156

Fish, B. J. (2017). *Art-based supervision: Cultivating therapeutic insight through imagery.* New York, NY: Routledge.

Ifrach, E. R., & Miller, A. (2016). Social action art therapy as an intervention for compassion fatigue. *The Arts in Psychotherapy, 50,* 34–39.

Plate 5 Supervision workshop participants (2017), Untitled response to the prompt, "The Ideal Supervisor", exquisite corpse 2 [oil pastels and markers]

Plate 6 Supervision workshop participants (2017), Untitled response to the prompt, "The Ideal Supervisor", exquisite corpse 4 [oil pastels and markers]

Plate 7 Blair Chase (2018), Untitled road [tape, colored pencil, and sequins]

Plate 8 Yasmine J. Awais (2018), Untitled [felt, tissue paper, and sequins]

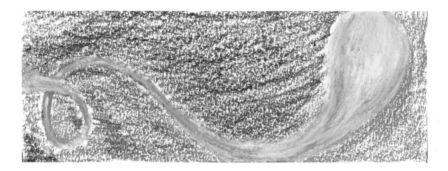

Plate 9 Julie Gotthold (2018), Untitled supervision orb [chalk pastels]

Plate 10 Group supervision participants (2019), Untitled deconstructed book [eraser stamp print on fabric]

Part 4

Locations, Places, and Spaces

Supervision Formats

This final part – with attention to differences in race, gender, and other identities – describes how different supervision formats influence the supervisory relationship from the standpoint of the supervisor and the supervisee. It includes three chapters:

- Individual and Dyad Supervision;
- Group Supervision; and
- Distance Supervision.

Within the chapters of this part, we provide working definitions for these supervision formats, consider the advantages and drawbacks of each type, review methods to incorporate arts-based supervision interventions, and describe reasons a supervisor or supervisee chooses (or is forced) to engage in one format or another. As supervisors and supervisees, we have experienced all three types of supervision formats and appreciate the distinct functions of each.

9 Individual and Dyad Supervision

Introduction

Shirley Riley (1992) described the traditional framework for art therapy supervision with students as a "discussion of theory and practice, metaphor and process, media and expression, projection and interpretation, and other issues to assist the art therapy intern to better achieve clients' goals set during the session" (p. 119). When infused with arts-based interventions and attention to differences in race, gender, and additional factors, we believe this description is quite accurate, and will remain valid and insightful throughout an art therapy career.

Individual or dyad supervision can take place on-site where art therapy services are provided (e.g., agency or hospital), or off-site, in locations such as a private practice or campus-based setting, separate from where the clinical work is conducted. Both of us started out as individual supervisors and have been in this role in many variations over the years. Our work as individual supervisors has included on-site graduate art therapy supervision as well as off-site professional supervision for art therapists and counselors. We have worked with supervisees who were seeking their credentials, and those who were looking for continued supervision after they received their credentials. Like all art therapists in training, we engaged in individual supervision as graduate art therapy students. We have also participated in providing off-site professional supervision and on-site supervision with non-art therapists.

This chapter provides an in-depth description of in-person, individual supervision. Dyad supervision is also included in this chapter, since dyads are often more similar to individual supervision than group supervision. We detail the nuances of various relationships. In particular, we examine the difference between required supervision and elective supervision. To better illustrate these supervisory relationships, strategies are shared from established best practices. We also highlight our experiences and the knowledge that we gained from our supervisees.

Defining Individual and Dyad Supervision

Individual supervision has a pretty straightforward definition: when one supervisor is supervising an individual clinician. In individual supervision, the tripartite model is clear, and consists of the supervisor, supervisee, and client. The supervision of dyads is when one supervisor is supervising two clinicians in a supervision session. The term should not be confused with the supervisor–supervisee dyad found in individual supervision. While the tripartite model may be clear in individual supervision, it is more complex with dyads, as it consists of the supervisor and two supervisees (who are the dyad), and the client(s). As described in Part 1, *How to Get the Most Out of Supervision*, there are different reasons one enters into supervision as a supervisee or becomes a supervisor. Furthermore, the decision to engage with individual or dyad supervision is also varied. Dyads typically occur in off-site supervision sought out by the supervisees; however, dyads do exist in work settings (e.g., two interns being supervised together with a supervisor).

Supervision dyads are generally more intimate than group supervision. They allow for additional attention and direct contributions from each participant, and have the added benefit of peer supervisee perspectives, which can create more context than individual supervision. See Vignette 9.1, which describes how Daniel approached the dynamics of a dyad for the first time. Ögren, Boëthius, and Sundin (2014) describe an expectation of all supervision participants to generate space for their "own training needs and at the same time allowing room and showing involvement in the others' needs" (p. 658). Whether through active listening, body language, or taking on a more nuanced role, being involved in a supervisory dyad can be especially powerful when working and exploring difference and privilege in the supervisory session.

Vignette 9.1 Defining Dyadic Supervision

Daniel's Story

The first time I was approached for contracted dyadic supervision I had been working in the field for about seven years. I was enthused by the idea yet cautious since I had never participated in nor led dyadic supervision. Is it small-group supervision? Is it individual supervision with an observer? Would this be a really tiny class? This was all in the midst of me really trying to find my foundation as an individual supervisor. In fact, the first few sessions probably did appear as an individual supervision with an observer who was rarely brought in while the other supervisee was presenting a case or an issue. In some ways I may have been unconsciously recreating the dynamic of an intern observing an individual art therapy session. Essentially a presence that is simultaneously trying to be invisible yet very physically present. Eventually the three of us found our footing and created an atmosphere that supported a flow of mutual conversation and observation. The observer role progressively became critical and transitioned to hold positions of active listener, entrusted participant, and committed examiner. This allowed my concerns of having a disruptive third wheel dissipate, and the supervisees rotated into engaging holders of the space, becoming crucial to the supervisory dynamic.

The Individual/Dyad Supervisory Session

As there is no one "right way" to do supervision, there is no one way to break up the 50-minute individual supervision hour. While we have suggested in Chapter 3, *What Supervisees Need to Know about Supervision*, that one can break supervision into thirds (i.e., one-third supervisor's agenda, one-third the supervisee's agenda, and the remaining third giving space to what comes from the items discussed), this format may not work in all situations. See Box 9.1 for factors to consider when determining how to use the time.

Box 9.1 Factors to be Considered When Determining How to Use the Time

1   What is the supervisor's theoretical framework or model?
2   What is the supervisee's learning style?
3   Why is the supervisee seeking supervision?
4   Developmentally, where is the supervisee in their therapeutic skills and style?

Regardless of whether in an individual or dyad supervision, the current demands related to the components of supervision – administrative, educational, and support (as introduced in Chapter 1, *What Is Art Therapy Supervision? Reasons and Expectations*) – determine the session structure. At times, the session will focus on one specific area, and on other occasions some combination of the three. It is also useful to establish exceptions to the rule of portioning the time. For example, we contract with our supervisees that crisis or pressing clinical concerns always takes priority over the set agenda. Mills and Chasler (2012) outline a nine-stage hierarchy of supervision priorities, with the most urgent being the suicidal or homicidal threats from the clients. Additional priorities on the continuum include: therapist conduct associated with potential client harm, dishonesty in supervision, resistance to supervision, supervisee acting out, and skill development with discussions of theoretical and technical subjects. Firmly establishing a framework of priorities provides permission for supervisees to step outside of the established agenda, and helps build the supervisory alliance.

For dyads in supervision, we recommend a clearly determined structure within the session so one supervisee does not monopolize the time and each supervisee has an opportunity to speak. One method we have utilized is to share the time equally – each half of the session is dedicated to each supervisee. Sharing time this way does not necessitate that the supervisee spend their entire time speaking. For example, in the first five minutes of their half of the session, a supervisee may pose an administrative difficulty, a question or concern about a group dynamic or an impasse with an individual client, or they might broach a specific topic such as privilege or intersectionality. The remaining time can be spent brainstorming various interventions or processing the issue through artmaking. Another method begins with a brief verbal or art-based check-in by all, including the supervisor, allotting the remainder of the session to one in-depth case presentation or theme introduced by one supervisee and equally discussed among all. With this format, supervisees may take turns presenting cases or themes during alternating sessions. See Vignette 9.2, which describes how a dyad used their shared time.

Vignette 9.2 Dyadic Supervision with Friends

Yasmine's Story

I (Yasmine) was originally seeing one supervisee, who worked in a public high school setting, for individual supervision. After about a year, she learned that a friend also needed supervision, and asked if she could join us to form a triad. We discussed this for several sessions – the benefits (e.g., lower cost for the supervisees) and potential drawbacks (e.g., sharing the time). After this discussion, I met with the new supervisee individually to see if it would be a good fit, and to discuss expectations of supervision, cost, and the signing of the supervision agreement. Furthermore, the new addition was working with a different age group and in a different setting. In our first dyad supervision meeting, even though I spoke with both individuals separately, we discussed how we would negotiate time and crises. We agreed that it would best to split the time in half – and that half of the supervision time would be dedicated to one of the supervisees' concerns, clients, or any topics they would like to raise, and the second half would be dedicated to the other's. We also agreed that if someone had a crisis, we would prioritize that person and they would go first. At first this 50/50 was difficult to manage – the supervisee I had a longer and therefore more established relationship with tended to take more space. However, we addressed this together and made sure to hold each other accountable for allowing this to happen and to be more equitable moving forward.

As addressed in Chapter 2, *What Supervisors Need to Know about Supervision*, maintaining a solid supervisory alliance is another type of priority. Enlow, McWhorter, Genuario, and Davis (2019) identified three concerns that threaten the strength of the supervisory working alliance: a mismatch between supervision style and developmental level, contextual factors impacting supervisee work performance, and unconstructive or unresponsive feedback. They provide recommendations and hands-on suggestions for best practices that are supervisor- and supervisee-specific to "foster a constructive and rewarding supervisory experience for both supervisors and supervisees" (p. 208). The three concerns can be amplified when working within a supervisory dyad, and require special attention to address the potential for contrasting developmental levels, contextual factors, and ability to give or receive constructive feedback.

On- and Off-Site Supervision for Individual and Dyads

Not only do pertinent supervision priorities change, the liabilities directly associated with supervision also differ between on- and off-site settings. Falender (2014) defines the differences quite clearly:

Supervision is distinguished from consultation by the power, responsibility, and liability the supervisor holds for the cases the supervisee carries contrasted to a consultation relationship, often between peers in which the consultant has no necessity for obtaining complete information about the case and the consultee has no obligation to enact the consultation suggestions.

(p. 9)

A growing field, art therapy provides wonderful opportunities for overlap and continued connections. Art therapists often know each other in different contexts, including supervisory ones. Vignette 9.3 excerpts part of the supervisory experience of a supervisee, Cindy, whose own path has crossed Yasmine and Daniel's multiple times, at different points in her career, as her supervisory needs transformed.

Vignette 9.3 Supervision Roots

Cindy's Story

Our work as therapists is shaped by so many personal and environmental factors; top among them is the supervision we receive. Today, I find joy in supervising art therapy students, interns, and professionals, cultivating the seeds planted by Daniel, Yasmine before him, and others. Some supervisors were wonderful, and some taught me how *not* to supervise. In the Practicum Supervision class I currently teach, I try to model presence with each student and I encourage a trust in their own instincts and abilities. I am continually impressed when students give constructive feedback and support to each other in the context of this safe learning environment.

Shortly after I graduated, I sought out Yasmine as a contracted supervisor while I was working as a consultant at an outpatient drug treatment program, because I had no colleagues from whom I could get feedback or support from at the agency. As a new professional, I saw Yasmine as someone I could come to with questions, share clinical experiences and client artwork, and obtain feedback from. I was very concerned with doing things "right", and her confidence in me and her gentle guidance shaped my development. Yasmine did this *not* by giving me answers, but by being curious about what I thought my next steps were, what I thought about the artwork or interactions with clients. She allowed me to find my own way and my own style, incorporating hers, while refining my own art therapist identity.

In 2012, I moved to Colorado from New York. I did not know Daniel well, but he supervised my supervisor when I was an intern, and Yasmine also spoke highly of him as she was supervised by him. I began my work with Daniel as a more experienced therapist in private practice. I was somewhat isolated, moving to a new location, and knew supervision was critical for me to both serve clients to the best of my ability and to grow professionally. In addition, I was ethically obliged to consult with an experienced art therapist about my work so that I was not working in a vacuum. I ended up working with Daniel for about three years, tackling issues such as boundaries, dual roles, clients' abrupt termination, self-disclosure, and working on my ability to sit in silence in client sessions. Daniel always modeled full presence, and I felt that he had faith in my abilities. He demonstrated humor and curiosity, and showed me how much wisdom there is in not (always) knowing. Daniel offered me his warm and assuring presence; his ability to be curious about the work in all its complexity and ambiguity inspired me. He modeled sitting with uncertainty, which I strive to integrate into my work with clients (and into my life in general).

When working with Daniel, I understood that "rightness" was on a spectrum, and I was dealing more directly with my own countertransference in a variety of circumstances, and addressing clinical situations that were particularly challenging to me. These topics included boundary extensions, not being able to reach a client I had worked with closely, working with trauma and suicidal ideation, and working with my anxiety around self-disclosing to clients that I had cancer. I remember one meeting in particular that will always stay with me – when I told Daniel that I had a recurrence of cancer, and expressed my anxiety about its impact on clients. I experienced such solid attunement from him, even in the emotional moments, and his presence and instincts were so well targeted. He offered me support as well as reality-testing, helping to allay my unwarranted fears that my clients would not see me as competent. Especially during this time, I relied on my supervision with Daniel to help me both think through how to talk with clients about my situation, and also help me process their responses. (See Figure 9.1.) For example, I was seeing a child whose mother was very ill with cancer, and it was helpful to think through how to handle the situation. Had I not had Daniel to discuss this with, I very well may have made a poor decision about how to proceed with the family.

Figure 9.1 Cindy Gordon (2015), Untitled supervision response art [mixed media]

Both Yasmine and Daniel, with their intelligence, grace, and openness, helped build my confidence as a budding therapist. They both provided a secure base necessary to become an astute, compassionate, and ethical therapist at different points in my career. And they both demonstrated that above all, solid presence is a critical quality to hold the space and nurture therapists at any stage in their career.

Daniel's Response

I began supervising Cindy shortly after her relocation from New York City and during the second of my five years of living in Colorado. The supervisory alliance was quick to build thanks to Yasmine's "stamp of approval" referral for each of us. It was easier to gain trust and build a productive supervisory rapport having known two of her previous supervisors and experiencing her as an educated participant of supervision. Living in a relatively small city, we eagerly put in the mandatory time to navigate multiple professional, social, and personal dual relationships. By the time Cindy announced a recurrence of cancer, our dual relationships were well established and boundaried. Since she chose to disclose this personal information in the professional context of supervision, the role of supervisor was my initial place of response. My personal reaction of fear and alarm, as a friend, had to wait. The focus of our work in supervision during this time was to design and navigate strategies for the best possible care and outcomes for her clients. This was best addressed through the supportive (e.g., acknowledging and partially holding the related anxiety) and educational aspects of supervision (e.g., concrete strategies for disclosing to clients) in addition to art. Continuously returning to the art was even more critical during this time of illness and healing, for Cindy and her clients. In hindsight, it would have been helpful had I made artwork as a more direct response to the situation. Cindy's ability to maximize boundaries, express vulnerabilities, rely on supervision to help own her expertise, and embrace the right of not (always) knowing were crucial to her professional success during this time.

On-Site (Required) Supervision

Some may argue required supervision, whether as a student or professional, is where the bulk of the art therapy training takes place. During their graduate education, students are required to take part in supervision. This individual supervision often takes place with an assigned, on-site art therapist, supported by on-campus group supervision (we discuss this and other forms of group supervision in Chapter 10, *Group Supervision*). Required individual supervision also occurs when working professionally as a clinician – the supervisor may be an art therapist or a clinician from another field, or may not be a clinician at all – and often takes place on-site.

Regardless, on-site supervision delves into accountabilities, consequences, and implications that are administrative in nature. Even if you *choose* your supervisor by actively seeking employment with a specific supervisor, this can change unexpectedly. As mentioned in the Preface, Yasmine was hired at a site anticipating Daniel to be her long-term supervisor – however, once he accepted a promotion to lead a different team she was paired with a new supervisor. For better or for worse, this match-up can impact job satisfaction and performance in unexpected ways. When the partnership is good, it can be very good and inspirational; when it is bad, let us just say it can be very challenging. When Yasmine was assigned a new supervisor with a drastically different style than Daniel, it required her to modify her expectations and alter her approach to supervision.

Being on-site influences the components of supervision. Specifically, the administrative component tends to take on a larger focus, potentially over-shadowing both the educational element for clinical development and the support role of attending to supervisees' work-related stress and emotional responses. The administrative portion of on-site supervision is often central, and contends with documentation, scheduling, and compliance, in addition to location-specific requirements (e.g., safety protocols, regulations, culture) and potential career advancement (e.g., completing educational requirements, promotion, more difficult clients, new skill acclimation) (Knapp & Vande-Creek, 2012). Interpersonal interactions in supervision, whether problematic or supportive, may be amplified when additional compulsory relationships are added, such as team dynamics, an on-site group supervision component, or multiple supervisors working in a single department with drastically different supervisory and communication styles. This places a tremendous responsibility upon on-site supervisors as they assume the primary role for "monitoring and providing evaluation" and "ensuring that clarity is achieved" when informing the supervisee whether they are "not meeting performance criteria and [are] being moved to a different status with remediation of identified competence areas" (Falender, 2014, p. 44). However, one of the benefits of supervising on-site is that it allows for direct observation of clinical work for a more comprehensive assessment. Even if one does not directly see a session take place, being proximate to sessions is often helpful for quick debriefs, and observing the supervisee pre- and post-session.

Students

The initial pairing of an intern with an art therapy supervisor can leave a substantial impression on their long-lasting relationship with supervision. All benefit when a supervisor aspires to the best practices and ideals shared in Chapter 2, *What Supervisors Need to Know about Supervision*, and a supervisee sets an intention to apply the best practices and ideals of Chapter 3, *What Supervisees Need to Know about Supervision*. Supervision with an experienced art therapist is one requirement for students in art therapy programs we enthusiastically support. The Accreditation Council for Art Therapy Education (ACATE) requires students to be supervised by art therapists who hold an ATR-BC while in the field (ACATE, 2019). This individual supervision typically occurs on-site, where the clinical art therapy practice is taking place. If a student does not have an on-site credentialed art therapy supervisor, the graduate art therapy program may provide the individual art therapy supervision.

Professionals

On-site individual supervision, typically with an assigned supervisor, is often the principal method of supervision for the art therapist. This required partnership regularly blends administrative, educational, and supportive supervisory interventions. Administrative management often includes tracking therapist productivity (e.g., number of sessions per week), grant or funding compliance, paperwork, agency expectations, time-off requests, and other non-clinical functions of the position that may challenge clinical supervision needs. On-site supervisors are also likely responsible for staff evaluations and assisting the supervisee in identifying and setting their work goals. Thus, the possibility exists for parallel yet conflicting paths of responsibilities for the supervisor.

Off-Site Supervision (Typically Chosen)

Why do people choose individual supervision? They may be compelled to find a supervisor in order to meet supervisory needs related to licensure or credentialing requirements. They may be seeking out expert advice, pursuing a certain skillset, or searching for a specific type of supervisory connection or cultural fit to reduce barriers of difference.

Off-Site, Individual Supervision of Students

Although students typically receive on-site supervision from an art therapist who is employed at the site of their field experience, there are cases where a student art therapist is not engaged with individual on-site art therapy supervision. For example, a student may introduce art therapy to a location that has never had art therapy. In this case, there is no art therapist on-site to provide supervision. A task or administrative supervisor is assigned, but is not providing art therapy supervision. When this is the case, the educational program secures an off-site individual supervisor.

There are benefits and challenges to this type of work unique to students. It may be difficult for the student to share all aspects of their clinical experiences, wanting to prove their competence or skills. Conversely, students may only focus on the difficulties and neglect to highlight the successes of their fieldwork. It takes an experienced supervisor to provide off-campus individual supervision for students, one who is not simply an experienced art therapist, but understands how art therapy is dependent on the student, placement itself, and persons they are working with.

> I've had experience with serving as both an on and off-site supervisor and there are more similarities than differences. The downside of not being able to assist and observe the student within the milieu can be offset by in-depth information gathering, a site visit or two if possible and interviews with milieu staff when necessary. Successful off-site supervision involves paring an intern who feels empowered by their developing therapeutic skill set, is self motivated, and assertive with a tenured therapist who has a strong foundation in providing direct service, some knowledge of the [site's] treatment and client population and who maintains an active relationship with the educational institution.
>
> (T. Dow, personal communication, October 4, 2019)

From the perspective of the graduate student receiving off-site, individual supervision there are also challenges and benefits:

> [Off-site supervision] required me to conceptualize my cases in a way that familiarized my supervisor with my clients and work environment … Challenges that I noticed while receiving off-site supervision were establishing a consistent time to meet with my supervisor and adding this to my own schedule as a full-time student and intern.
>
> (K. Wuebbling, personal communication, October 10, 2019)

Professionals

Early-career art therapists often seek supervision to obtain credentials or licensure, while Intermediate or Advanced art therapists may seek out supervision to work on specific skills or conceptualize a particular case. A well-experienced art therapist expressed the differences between supervision as a new professional and as a more seasoned professional:

> Supervision was critical to my growth as a new therapist as it allowed me to navigate through clinical and ethical decisions that felt challenging in the beginning of my career. However, I always felt like limited time and money prevented me from continuing supervision after I received my BC and LPC.
>
> (B. Asch, personal communication, September 27, 2019)

Unless one is in private practice, a supervisee is most likely receiving on-site supervision as well as the supervision they are seeking off-site, and must work with each supervisor to define the intent of each supervisory relationship. Blair's story (see Vignette 9.4) describes different types of individual supervision he has received, both on- and off-site.

Vignette 9.4 Differences between On-Site and Off-Site Individual Supervision

Blair's Story

I have had the pleasure of working with all different types of supervisors, who came from different backgrounds not only clinically but ethnically, spiritually, and economically. As we know, the mental health world is dominated by white women, and that was mirrored in my experience. While I did have two white male supervisors to date, I did not receive a sense of comfort from them, which I would have benefited from, as I was the only male in my cohort during this time. Although their insight was fruitful, I felt disconnected from them in many ways. Personally, they did not acknowledge how my Blackness, my being a male, and my culture affected my ability to provide therapeutic services. It was never brought up by either myself or my supervisor, and maybe that was a mistake. As a young and upcoming therapist, my only goals were to gain experience and be seen as useful and competent. I did not want to stir the pot, out of fear that I would be rejected due to my lack of experience in comparison to theirs. Looking back, I believe that perception of power played a role in my inability to engage in conversation around my feelings of being uncomfortable. It may have helped if a conversation was had around our ethnic differences, but I cannot say for certain that I would have been honest about my feelings. Questions in culture, beliefs, and overall views on life arose that I felt none of my white supervisors could provide the answers to.

As a result of these experiences, I have since made conscious efforts to seek out Black supervisors, in hopes of understanding more about our struggles as the minority in our field. My rationale was that a Black supervisor would not only teach me how to find my authentic self as a Black therapist, but their high position was also proof that they learned how to successfully navigate through a profession where Black people (especially men) are seldom seen in higher positions. In my mind, if they were able to make it to that role, they would be able to provide me with the tools to do the same.

Currently, I am supervised by two female therapists; one who is Black and the other who is a person of color. The supervisor who is Black was assigned to me due to my position – she holds a master's in Social Work and specializes in Functional Family Therapy (FFT). However, my goal was to find a Black art therapist who was also a Licensed Professional Counselor so I could obtain the ATR, ATR-BC, and LPC credentials – a needle in a haystack.

When I first began my search, I started internally at my full-time job, as the employees are predominantly Black. I also was concerned about cost and wanted to avoid having to pay for supervision. When I realized that the individuals within my organization were either licensed social workers or licensed marriage and family therapists, I knew that I would have to do more research outside of my organization. Eventually, and luckily, through a Creative Art Therapists of Color (CATs of Color) networking event, I was able to meet a person of color [Yasmine] who carried both licenses that I was seeking. While she was not Black, she did have the other requirements I was looking for – two out of three ain't bad.

These two supervisors are very different – not only in their supervisory roles, but also in their clinical observations. While those differences make up a part of why these supervisions are night and day, it is the personality of each of these supervisors, and their approach to supervision, that truly distinguishes each experience. My FFT supervisor uses a mixture of FFT skills and personal observation in regard to me as a person and how this work connects to me as a Functional Family Therapist. Her supervision starts off very structured: she will ask me to pick one case and give background information in the individual. Then, depending on which phase of FFT we are in, we will go down the list of questions that helps her paint a clear FFT picture: what are the risk and protective factors of the child and family, theme hints that bring the family together, the family's relational functions (are they autonomous towards one another, contacting, or in the middle), what FFT skills did you use to change meaning around the family conflicts and build hope, what is the family's behavior pattern (what is the overall series of events that keep occurring on a day to day basis that results in their negative interaction), and what are your plans for the next session? In the mist of all of those questions, she inquires about my personal life to create a parallel between my life history and my clinical struggles with my families.

With my art therapy supervisor, there is more of a dialogue in regard to all of my clients at once, and a heavy emphasis on maintaining my art therapist identity. Our conversations are more free-flowing and there is more of a collaborative brainstorm of ideas in regard to a clinical assessment of my clients, how art therapy can benefit their specific struggles, and how me partaking in my own art therapy may help clear clouds of frustration and doubt in terms of my client's ability to grow and be successful in treatment. This focus on the client gave me the ability to grow as a clinician and art therapist, working on skills that revolve around critical things about the client, what I observed, and how those assessments can be transformed into an art therapy skill when the time comes.

The irony of it all is that the dynamics of how I expected my experiences to be were completely different, which was based on the fact that I was in control of who I picked for one supervisor vs having no control over who my supervisor was at my full-time job. Working with my FFT supervisor, I expected a very formal and professional relationship, simply based on past relationships with supervisors who were connected to employers. Working with a supervisor I specifically sought out, I expected there to be more of an informal relationship, as time and effort was put into picking out that supervision; it was the complete opposite experience for me. I found that, while working with my supervisor from work, we developed a very personal relationship in which I was able to recognize similarities and differences not only externally, but internally as well. This gave me the space to be vulnerable and put more emphasis on myself and how my personal being effects how I interact with my families. In addition, since FFT is a very specific model, there was little wiggle room for creative space clinically. On the other end of the spectrum, working with a supervisor who I sought out turned out to be very formal and business-oriented. This gave me the space to not only think outside of the box clinically, but also, as an art therapist, to learn how my own artist journey plays a role in my mood when working with families. This could also be due to the fact that I am paying for her services, so she feels an obligation to make sure I am receiving the most "bang for my buck". In addition, while the goal was to find a Black therapist with their LPC and ATR-BC, I found a person of color instead and the outcome was not as expected. My intentions with finding a Black art therapist were for personal satisfaction and a need for representation; to prove that Black people can grow up how I grew up (low-income and in the hood), maintain that identity (i.e., not "white wash"), and become successful art therapists. My ideal chosen supervisor would speak slang, curse, be current with current Black news/events, have developed a personal relationship with me (and vice versa), would be able to challenge me clinically around cases and my own personal life views and choices, and be an amazing artist. I did not necessarily care about their clinical background as long as they were Black because, if they made it this far being Black, they have to be amazing by default. However, I found someone who was, instead, a person of color (still unsure about her ethnic background), has not sworn during supervision, has not spoken any slang, and has not shown that she is current in Black news. Despite not displaying these actions, she has given me something much more important than anything I could have asked for – she gave me back my art identity.

Overall, the biggest difference between myself and my supervisors was how their supervisory styles connected with my specific needs as someone seeking supervision. While it is important for me personally to feel understood as a human, it is equally as important to feel validated as a clinician. As a clinician, I personally feel as though my worth is gauged on my ability to make accurate assessments and create a plan, based off that assessment, that will best benefit the families and clients that I work with. I also personally believe that my work is based on perspective – my ability to take in perspective affects my ability to give the best treatment possible. Since each therapist has their own perspective, there is never a "right answer" in therapy; there is only your perspective and how you work with the client to best benefit their growth. Keeping that in mind, it is extremely important for a supervisor to not only validate their supervisee's perspective, but to also challenge it and to give different perspectives. If supervisors do not learn how to help/encourage a supervisee to be confident in their own assessment/perspective while also teaching them how to absorb other perspectives, the supervisee can come out of supervision either unconfident, too cocky, or stagnant in their growth.

Finally, it seems important to note there is a feeling that, being a person of color, and knowing how hard it is to be accepted in the professional world the higher up you go, there is a sense of responsibility among us. We are able to do all of the things stated above, but we also hold each other accountable for what is done outside of supervision. We may be able to use slang with one another, but we know how we should speak to the CEO and others outside of our circle. The desire to see one another succeed while being true to ourselves plays an important role in our identity as therapists – not only how we work with our clients, but also how we supervise in the future.

Yasmine's Response

Although I (Yasmine) strive to share my identities with my supervisees, particularly those who are therapists of color, I did not realize until working on this vignette with Blair that I never explicitly named my South Asian and South East Asian identities. Perhaps I thought I shared this in the CATs of Color meeting; however, even if I did, that is no replacement for having explicit discussions about race, ethnicity, and identity in supervision. While I have had colleagues of color in clinical settings, I have had limited experience with supervising therapists/therapists-in-training of color, or being supervised by therapists of color. I may have been enacting anti-Blackness behaviors by not explicitly naming my identities, how I have personally benefited from racism (including the model minority myth which lifts Asian Americans while reinforcing negative Black stereotypes), and not having overt discussions about racism in the fields of art therapy and mental health counseling. Fortunately, we were able to discuss this – I asked Blair why he never asked about my racial identity after reading his vignette submitted for this book. And I learned, once again, the importance of explicitly discussing race and intersecting identities.

Supervision of Supervision

Supervisees may seek out supervision to learn how to become supervisors themselves. This type of supervision is often referred to as *supervision of supervision*. As described in Chapter 1, *What Is Art Therapy Supervision? Reasons and Expectations*, individuals with extensive experience and expertise in supervision can obtain specific credentials such as the Art Therapy Credentials Board's Art Therapy Certified Supervisor (ATCS). Supervision of supervision can occur as naturally as supervising an art therapist who has decided to supervise their first intern. Or it can be more layered. As an example, at one point I (Daniel), as a director of mental health and substance use, was collaborating with direct reports (associate directors) in supervision on how to best work with their direct reports (coordinators and staff clinicians) on how to constructively and supportively supervise interns.

In supervision of supervision, although client outcomes maintain significance, the focus shifts and expands to include the performance of the supervisee as a supervisor, and their direct reports of working directly with the client. This creates a secondary triadic relationship with the supervisor's supervisor, the supervisor, and the art therapist.

Unless a conscious tenacity is applied to training supervisors, supervision of supervision can easily perpetuate the common cycle of successful art therapists becoming untrained supervisors. The three components of supervision identified by Kadushin and Harkness (2014) – administrative, educational, and supportive – apply here as well, and assist the supervisor in developing well-trained supervisors. Yes, the administrative aspects are critical to maintaining a multitude of compliances and meeting goals, alongside the supportive function of assisting with the stressors of being a supervisor. However, we find the educational component is most critical to actively teaching someone how to be a better supervisor.

Termination Considerations

Analogous to the therapeutic relationship, we recommend supervisors and supervisees consider termination or the ending of the supervisory relationship. Termination is often activating for clients, supervisees, and supervisors. Blindly entering termination can be detrimental to all involved and represents a missed opportunity to transparently review gains and challenges in order to implement timely strategies for maintaining and nurturing growth. When a supervisee has properly addressed and prepared for termination within the supervisory relationship, they are able to properly focus on termination concerns and opportunities within the (a) client–therapist relationship, (b) relationship between the supervisee and supervisor; (c) relationship between the supervisee and the site, and (d) transference and countertransference connections.

In forced termination, such as the completion of an internship, interns find these terminations demanding and "require further knowledge and skills and significant support in negotiating this complicated passage for themselves and their clients" (Gelman, Fernandez, Hausman, Miller, & Weiner, 2007, p. 89). As such, we find it useful to speak about the ending of supervision at the start of supervision.

For contracted or private supervision, the first mention may be listed in the supervisory contract, which outlines how the supervisor and the supervisee decide when supervision will end. The first session may also include a discussion – will supervision end when clinical hours are met, after licensure paperwork or credentials is/are submitted, or once licensure or credentials is/are obtained? Or perhaps supervision will end after a difficult case has been closed. For campus-based supervision, the ending of supervision typically follows the academic calendar – finishing at the end of a term or academic year. Even though all parties know the end date, it is still useful to discuss it up front.

In termination, goals are a critical part of the process to provide a framework during a complicated time, as supervision termination often coincides with other major life changes. Levendosky and Hopwood (2016) identified the following goals for supervision termination: (a) consolidate growth of the student/trainee, (b) active repair of ruptures between supervisors and the student/trainee, (c) acknowledge the meaning of the supervisory relationship, and (d) express authentic feelings associated with termination. Although student-focused, they apply easily to professional supervisory terminations. Goals such as these cannot be completed quickly, and prompt the discussion and act of termination to occur over the last month or so of the supervisory relationship.

Prioritizing Artmaking in Termination

Having discussions about termination, endings, loss, moving on, and transformation is important; however, as art therapists, it is profoundly important to process through artmaking. Engaging artmaking during termination is much easier if art has previously been part of the relationship. When artmaking occurs towards the end of a supervisory relationship, different imagery can emerge, or familiar themes can reoccur. Some art therapy supervisors are more comfortable with providing a prompt, such as asking the supervisee to draw a road that is a metaphor for change, growth, and journeys ahead. Art therapists who are more comfortable with the process may want to encourage the supervisee to consider what they have learned about themselves and their clinical work through the supervisory process and make an image from there. As we have noted before, supervision is a relationship, and the supervisor may have grown and changed as well from the supervisory relationship. For those art therapists who are comfortable with creating *with* their supervisees, creating art during the supervisory session can allow for a rich discussion of how the relationship has transformed both parties. See Color Plates 7 and 8 for examples of artwork created in individual supervision by a supervisee (Blair) and supervisor (Yasmine).

Presuming the supervisor has the clinical and supervisory skills to incorporate artmaking, off-site supervision with an art therapist can be an ideal place for artmaking during termination. One benefit of off-site artmaking is that the administrative duties present during on-site supervision are notably absent, such as coordinating client care with other clinicians, managing crises, caseloads, etc. Of course, administrative responsibilities exist, but are minimal in comparison to on-site supervision. Despite the benefits of artmaking during termination with off-site supervision, it often does not happen. While there is evidence (Deaver & McAuliffe, 2009) and support (Deaver & Shiflett, 2011; Fish, 2017, 2012; Miller, 2012) for including artmaking in individual supervision, the creative process often gets left out throughout termination. One reason this happens is time. We have heard this again and again over the years. The lack of time is ever-present within the boundaries of 50 minutes – so many clients to discuss, so many questions during termination! There is never enough time to do it all.

Takeaways

- Individual supervision is often required at the workplace, but can also be optional. Optional individual or dyadic supervision often occurs to meet art-therapy-specific credentialing or licensing requirements for early-career professionals, and for in-depth skill-building and case conceptualization for Advanced Therapists.

- Consider artmaking throughout the individual or dyadic supervisory relationship, including during the process of termination. Termination considerations may be more complex for professionals, as leaving can be staggered. For students, beginnings and endings tend to follow the academic calendar.
- One advantage of individual and dyadic supervision is individualized attention. The pair or trio gets to truly dive deep into the work with minimal distractions.
- One disadvantage to individual and dyad supervision is the absence of diverse opinions. It may be difficult to recognize varying perspectives if there is conformity within the supervisory relationship; likewise, it may feel adversarial or uncomfortable to challenge a viewpoint of a supervisor or supervisee without others.

Practice Prompts

Role Clarification

Clay can be a useful medium to enhance role clarification and understanding in the supervisory alliance.

- Provide a portion of clay (or clay substitute, such as Model Magic or other modeling material) to each participant – supervisor and supervisee(s). During ten minutes of silence, participants create clay images reflecting on their role(s) in the supervisory alliance.
- After the images are completed, arrange the clay pieces on a 10 in x 14 in sheet of paper. Do this part for five minutes, in silence.
- Next, allow five minutes for response writing to the artmaking process and the final art.
- Finally, verbally discuss physical connections, distances, and overlap of supervisory roles using the metaphor of the final clay image.

Bridges as a Metaphor of the Supervision-of-Supervision Transition

- Create a piece of art containing a bridge that connects the "supervision of art therapist shore" to the "supervision of supervisors shore".
- Focus on the bridge as a symbol marking your shift in role, responsibilities, and priorities as a supervisor.
- Free write for five-minute in response to each shore of the bridge and the bridge itself. Share art and self-reflections in supervision.

Farewell Box

The supervisee(s) and supervisor work together to create a found object farewell box during the last few weeks of supervision. The box can be a wooden cigar box, cell phone box, or other small, sturdy box, and is completed by the supervisee(s).

- The exterior of the box represents the supervisee's therapist self while the interior represents the role and support of supervision.
- The supervisor and the supervisee(s) create small art pieces or found objects to represent strengths, messages, lessons learned, etc., in supervision. If a dyad, the supervisees create gift art for each other as well.

References

ACATE. (2019). Handbook for completing a self-study for Initial Accreditation. Retrieved from www.caahep.org/CAAHEP/media/CoADocuments/Self-Study-Handbook-2019_1.pdf

Deaver, S. P., & McAuliffe, G. (2009). Reflective visual journaling during art therapy and counselling internships: A qualitative study. *Reflective Practice, 10*(5), 615–632. doi:10.1080/14623940903290687

Deaver, S. P., & Shiflett, C. (2011). Art-based supervision techniques. *The Clinical Supervisor, 30*(2), 257–276. doi:10.1080/07325223.2011.619456

Enlow, P. T., McWhorter, L. G., Genuario, K., & Davis, A. (2019). Supervisor-Supervisee Interactions: The Importance of the Supervisory Working Alliance. *Training and Education in Professional Psychology, 13*(3), 206–211.

Falender, C. A. (2014). Clinical supervision in a competency-based era. *South African Journal of Psychology, 44*(1), 6–17.

Fish, B. J. (2012). Response art: The art of the art therapist. *Art Therapy: Journal of the American Art Therapy Association, 29*(3), 138–143. doi:10.1080/07421656.2012.701594

Fish, B. J. (2017). *Art-based supervision: Cultivating therapeutic insight through imagery.* New York, NY: Routledge.

Gelman, C. R., Fernandez, P., Hausman, N., Miller, S., & Weiner, M. (2007). Challenging endings: First year MSW interns' experiences with forced termination and discussion points for supervisory guidance. *Clinical Social Work Journal, 35*(2), 79–90.

Kadushin, A., & Harkness, D. (2014). *Supervision in social work.* New York, NY: Columbia University Press.

Knapp, S. J., & VandeCreek, L. D. (2012). *Practical ethics for psychologists: A positive approach* (2nd ed.). Washington, DC: American Psychological Association.

Levendosky, A. A., & Hopwood, C. J. (2016). Terminating supervision. *Psychotherapy, 54*(1), 37.

Miller, A. (2012). Inspired by El Duende: One-canvas process painting in art therapy supervision. *Art Therapy: Journal of the American Art Therapy Association, 29*(4), 166–173. doi:doi: 10.1080/07421656.2013.730024

Mills, J. A., & Chasler, J. K. (2012). Establishing priorities in the supervision hour. *Training and Education in Professional Psychology, 6*(3), 160.

Ögren, M. L., Boëthius, S. B., & Sundin, E. (2014). Challenges and possibilities in group supervision. In C. E. Watkins, Jr. & D. L. Milne (Eds.), *The Wiley International Handbook of Clinical Supervision* (pp. 648–669). Chichester, UK: Wiley.

Riley, S. (1992). Supervision and the issue of case management. *Art Therapy, 9*(3), 119–120.

10 Group Supervision

Introduction

This chapter draws on the literature and our many experiences as members and leaders in group supervision, including campus-based art therapy groups, off-site group art therapy for professionals, peer supervision groups, and on-site group supervision for clinicians from various backgrounds. Group supervision is more than several clinicians meeting together to discuss "the work". Group *feedback* is what makes it distinct from individual supervision (Smith, Riva, & Cornish, 2012). In our experience, although group supervision can be the primary mode of supervision, group supervision is more often used in conjunction with individual supervision. For example, art therapy students are required to be engaged in on-campus group supervision and on-site individual supervision (Commission on Accreditation of Allied Health Education Programs [CAAHEP], 2016). Group supervision for students is particularly notable as the triadic relationship shifts. While the dynamics of the student therapist, supervisor, and client remain present, there is an additional triadic relationship, which involves the campus group supervisor, the art therapy student, and the site supervisor (Sweitzer & King, 2018).

Group supervision can be discipline-specific, composed of only art therapists, or multidisciplinary. For many students, group supervision on campus consists of all art therapy students with a credentialed art therapy group supervisor as an art therapy program requirement (CAAHEP, 2016). However, group supervision for professionals can include other mental health professionals, depending on individual licensing requirements or the composition of the workplace.

This chapter will focus on various formats of group supervision: on-campus group supervision for graduate art therapy students, private group supervision composed of only art therapists, and on-site group supervision for mixed modalities or disciplines. Case examples from supervisees will also be included to illustrate the power of group supervision.

Another type of group supervision discussed in this chapter is peer supervision. According to Rubin (2011), "no matter how experienced you are, a more objective person can always help you to do your therapeutic or supervisory job better" (p. 202). This is supported by Moon's (2019) statement that "No art therapist ever knows all there is to know about art therapy and no individual therapist can ever have sufficient skills and range of experiences to treat every type of client" (p. 120). Peer supervision, sometimes referred to as a consultation group, is useful for experienced art therapists as well as new professionals who work in isolation and desire clinical connection and the support of other art therapists. Specific types of peer supervision models have been promoted for students as well. Generally, peer supervision models allow for the sharing of expertise without an overarching leader or expectation that one person holds the role of clinical expert.

We will highlight the triadic and group supervision models in this chapter. For more information on individual or peer supervision in a dyad, see Chapter 9, *Individual and Dyad Supervision*. Note that for licensure purposes, dyad or group supervision may only constitute part of the required supervision experience – please check your state licensure board for details.

Considering Developmental Stages of Supervisees in Group Supervision

As clinicians, we understand individual therapy is different than couples, family, and group therapy formats as the dynamics are shifted due to who is in the room and what their relationships are. Similarly, group supervision is different than individual supervision in that feedback is given from multiple perspectives. Learning is shared by all participants, which can be enhanced or diminished by all members of the group.

Understanding the needs of the supervision group can inform the structure of the group. School-based supervision on campus is more homogenous regarding developmental needs than group supervision for professionals. While group supervision is required for accredited art therapy programs (CAAHEP, 2016), how the supervision is structured is left to the individual program or supervisor. Some groups are task-oriented, particularly when working with students who are initiating their clinical experiences. Groups tend to be more diverse outside of the educational setting – whether contracted or on-site – since educational and experience levels are more varied. Because of these differences, we briefly review developmental considerations.

According to Lambie and Blount (2016), Introductory Therapists desire concrete instruction and direction, as there is a general lack of awareness of understanding when they need supervision, they may lack self-efficacy or not want to appear unknowledgeable, and they may lack confidence in how to approach a supervisor. However, when working with supervisees who have more experience, such as Intermediate Therapists or student interns, who are transitioning from being supervisor-dependent to more independent clinicians (Lambie & Blount, 2016), highly structured supervision may not be as useful. Proficient and Advanced therapists do not exist in the typical master's-level school-based group supervision setting, as both of these developmental levels require extensive clinical experience. However, advanced post-master-level clinicians in on- or off-site group supervision may participate in group supervision. Outside of the educational context, it is likely that participants in group supervision will have a varied range of experiences and expertise.

Sharing Space

One challenge of group supervision is how to structure the time. Individual supervision can be easier to manage, as there are only two individuals involved – the supervisor and supervisee. With the addition of more participants, the rule of thirds is not easily realized (see Delano, 2001). Furthermore, when wanting to ensure artmaking takes place, it can be difficult to know how to make room for all that is brought up in the group setting. When discussing how group supervision will be structured, the group should also discuss when the schedule may shift.

Taking Turns: Early Developmental Stage

For students, particularly those in their first clinical experiences, taking turns through case presentations or other structured formats can be useful. It is difficult for students in the Introductory Therapist stage to know exactly what to present. Also, some students may strictly be observing sessions, so they do not have a choice in what clinical cases they have access to. In other words, if a student therapist is shadowing their supervisor or another clinician, they can only discuss in supervision what they have had the opportunity to observe. Introductory Therapists have fewer clinical experiences to draw from and have not seen or given case presentations. There is also a desire for concrete instruction, in that they may need a supervisor to tell them exactly what to do, and inform them when they are doing something "correctly" or "wrong". When the group is first being formed, there may also be the need to perform for the supervisor and to peers in the group. In the early stages, the lack of self-efficacy, or wanting to appear like a competent art therapist, may prevent students from sharing difficulties or mistakes. In addition to taking turns, providing a framework for what to share during the supervisee's allotted time is useful. See Appendix B for suggestions on how to structure case presentations.

Similarly, it may be difficult for other members of the group to understand how to provide feedback to a case. Introductory Therapists may not know what to ask or look for in a case. They may be focusing solely on interventions or outcomes, missing relational or other aspects of the therapeutic experiences discussed. See Appendix F for guidelines on how to help new therapists ask critical and observational questions to their peers during case presentations.

For the supervisor, goals for Introductory Therapists include increasing members' observational skills, gaining confidence in presenting and giving feedback, and helping supervisees get comfortable in sharing difficult materials (as opposed to sharing only successes). The supervisor can aid the group by sharing guidelines and expectations for presenters and members who are expected to give feedback. Also, monitoring the time is important part of group supervision, and ensures presenters have enough time to present and peers have enough time to give feedback. We suggest allowing at least twice as much time to give feedback, meaning if the "presentation" portion is 20 minutes, allow 40 minutes for a response from the group, for a total of 60 minutes for the entire case presentation. The response time includes all forms of feedback – verbal, written, and artistic.

Learning How to Prioritize

Intermediate Therapists, such as interns and new professionals, are becoming more independent in their clinical practice. They have achieved basic therapy skills, but are still working on advanced concepts such as case conceptualization and reflection of meaning (Lambie & Blount, 2016). For clinicians in the Intermediate stage, taking turns presenting cases may be helpful to set the norms of the group. However, once the group is established, the structure may become more fluid to encourage more independence and mirror what is happening in their clinical experiences. Structuring group supervision can be difficult for the supervisees and supervisor. On one hand, supervisees may be hesitant to discuss cases because they do not want to take up space in the group, feeling their case is not important enough. Similarly, some supervisees may monopolize the space and bring up issues every week. Without proper organization and facilitation, the group can easily become lopsided in participation.

As with any clinical therapy or supervision group, learning how to prioritize starts with establishing group norms. In my (Yasmine's) group supervision with interns, a group agreement is created. While each group agreement differs, as the norms are created by the members themselves, there are some rules I introduce to each group:

1. We start each group supervision with a "check-in" to determine what each individual is bringing into the space, and to identify any

common themes or concerns. This check-in can be verbal, artistic, or incorporate aspects of both.

2. If any member has a clinically pressing issue, that person becomes the priority.
3. Members should consider "stepping up and stepping back". Meaning, if you are a person who tends to remain quiet about clinical cases, step up and share. If you are a member who normally speaks first and often, or has already received feedback on your case, consider stepping back and allowing another member to speak about their case.

While these three rules are quite basic, part of the job of the group as a whole is determine how to enact them. How do we best check-in with each other? What constitutes a clinical pressing issue? How does each person measure if they have not stepped up and shared enough or have over-shared and need to step back?

Considering the Impact of Difference

Just as in group therapy, there are group dynamics to tend to in group supervision. The following vignette (see Vignette 10.1) illustrates a session where race influenced group membership and participation.

Vignette 10.1 Racial Differences in Group Supervision

Blair's Story

Being in group supervision where I am one of the only clinicians of color (versus being in group supervision where there are multiple clinicians of color) is a situation that creates its own interesting dynamic. On one end of the spectrum, sitting in a room full of clinicians who do not look like me can be uncomfortable. That uncomfortable feeling comes from not knowing if they accept me as competent or "good enough". The other side of this uncomfortableness is not being able to be my authentic self in the room. There is always a feeling that I have to "white wash" my personality and that, if they are to see the authentically "Black" me, they will judge me and see me as unprofessional, despite my resume or credentials. It is almost as if I am in a constant battle to prove my worth despite having already proven that I am qualified through my clinical qualifications and job history. It is an assumption that my culture is seen as "unprofessional" and that there is a professional handbook that does not accept my truth and my culture.

On the flipside, when being in group supervision where a majority of the clinicians are people of color, there is this air of acceptance. I can make statements or references that will actually make sense in the room. For example, while staffing a case, I can mention an episode of *Insecure* and not have a majority of the room ask me, "What is that?" Also, it is acceptable to use slang or speak broken English without feeling as though I am being viewed as less than or unintelligent.

Formats

Like individual supervision, group supervision can be required or optional. School-based supervision is typically a mandatory course. Places of work, including field placements for students, may also have required group supervision. Peer supervision is another type of group supervision that tends to be voluntary or sought out. Off-site group supervision may be considered voluntary.

School-Based Group Supervision

As noted earlier, art therapy master's programs are required to hold group supervision for students, with a group size to maximize mastery of entry-level clinical competencies (Accreditation Council for Art Therapy Education [ACATE], 2019), and a supervisor with art therapy board certification credentials (ATCB). School-based groups are essentially an off-site group supervision experience, as everyone from the group is obtaining training at a different clinical placement.

The following vignette is from Julie (see Vignette 10.2), a student enrolled in an on-campus group supervision course while in a master's program for art therapy. The group was for students in their first practicum placement.

Vignette 10.2 Flexibility in Structure, On-Campus Group Supervision

Julie's Story

It was nearing the end of my field placement and I was coming into my art therapy group supervision on campus with heightened emotions that were more than the usual stress of the week. That morning, I was planning to give a case presentation to the group, but I was very distracted over what happened at my field placement a few days prior. During our check-in at the start of the supervision, I told the group that I found out my on-site supervisor had put in her two weeks' notice and she was handing me off to another art therapist for the remainder of the placement. This was without acknowledging how this may affect my learning experience. I further explained that throughout the time spent at the placement, my on-site supervisor spoke to me about her dissatisfaction with the management system, pointing out the burnout statuses of other staff, and appeared to be verbally irritable when with the patients. She never mentioned to me that all of these frustrations were possibly making her question whether she should remain in her position at the site, yet I had often wondered to myself if this was emerging burnout. Although my assumptions and speculations were correct, I felt as though I needed further explanation of her decision process. In particular, her acknowledgement of being my on-site supervisor, in which she was responsible for my supervision and learning about this particular population, was completely down-played. My part in her process was left unanswered and I needed more clarity and input to help with the sense of not knowing.

Overcome by the feelings of frustration and abandonment, I began to cry after sharing this in group supervision. I viewed my on-site supervisor's leaving as disrespecting my education. I considered the finances and time put into the field placement. I was only at this site for a short period of time and she scheduled her last week of work one week before my last day. She told me one week before she left that she gave her notice, even though she gave her notice two weeks prior. I felt that she had overlooked my presence, and it made me question if I had been paid any attention at all during the entirety of my time at the placement. I felt completely in the dark about her reasons for quitting and her experience of my learning under her supervision.

My group supervisor and classmates were supportive while they listened and watched me. They asked some questions to help me explain what I was feeling, and offered me paper towels to dry my tears.

After I settled down, I insisted I would be okay to present my case as originally scheduled. I had felt that my learning experience from the field placement was shortened and I did not want to miss on more learning in group supervision because of it. With my wavering ability to maintain composure, my group supervisor stepped in and asked if we could process what had just happened through some artmaking. In that instance, I felt some relief at the suggestion, because my group supervisor was addressing what I desperately needed to process in the moment, and it gave me assurance that I could find some closure in the situation. This opportunity of artmaking made me feel understood when I felt like I could not speak about the situation anymore, but the feelings remained. While we made art, I was so intently focused on what I was doing that I did not look up to see what my classmates were processing. I typically like to experience the group as a whole during group supervision by noticing and observing what my peers are creating, but that day it was nice to pay attention to only myself.

Once we were finished, we went around the room and shared the art and our thoughts. Looking at my classmates' and supervisor's art and process, I felt validated. My classmates and supervisor spoke about their frustrations towards my situation, wanting to comfort me while I cried, and how they were unhappy with my on-site supervisor's decision. I identified that my own artwork helped me get through my emotional processing as well as the transition of settling down after the news I shared with the group. I drew an image of a vibrant orb-like object stretching across the paper, it moved out from the dark and reached a place with a similar color to its own form (see Color Plate 9). I specified that I purposely made use of different colors than I usually do not use to help me think in a new perspective on the placement experience. As my perspective shifted, I noticed my supervision group felt immensely comforting as I realized I could go to them for support I could not get from my placement supervision. [On-campus] group supervision provided ample space to share this news, as it was flexible with the needs I had for that day, and my classmates and supervisor showed that they understood what I was going through.

Yasmine's Response

There were many factors that allowed for this experience to happen for Julie and the group as a whole. To start, the space was safe enough for Julie to share her hesitations with her supervisor, and this was not her first time sharing her concerns. Part of the safety may be the boundaries of confidentiality within the school structure of group supervision. Of course, confidentiality in group supervision relates to clients – not sharing identifying information of people that they are working with in session, such as name, admission or discharge date, where they live, or any details that may make it easy for group supervision members to know who the client is. While our school is located in an urban area, the community that receives treatment is quite small. So small that sometimes students may treat the same individuals. In addition to paying attention to the confidentiality of clients, we also tend to supervisors' and supervisees' privacy. The treatment community is small, but the art therapy community is even smaller. Many of the supervisors graduated from the program that my same group supervisees have attended, with most supervisors and supervisees being only one or two degrees away from each other. Being sensitive to this does not mean that we do not use the names of supervisors in session, but I make a commitment to the group that I will not share any details about their complaints or celebrations about their supervisors to my colleagues. If a student does bring up an issue that I think requires the intervention of our school's field coordinator, this is discussed with the student first and not discussed without their knowledge. Because of my own supervision experiences as a student and professional, I am sensitive to the need for supervisees to share hurtful or negative supervision experiences. I have shared some of my own negative supervision experiences with my students as a way to model how to use supervision, grow from experiences, and provide encouragement.

Besides the holding environment of the space, Julie was aware and knowledgeable enough to know that she should bring up this issue to the group. As noted earlier, it is developmentally appropriate for Introductory Therapists to lack awareness and confidence. While Julie initially did not want to take space in talking about her relationship with her supervisor and wanted to stay on task by presenting her case, it was clear what she presented was worth exploring further. Her affect showed she was hurt by this experience and attempting to avoid deeper discussion. I felt she originally wanted to present her case because she was scheduled to do so, not because there was a pressing clinical question. Furthermore, going through with the case presentation may have been a way to avoid the feelings beneath the interaction that occurred with her and her supervisor. I felt there was the potential for growth for Julie as well as for the other group members, who empathized with Julie's situation.

Instead of risking negative talk about the supervisor or intellectualizing and providing verbal support to Julie, I asked the group to create in silence an art response to what Julie shared. After working, we all looked at each other's work and verbally processed from there – identifying themes in subject matter, colors, and our own affective responses to Julie's telling of her story.

Off-Site Group Supervision for Professionals

The members of off-site group supervision are often from differing places of work, with different clinical populations and different types of settings, and working in different teams. An additional concern with a professional group is that the group members may have different levels of experiences. Some may be new graduates with no credentials, while others may be seasoned professionals; members may be working from different theoretical frameworks or disciplines entirely. Sometimes off-site group supervision for professionals is restricted to only one discipline (e.g., art therapists only) or developmental level (e.g., only those seeking credentials or only those with extensive clinical experiences), but this is not a requirement.

The group must determine how to prioritize and structure their time. Will cases be presented formally, and will that be on a rotating basis? Will artwork be made in group? Will members bring in their own supplies or will the supervisor provide materials and storage space? If group membership is open, meaning members can join and leave at any time, it is beneficial for introductions to happen whenever a new member joins. Each member can artistically introduce themselves, their workplace, and their theoretical orientation or way of conducting therapy. Existing members can share what they are currently working on in group supervision, and new members can share what they are anticipating or hoping to gain from the group.

Another factor to consider is endings (discussed in detail below). As the group is composed of professionals from different agencies, hospitals, or other places of work, membership may be rolling, with individuals leaving the group at different times. The group will have to negotiate how to address its shifting nature. Because this is an off-site group for professionals, members tend to choose to attend and are not forced by their school or workplace. What type of rituals will the group want to use when someone announces their departure? How will the group address each other if someone leaves without notice?

On-Site Group Supervision

This type of group supervision, usually at a work site, may also contain therapists from different disciplines and different levels of clinical experiences, sometimes including student interns. However, this type of group supervision may be required. They may come from different units or all work in the same department. While ideally the group as a whole should discuss together how to structure the session, the nature of the location may not allow this. For example, some settings may have an existing rotating leadership structure or have guest facilitators, or the supervisor may run the group. Furthermore, on-site group supervisions tend to have some type of administrative component.

If the supervisor is responsible for structuring the group supervision, the rule of thirds may come in handy – the supervisor can set one-third of the agenda to meet whatever needs they have, such as any administrative policies or other business aspects. Another third of the agenda could be for the group to determine what clinical aspect they would like to address. And the final third can be processing of any session material.

Peer Consultation Groups

Peer consultation groups can occur for professionals or during training, and may happen on- or off-site. These groups generally meet on a regular basis to discuss a range of topics such as challenging clinical work, self-care, impact of privilege and difference, and ethical concerns. They are typically leaderless or have collective shared leadership "without the hierarchical presence of a more expert facilitator" (Nelson, 2014, p. 322) for an exchange of expertise and support. Peer consultation groups are not limited to in-person meetings, and can be facilitated by teleconference, or for "large groups via electronic mailing lists and Web forums" (Rousmaniere, 2014, p. 245). When forming a peer or consultation group, it is recommended the goals, structure, leadership model, and number of participants be considered (Borders, 2012).

Recognize that peer consultation and group supervision are distinctly different. In a peer consultation setting, the peer receiving the assistance is not obligated to implement the recommendations, while the peers providing the guidance are generally not legally or ethically responsible. It must be understood that in peer consultation "no group member has authority or responsibility in relation to the other members" (Watkins & Milne, 2014, pp. 685–686) to reduce legal responsibility. See Vignette 10.3 for Yasmine's experience in a peer consultation group for psychotherapists who were providing pro bono work for children and young people impacted by foster care. If joining or establishing a peer consultation group, consult legal advice to clarify responsibility and liability. For example, who is liable if a client sues after their therapist implements advice from a peer consultation group.

Vignette 10.3 Off-Site Peer Supervision

Yasmine's Story

I participated in a peer consultation group open to clinicians who were providing pro bono psychotherapy to youth involved in the foster care system. The group was homogenous in regard to mission and clients served – the majority of the members were seasoned professionals, many with clinical/practice doctorates (i.e., PsyD), and primarily worked in private practice. At times, all members were actively seeing pro bono cases; at other times, only a few members were.

While there was a lead organizer, the leadership model was collective. At the start of each session, each member would check-in regarding their pro bono case, particularly if the client had attended sessions, as high no-show rates were common. Over the three years I was a member of the peer consultation group, we shifted the days that we would meet, frequency (from twice a month to once a month), and how we would communicate with each other between groups if the need arose. The group together decided on these changes, not the lead organizer, which allowed us to create the norm and structure of our unique peer group.

The peer consultation group was extremely helpful – I was the only art therapist in the group and did not have much experience working with young children. I was hesitant to take a case with a younger child as I felt inexperienced and originally wanted to work with teens or youth who had aged out of the foster care system. With the support of the peer group, I worked with a child and foster family for over three years. The group provided critical feedback and challenge to my interventions. For example, after voicing frustrations about difficulty connecting with the client using art, I was encouraged to explore sandtray, which gave my client the ability to direct play. Sandtray is a non-verbal play technique that allows clients to create their own worlds in a box (or oftentimes, two boxes – one filled with wet sand and other with dry) utilizing miniatures. I received this suggestion as an invitation because of the holding structure of our group. I shared many pieces of art in peer consultation, and discussed why I felt these works were superficial and not beneficial to the therapeutic work. As a group we struggled together, and discussed various materials and ways of entry to build rapport with a client who had every right not to trust adults or the system. As several of the peers utilized sandtray in their practice, and our organizer had advanced training, the suggestion was welcomed and felt well thought through. Utilizing the process of sand transformed my work with the client – how I saw him and his relationship to his new family, how he interacted between the worlds of fantasy and reality.

When I was no longer able to work with the client, I knew they would continue to require therapy. It was comforting to know the case would be transferred to a peer who was intimately familiar with the case as well as the overall needs of youth in foster care. The peer consultation group was a valuable holding container. We also discussed how to process termination and change with the client. Of course, we also terminated our work together as a peer consultation group as my concluding the case meant my time in the peer group was also ending. While the group would continue on without me, an acknowledgement of our ending (through a lovely breakfast) marked a shift in the group membership.

Process Recordings, Sketchbooks, and Other Tools

One of the benefits of supervising groups, particularly an off-site supervision group, is learning about many different clinical settings – how treatment is provided, how systems work (or do not work) for those receiving services, etc. Since it is not realistic for group supervisors to intimately know every site a member is clinically working in, there are various methods to learn about these sites. The best way to better understand the nuances of a site is to visit. If this is possible (ethically and logistically), a supervisor can see first-hand what the supervisee has been raising and experiences on-site. Another method to better understand the placement, especially for on-campus group supervisors, is to speak with the on-site field instructor or supervisor. For those who cannot visit the clinical site, audio or video recordings are useful, again, if ethically allowed at the supervisee's site. These recordings can be used in group supervision for case presentation purposes. In all methods, as a supervisor, remember to experience the site from your supervisee's distinct perspective.

Sketchbooks and/or journals are another way to "enter" the supervisee's experience. This is not as direct as visiting the site or listening/viewing a recording of a session, but provides valuable experiences from the supervisee's perspective. Directives can be given to supervisees to better learn about the site:

1. Draw the art therapy studio. Understanding the space in which art therapy is conducted is vital. Are tables or easels used? How much

room is available? Is the space accessible to wheelchairs, walkers, or other adaptive devices? Show how materials are stored and offered to participants. How is completed artwork stored or displayed?

2. Draw the layout of the floor/unit/office. Asking for a map of the unit/floor/office is helpful in understanding how systems work. In the case of students and professionals, do they share an office with others or have their own space? What is their proximity to administration? How far is the area from where art therapy is conducted?

Process notes (see Chapter 2, *What Supervisors Need to Know about Supervision*; Chapter 8, *Disciplinary Differences: When Your Supervisee Is Not an Art Therapist*; and Appendix A) allow the supervisee to "enter" the setting through the eyes of the supervisee. Process notes are not shared with the other group members, and are shared only with the supervisor.

Termination Considerations

As discussed in Chapter 9, *Individual and Dyad Supervision*, supervisors and supervisees engaged in group supervision should also consider the ending of their work together. In groups, it is particularly useful to speak about termination at the start of supervision and every time a new member joins if the group has rotating membership. Again, for contracted or private supervision, the first mention may be listed in the supervisory contract, which outlines how the supervisor and the supervisee decide when participation in the group will end. Each time a new member joins the group, a discussion should occur that welcomes the new member and addresses the norms and culture of the group, including any rituals when someone leaves. Even though campus-based group supervision predictably follows the academic calendar, it is still useful to discuss up front. Having discussions about termination, endings, loss, moving on, and transformation is important; however, as art therapists, it is profoundly important to process through artmaking. See "Prioritizing Artmaking in Termination" in Chapter 9 for a more in depth discussion.

Yet termination in groups requires special attention because each individual in the group carries with them a different association with endings and transitions. For example, in the classroom, on-campus group supervision setting some students may feel readier to leave if they have a job or other opportunity lined up, and others may feel less prepared or even inadequate if they do not. We suggest focusing on the closure of the group as a whole rather than solely on outcomes such as securing a job. Utilizing artmaking is one way to acknowledge this ending. See Color Plate 10 for an example of a deconstructed book that was created during the final, on-campus group supervision. Each participant created two stamps, carved out of vinyl erasers using X-Acto blades and linoleum cutters. After creating the stamps, each member of the group supervision stamped a small piece of fabric. At the end, each individual had their own stamped pages plus two pages from each group member.

Takeaways

- Group supervision may be required or optional. Required groups include those found in graduate art therapy program or obligatory group supervision at the workplace. Optional groups tend to be off-site supervision groups for professionals and peer consultation groups.
- Group supervision for students tends to have members in early developmental stages of learning. Professionals engaged in group supervision off-site, on-site, or in peer supervision may be in the Intermediate or Proficient/Advanced stages of their practice.
- Termination considerations may be more complex for professionals than in student groups, as membership entry and leaving can be staggered, though this makes those leavings no less intense. For students, beginnings and endings tend to follow the academic calendar.
- Advantages to group supervision are obtaining multiple and diverse perspectives.
- A disadvantage to group supervision is having to negotiate time and structure.

Practice Prompts

Understanding the Art Therapy Studio

It is vital to understand the locations, places, and spaces where art therapy is conducted from varied perspectives. Are tables or easels used? How much room is available? Is the space accessible to wheelchairs, walkers, or other adaptive devices?

1. Draw or use 3-D material to recreate the art therapy studio or where the art therapy sessions are held. Show how materials are stored and offered to participants. Specify how completed artwork is stored or displayed. This can be completed within the supervision group, or as an assignment, and then brought into session.
2. Discuss similarities and differences in the perspectives of the supervisor and the supervisees, and how clients may perceive the space differently.

Comprehending Systems and Locations

1. Draw the layout of the floor/unit/office. A map of the floor/unit/office is helpful in understanding how systems work. Are offices and clinical

spaces shared? What is their proximity to administration? How far is the office area from where art therapy is conducted?

2. Discuss locational impact on the supervisor, the supervisees, and different client populations.

Creating Something Together

Creating something that each individual can take with them can hold significant symbolic meaning. I (Yasmine) still have the small purple bead that I received from my group supervision with Barbara Fish over 20 years ago. As the group supervision process is a relationship between each member, a collective building of knowledge, I like recreating this as metaphor.

- *Round Robin:* For the last supervision group, give each supervisee a piece of paper and various art materials. To start, each person creates an image of what they treasure from group supervision. After five minutes, pass the paper to the person next to you. Start creating on this new piece of paper, for two minutes. After the two minutes are up, pass again. Continue to pass the paper until you receive the paper you started with. Spend five or ten minutes for this final pass. A timer is useful for this exercise. Adjust the time to ensure that each group supervisee has time to create, ensuring that the first and last passes have more time than the other passes to allow for a strong base (start) and final product.
- *Accordion books:* Create simple accordion books in the last supervision book, ensuring that there is one page for each participant. Allow each supervision member to make an entry for the book's owner. The cover can be created by the owner of the book before passing it to other group members or after the members have finished.

References

ACATE. (2019). Handbook for completing a self-study for Initial Accreditation. Retrieved from www.caahep.org/CAAHEP/media/CoADocuments/Self-Study-Handbook-2019_1.pdf

Borders, L. D. (2012). Dyadic, triadic, and group models of peer supervision/consultation: What are their components, and is there evidence of their effectiveness? *Clinical Psychologist*, *16*(2), 59–71.

CAAHEP. (2016) Standards and guidelines for the accreditation of educational programs in art therapy. Retrieved from www.caahep.org/CAAHEP/media/CAAHEP-Documents/ArtTherapyStandards.pdf

Delano, F. (2001). If I could supervise my supervisor: A model for child and youth care workers to own their own supervision. *Journal of Child and Youth Care*, *15*(2), 51–64.

Lambie, G. W., & Blount, A. J. (2016). Tailoring supervision to supervisees' developmental level. In K. Jordan (Ed.), *Couple, marriage and family therapy supervision* (pp. 71–86). New York, NY: Springer Publishing Company.

Moon, B. L. (2019). *Ethical issues in art therapy* (4th ed.). Springfield, IL: Charles C Thomas.

Nelson, M. L. (2014). Using the major formats of clinical supervision. In C. E. Watkins & D. L. Milne (Eds.), *Wiley international handbook of clinical supervision* (pp. 308–328). Chichester, UK: John Wiley & Sons.

Rousmaniere, T. (2014). Using technology to enhance clinical supervision and training. In C. E. Watkins & D. L. Milne (Eds.), *Wiley international handbook of clinical supervision* (pp. 204–237). Chichester: UK: John Wiley & Sons.

Rubin, J. A. (2011). *The art of art therapy: What every art therapist needs to know.* New York: Routledge.

Smith, R. D., Riva, M. T., & Cornish, J. A. E. (2012). The ethical practice of group supervision: A national survey. *Training and Education in Professional Psychology, 6*(4), 238–248. doi:10.1037/a0030806

Sweitzer, H. F., & King, M. A. (2018). *The successful internship: Personal, professional, and civic development in experiential learning* (5th ed.). Boston, MA: Cengage.

Watkins, C. E., & Milne, D. L. (2014). Clinical supervision at the international crossroads: current status and future directions. In C. E. Watkins & D. L. Milne (Eds.), *Wiley international handbook of clinical supervision* (pp. 673–696). Chichester, UK: John Wiley & Sons.

11 Distance Supervision

Introduction

This chapter discusses distance supervision, which is primarily defined as supervision performed by means of videoconferencing, which "involves a trainee at one site securely videoconferencing (VC) with a supervisor at another site" (Luxton, Nelson, & Maheu, 2016, p. 97). Distance supervision is complex and its own art. It is not simply a different form of supervision. The utilization of distance supervision increases options available to art therapists who embrace technology for the purpose of art therapy services, consultation, and supervision (Orr, 2010). Due to the newness of the burgeoning field of telemental health, there is an equivalent development of distance counseling, training to conduct distance counseling, and distance supervision. While we understand distance supervision in art therapy can also include telephonic supervision, or supervision via telephone, as art therapists we favor and focus on videoconferencing as this allows for ease of face-to-face contact and reviewing of artwork.

Our environment is ever-changing, and as such, our work transforms with it. In-person clinical supervision and therapeutic best practices have been adapted and revised over the years. However, of all the chapters in this book, this chapter contains content that will continue to rapidly change regarding technology, best practices, ethical concerns, and jurisdictional oversight. In fact, since the technology is changing as we are writing today, by the time you read this, this chapter will most likely already be outdated. Though change can be daunting, it can simultaneously be energizing as we have the opportunity to apply significant advances in telecommunications technologies in the provision of effective telemental health services (Baker & Bufka, 2011; Brandoff & Lombardi, 2012; Glueckauf et al., 2018; Kanz, 2001; Luxton et al., 2016; Orr, 2010; Rousmaniere, 2014). While this is an exciting time, it is also a time for attentiveness and planning, "in light of the myriad federal and state laws and regulations, payer policies, technological challenges, and heightened privacy concerns triggered by telehealth practice" (Baker & Bufka, 2011,

p. 410). Even the nomenclature is fluid and inconsistent. For example, telemental health has also been referred to as telepsychology, telehealth, telemental health, online counseling, e-health, e-counseling (Barnett & Kolmes, 2016), and technology-assisted counseling (TADC) (Dawson, Harpster, Hoffman, & Phelan, 2011), among other terms.

Within this rapidly changing world of technology applied to therapy, the options for distance supervision through electronic means is expanding and can feel overwhelming, in part due to possible challenges (Rios, Kazemi, & Peterson, 2018), particularly regarding questions and concerns of confidentiality, ethics, and legal responsibilities (Brandoff & Lombardi, 2012; Fish, 2017; Glueckauf et al., 2018; Orr, 2010; Rousmaniere, 2014). This chapter addresses the need to establish and maintain a distance supervisory relationship "in compliance with state and federal laws including [the] Health Insurance Portability and Accountability Act (HIPAA)" (Fish, 2017, p. 176), and explores best practices for technology-facilitated supervision. In addition, supervisors engaging in distance supervision need to fully understand the intricacies of conducting distance supervision as well as effectively and ethically explaining the process and risks to potential supervisees. We also cover reasons for engaging in distance supervision, issues related specifically to distance supervision, and technology considerations.

Reasons for Engaging in Distance Supervision

There are several factors to consider when deciding to whether to engage in distance supervision. Access to competent supervision may be the primary incentive. For instance, geographical isolation may prevent traditional face-to-face art therapy supervision to secure expected credentials and further professional development. Additional considerations may be due to a combination of location, clinical focus, or supervisory compatibility. Furthermore, convenience and the managing of self-care and burnout prevention may be reasons to engage in distance supervision.

Access

Art therapy is a small field compared to other mental health professions – there are significantly fewer graduate programs in art therapy than counseling or social work, which also have the master's degree as the entry level for clinical practice. As a result, there are fewer practitioners, and art therapists who are able to supervise may not be available in all locales. In the United States, art therapy programs tend to be located in metropolitan areas on the coasts, with tremendous distances between programs in the middle of the country. There are also very few programs internationally, and most of those are concentrated in the United Kingdom. Because of the lack of programs, students often relocate for their art therapy education. As Orr (2010) highlighted, art therapy programs in the

United States educate and graduate a number of international students, and many return to their home countries with little in the way of an established art therapy community, and require continued support and supervision. This may also be true of those in the United States who return to isolated art therapy areas post-graduation. This highlights the reality that distance supervision may be the only option for some art therapists. For those who are expanding the reach of art therapy, there may be no supervisors in the areas where they practice.

The financial burden of travel costs and the inconvenience of travel time have also been identified as contributing factors that lead someone to seek distance supervision (Abbass et al., 2011; Fish, 2017; Schank, 1998). However, it has been argued that distance supervision "should be used only when it is in the best interest of clients and supervisees, and never solely for the convenience of supervisors" (Rousmaniere, 2014, p. 216).

Supervisory Fit

Even when supervising art therapists are practicing nearby, there may be complexities such as scheduling, fee negotiation, dual relationships, and/or differing theoretical approaches and specialties. In tightknit communities, distance supervision reduces the intersection of professional, personal, and community interactions and in turn decreases potentially delicate dual relationships. Reducing dual relationships through distance supervision can allow for clearer, less muddied roles in the supervisory relationship.

Separate from clinical focus and theoretical approach is a supervisor's temperament and style of engagement. Compatibility interviews are an excellent chance to experiment with the distance supervision format and potential technologies. This test run helps determine fit and provides important details regarding videoconferencing approaches and comfort level between the potential supervisor, format, and supervisee. Witnessing and experiencing individual engagement ability, interpersonal dynamics, teaching style, and the ability to articulate theory and practice by means of a videoconference can help to determine whether distance supervision is the right choice for the participants. See Box 11.1 for a circumstance exploring distance supervision as a viable option.

Box 11.1 Considerations of Distance Supervision

What Should Alejandra Do?

Immediately after completing her graduate art therapy program in a metropolitan area, Alejandra was hired at her internship site to continue working with elementary-aged children. On-site she received comprehensive and effective weekly individual supervision by a licensed clinical social worker and sought supplemental bi-weekly group supervision with a local ATR-BC (board-certified, Registered Art Therapist), ATCS (Art Therapy Certified Supervisor) credentialed art therapist. The supervision group consisted of six art therapist members and the supervisor. The supervisor had over 20 years of experience of implementing and restarting numerous art therapy programs over the years, and the members ranged from new professionals to those with over eight years' experience.

After two years of employment and obtaining her ATR-BC, Alejandra relocated to a rural and isolated area to work within an upscale, inpatient drug treatment facility serving young adults from 21–35 years old. Although the facility was excited about the return of art therapy for its clientele, Alejandra was the first art therapist it had had in three years. Alejandra's clinical supervisor has extensive experience with the population; however, he is new and has never supervised an art therapist. On-site, Alejandra will receive one hour of individual supervision covering clinical and administrative issues and monthly, interdisciplinary clinical team group supervision.

Previously, Alejandra successfully worked in well-established counseling teams with extensive understanding and integration of art therapy interventions. At her new place of employment, she will essentially be developing a new art therapy program. There are minimal art materials, no manual that outlines effective interventions, nor any other historical art therapy information at her new site other than group titles.

Supervision Considerations for Alejandra

If Alejandra opts for distance supervision, she would need to consider the legal and ethical concerns, technology, cost, expertise, and compatibility.

Alejandra could reach out to her former ATR supervisor for distance supervision. However, Alejandra would need to research the ethical and jurisdictional laws and regulations of the state they practice in. Furthermore, if permissible, Alejandra would have to inquire and see if her former supervisor currently offers or would consider offering this distance service. They would have to negotiate a time and fee, determine the technology to be used to maximize confidentiality, and determine the scope of the supervision to complement, not compete with, the on-site supervision.

Clinical Focus

Art therapists often pursue distance supervision to gain specific clinical expertise (Fish, 2017) when only a small number of regional experts exist in a particular area of specialization (Luxton et al., 2016). Orr (2010) identified "the increased breadth of the possibilities for art therapy placements, populations, or procedures also has created sub-specialties in art therapy", affirming access "to supervision with a person who has specialized knowledge of a particular population, media or placement may be needed and would provide more appropriate supervision" (p. 106). For instance, a client may present with unfamiliar clinical or cultural circumstances, necessitating specialized clinical expertise and understanding attained elsewhere. This may well happen through ongoing or time-limited distance supervision, depending on the needed skills and knowledge. Vignette 11.1 shares an example of seeking distance supervision for population-specific art therapy expertise.

Vignette 11.1 Gaining Expertise through Distance Supervision

Daniel Supervising Lamar

Lamar, an art therapist, began employment at a non-profit agency with on-site supervision provided by a licensed mental health professional. The on-site supervisor was experienced, knowledgeable, and clinically astute in the agency mission and subsequent client needs. However, as a new professional Lamar sought distance supervision with me (Daniel) since I have extensive art therapy experience with the population Lamar was working with. In-person supervision was not an option as we lived in different states. Additionally, our supervision would count towards obtaining his art therapy credentials, while only half of the hours he was obtaining with his on-site supervisor would count. As Lamar began to build a trusting and productive supervisory relationship with the on-site supervisor, we dove into the art aspect of his clinical work via video conferencing. The art was the main focus and intention of our supervision, and incorporated interventions and theory, the exploration of the artmaking process, the completed art, and his response art. In addition to exploring issues related to race, gender, and privilege, we also had the luxury of examining his acclimation to the agency, personnel, and protocols, and his professional boundaries in a way that may have been difficult with an on-site supervisor.

Self-Care and Burnout

When barriers to competent supervision exist, ongoing or episodic supervisory engagement helps decrease burnout and job turnover; lack of competent supervision can also lead to poor job satisfaction (Fish, 2017; Kanz, 2001). The intense therapeutic and empathetic attendance of the art therapist is demanding and can be emotionally exhausting. "This focused, empathic response to client concerns is critical to effective client care and may act as an emotional drain on counselors who do not adequately attend to their own self-care" (Warren, Morgan, Morris, & Morris, 2010, p. 110). In person, there are a number of cues that indicate burnout or drain. The ability to recognize burnout during distance therapy can be more challenging. The more nuanced encounters which indicate burnout in person, such as casual observations, "hallway" client conversations, or routine interactions with team members, are limited or nonexistent for long-distance supervisors. Even seemingly innocuous interactions such as walking into supervision are eliminated in the virtual space, although there can be a time when a supervisor and supervise informally "check-in".

Practicing self-care in supervisory sessions and obtaining "training in identifying the signs of primary stress reactions, secondary trauma, compassion fatigue, vicarious traumatization, and burnout" (Center for Substance Abuse Treatment, 2009, p. 19) solidifies and models the worth of self-care by structurally incorporating the practice of self-care within distance supervision. Videoconferencing by nature adds a technology concern and promotes an on-camera performance element unique to this format that reflexively encourages us to put our best face forward. Supervisors must routinely probe and make space to directly address self-care through awareness of symptoms related to burnout, compassion fatigue, and the like. Simple acts of asking about moments of stress, or lingering heaviness after client interactions, or asking what self-care activities have been prioritized since the last supervisory session, can help decrease the distance of the relationship.

Distance-Supervision-Specific Matters

Art therapists and other mental health practitioners who engage in distance supervision are required to adhere to all applicable ethical codes, conduct policies, and practice guidelines equally as for in-person supervision sessions (Abbass et al., 2011; Glueckauf et al., 2018; Luxton et al., 2016; Rousmaniere, 2014). Distance supervision inherently presents certain uncertainties warranting heightened awareness, such as supervisor availability, engagement, role definition, and a host of ethical and legal uncertainties, so it is essential distance supervisors are aware of possible unintended consequences, and "the potential impact of the technologies on clients/patients, supervisees, or other professionals" (American Psychological Association [APA], 2013, p. 793). As simple as it sounds, to prevent or moderate some of these concerns a supervisor "can best contribute by being highly engaged and comfortable with the supervision structure" (Abbass et al., 2011, p. 116).

Supervisor Availability

A distance supervisor has a greater likelihood of not being easily accessible. They not even be in the same time zone as a supervisee (Orr, 2010) or may be fast asleep during a time of need. This may be a significant concern for a supervisee without proper forecasting. A clear communication plan may include defining levels of need, including emergencies, and how they dictate acceptable and expected response times as well as preferred methods of contact. Being cognizant of communication styles is relevant, as some persons may be used to more immediate responses or text messaging as a form of communication (Rousmaniere, 2014). It may be useful for the supervisor and supervisee to determine how communication will occur between scheduled supervision sessions (e.g., text, email) and when to expect a response. Once the method and timing is determined, Thomas (2007) notes that "it may be helpful for supervisors to provide their supervisees with guidelines regarding the types of events, personal experiences, and problems about which they want to be informed" (p. 227). All of these considerations can be included in the supervision contract and should also be discussed during the first supervisory session.

Even on-site supervisors are not always readily available, yet there is comfort and confidence knowing they are nearby and most likely have a physical sense of the geographic area, which allows for an intimate awareness of local resources, collaborations, and cultural influences. To counter the lack of local area knowledge, an important role of the distance supervisor is to work preemptively with the supervisee to gain a solid understanding of local resources and arrange for an ongoing backup plan for when the supervisor is routinely unavailable. Ideally, this includes access to a local supervisor (Abbass et al., 2011; Glueckauf et al., 2018; Rousmaniere, 2014).

Technical Difficulties

Technology is not faultless, and there will be disruptions in communication (Orr, 2010; Rios et al., 2018; Rousmaniere, 2014). We suggest that you proactively plan for unexpected difficulties and develop a contingency plan before they arise and prepare "for potential of loss of sound, video, or Internet connection during sessions, and have the ability to troubleshoot difficulties that may arise including loss of Internet connection or other interruptions of service" (Barnett & Kolmes, 2016, p. 56). Even though Brandoff and Lombardi (2012) experienced such unpredictable communication interruptions, which resulted in frustrating times of rescheduling or significantly adapting sessions, they found that overall these inconveniences did not "negatively impacted the trajectory of supervision" (p. 94).

Ethical and Statutory Considerations

Brandoff and Lombardi explain "that professionals must consider best practices and their ethical responsibilities before offering or participating in distance supervision" (2012, p. 95). In part, this means distance supervisors are accountable for the legal and ethical consequences of the supervision provided to supervisee(s) in differing physical locations, and required to follow the ethical standards and relevant laws at each location and credentialing body (APA, 2013; Brandoff & Lombardi, 2012; Glueckauf et al., 2018; Orr, 2010; Rios et al., 2018; Rousmaniere, 2014). The criteria vary widely between states, jurisdictions, and credentialing bodies. To avoid misrepresentation, misunderstanding, and frustration, the supervisor and supervisee should firmly establish the eligibility of supervised hours intended for licensure, certification, and other credentials before supervision begins (Fish, 2017; Orr, 2010).

Supervision Contracts and Informed Consent

As discussed in Chapter 5, *Confidentiality and Informed Consent*, confidentiality, supervision contracts, and informed consent are critical elements in supervision, but require additions specific to distance supervision (APA, 2013; Art Therapy Credentials Board [ATCB], 2018; Brandoff & Lombardi, 2012; Glueckauf et al., 2018; Kanz, 2001; Orr, 2010; Rios et al., 2018). Informed-consent materials help those engaged in supervision "articulate and thereby fortify their commitments to supervisees" (Thomas, 2007, p. 230). Additionally, supervisees "learn what to expect, what will be expected of them, and what they must do to succeed" (Thomas, 2007, p. 230). Particular additions are raised by Brandoff and Lombardi (2012):

> The provision of distance supervision should be included in all relevant contracts and should articulate methods that will be used to establish supervisory rapport, technical requirements and limitations, protocols for dealing with ethical and professional issues, methods for securing and maintaining privacy and confidentiality, and methods for meeting the requirements of the U.S. Health Insurance Portability and Accountability Act and/or other legal rules for protecting client information.
>
> (p. 95)

Electronic communications should also be considered in supervision. In regard to electronic communication and working with clients, the ATCB's *Code of Ethics, Conduct, and Disciplinary Procedures* (2018), states, "Art therapists shall seek business, legal, and technical assistance when using technology applications for the purpose of providing art therapy services, particularly when the use of such applications crosses provincial, state lines or international boundaries" (p. 10). Although originally written from the perspective of the art therapist and client, we have modified them for supervisors and supervisees to consider:

- Clearly inform supervisees of the complexity of electronically based confidentiality and communications, and the obstacles and unfeasibility of removing any electronically posted images and information if permission is later withdrawn.
- Notify supervisees of any persons, including information technology personnel, that have potential sanctioned access to electronic transmissions.
- Advise supervisees that with technology-assisted distance supervision there may be unauthorized access to the supervisee's personal information in addition to the supervisee's or client's artworks shared in the therapeutic session.
- Tell supervisees of germane legal rights and limitations prevailing over the practice of the art therapy (or related) profession between jurisdictions or international borders.
- Convey to supervisees that encrypted Internet sites and email communications will be utilized, but there are encryption software limitations to ensure confidentiality.
- Notify supervisees when encryption is not possible, and engage in only general communications without sharing electronic transmissions containing client-specific data.
- Advise supervisees of how records will be kept that document the supervision hours and dates.
- Review the prospect of technology malfunction and substitute service delivery systems.
- Let clients know of emergency procedures when the supervisor is not available, such as contacting a local supervisor.
- Discuss the impact of differing time zones and cultural or language variances on service provision.
- Inform supervisees that some jurisdictions do not allow any distance supervision, or only some distance supervision, to count towards licensure or credentialing hours.

Additionally, when engaged in distance supervision, it is best practice for the supervisee to directly discuss this with their client, and have the clients' informed consent reflect and address this supervisory format.

Specifically, the supervisee should advise their client on the potential use of the Internet to transmit the client's confidential information (Kanz, 2001; Rousmaniere, 2014) and art images. Rousmaniere (2014) indicates the client's "informed consent should state the technologies and security measures utilized, in as clear language as possible" (p. 214) for transparency, and suggests a test of "whether supervisees or clients can clearly describe those tools and procedures" (p. 216) to confirm understanding.

Supervisor Qualifications

When considering the complexities of distance supervision, perhaps this might not be the best entry point for a first-time supervisor. However, even a seasoned supervisor is of less value when technology becomes a limitation. A balance should exist between clinical experience and a comfort and an ease with the technology being employed. Brandoff and Lombardi (2012) go as far as to "recommend that individuals planning to engage in distance supervision obtain training in selected technology. A lack of familiarity with the methods and capacities of technology can hinder the learning process and expose practitioners to risk" (p. 95). As a best practice for supervisor experience, we recommend a distance supervisor meet the qualifications of the ATCB's ATCS. This provides some assurance that the supervisor has gained additional clinical *and* supervisory experience, and has begun to gain confidence as an expert. Rios et al. (2018) remind distance supervisors to only work within your "scope of practice and possess the appropriate technology skills" to effectively participate in distance supervision or "have the means of technology support to assist you" (p. 285).

Supervisee Performance and Gatekeeping

Supervision of any format can be anxiety-provoking for the supervisor and the supervisee. The additional "on camera" performance element can create even more heightened apprehension in some supervisees. This needs to be addressed and considered early on when the supervisor is assessing performance and acting as a gatekeeper. It is important to distinguish between being a good candidate for distance supervision and being a competent art therapist. "Authority rests with the gatekeeper to apply the criteria and so to allow, or not allow, passage. The gatekeeper must take responsibility for that decision" (Behnke, 2005, p. 90). In the context of the supervisor, gatekeeping is the responsibility to objectively assess supervisees' competence of the expected professional skills and performance for academic or professional endorsement. The often ambiguous definition and difficult nature of gatekeeping is potentially amplified by distance supervision. "This lack of clarity combined with the threat of legal liability makes gatekeeping an unwelcome task for many supervisors of counselors-in-training. Legal precedents indicate that effective gate-keeping is as much a legal as an ethical issue" (Bhat, 2005, p. 402). This combination of technology and distance offers many opportunities, yet may unintentionally create obstacles in detecting benchmarks of impairment. Any missed areas of impairment potentially violate ethical and legal guidelines designed to protect clients from comprised therapeutic services. Consequently, it is crucial to be in agreement and have a clear understanding between the supervisor and the supervisee of the evaluation methods and tools that will be utilized to gauge performance and knowledge.

Client Considerations

To best monitor a supervisee's performance with a nod towards gate-keeping, a supervisor can learn a tremendous amount by gaining understanding of what is happening within the client session. Unfortunately, a distance supervisor does not often have the luxury of quick debriefings immediately following a session when the supervisees' experience is fresh, possibly less filtered, and their post-session body language and emotional state can be witnessed. The distance supervisor tends to rely on more supervisee self-reports. As mentioned earlier, it is important to modify clients' informed consent if Protected Health Information (PHI) is transmitted during distance supervision.

There also needs to be a backup plan, as mentioned earlier, that includes a strategy for when the immediate session requirements move beyond the supervisee's current level of expertise. These "red flag" moments may typically include a request for the on-site supervisor to join the session or for a momentary supervisory debriefing to gain additional support or crisis intervention. For example, when in-person, on-site supervision is utilized, a supervisee may momentarily step out of session to discuss a client's suicidal ideation or abuse disclosure. In distance supervision this is not possible, and an appropriate plan pre-determines next steps.

Technology Options Modes of Communication

To bridge the lack of physical proximity inherent to distance supervision, the hardware, the actual equipment (e.g., desktop or laptop computer, smart phone, tablet), and software, the tool for audio and visual communication (i.e., a videoconferencing program), are used. Not only must the hardware and software be available, a confidential setting is required. Time is another consideration that impacts software. While this chapter discusses synchronous communication, which "allows involved parties to see and/or hear each person at the exact same time", there may be times when asynchronous communication may occur (Lustgarten & Colbow,

2017, p. 159) in tandem or independently. Sketchbooks, audio or video recordings, etc., are all examples of asynchronous communication that can enhance supervisory communications. At times, supervisees may upload and share images or videos into a secure drive where the supervisor can review client artwork, videos, and supervision response art before and/or during session. Luckily, there has been a significant surge in HIPAA-compliant synchronous communication videoconferencing programs designed specifically for medical and mental health providers. The program list changes often, and it is the responsibility of the supervisor to ensure that the program is currently HIPAA-compliant. At this writing, HIPAA-compliant videoconferencing programs include Doxy.me (https://doxy.me), Theranest (https://theranest.com), and Vsee (https://vsee.com). However, we must stress that due to the inherent nature of technology, these programs may or may no longer be currently compliant and all readers should do independent research on their viability. Furthermore, there are likely other products available for use that may be compliant.

Preparation and Setting

Once you have identified a videoconferencing program, it is imperative that a supervisor practice, problem solve, and understand the program well enough to guide a supervisee through the process. As mentioned earlier, there will be glitches with the Internet, the program, and the users. Videoconferencing allows for a tremendous amount of freedom since it can potentially be implemented anywhere there is a solid Internet connection. This means that supervision is no longer contained to the office or studio, opening up locations as varied as a hotel room or home, among many others. Regardless of location, a private setting is required, as confidential material will be discussed. It may be tempting to have supervision in a coffee shop due to convenience, but a public space does not meet HIPAA or ethical standards. To safeguard confidentiality, the space must be carefully considered from the perspective of unintended and random intrusions by children, pets, or even hotel staff, as well as troublesome noise, or the potential for being overheard due to inadequate soundproofing. Other conceivable disruptions include the possibility for the environment to be more intimate if at home or a hotel room. For example, unintended visual distractions may include an unmade bed, or mirrors.

Security Measures

Rios et al. (2018) highlight that "service providers must take into account many security matters, such as encryption, virus safety, and security compliance that accompany the transfer of data" (p. 278). The central emphasis is to prevent "unauthorized or unintended disclosures of confidential patient information" with meticulous consideration devoted to risks distinct to distance services (Baker & Bufka, 2011, p. 408). This is in alignment with the APA's Guideline 5 compelling distance providers to "take reasonable steps to ensure that security measures are in place to protect data and information related to their clients/patients from unintended access or disclosure" (2013, p. 797). This is complicated by the fact that secure technology legislation is "evolving rapidly, and service providers must ensure that their decisions are in compliance with the emerging laws" (Rios et al., 2018, p. 278).

Encryption

APA's guidelines expect that distance providers "make reasonable effort to protect and maintain the confidentiality of the data and information relating to their clients/patients" (2013, p. 796) and that distance providers are to inform clients of the intrinsic risks associated with maintaining confidentiality when applying telecommunication technologies. Encryption is one manner of protection. Rios et al. (2018) defines encryption as "the process of encoding materials so that only specific individuals have access to it by way of a unique password" (p. 282). This is important for data that is stored "locally or in a cloud, it is important that all storage devices are encrypted" to restrict authorization to the stored information (Rios et al., 2018, p. 282).

Storage

Secure data storage is another fundamental requirement (APA, 2013; Baker & Bufka, 2011; Brandoff & Lombardi, 2012; Cooper & Neal, 2014; Glueckauf et al., 2018; Luxton et al., 2016; Orr, 2010; Rios et al., 2018; Rousmaniere, 2014). Distance providers utilizing cloud storage in the United States must guarantee the hosting company is a HIPAA-secured environment that provides a Business Associate Agreement (commonly known as a BAA) before implementing it in their practice (Luxton et al., 2016; Rios et al., 2018). Additionally, APA guidelines identify the need to "make reasonable efforts to dispose of data and information and the technologies used in a manner that facilitates protection from unauthorized access and accounts for safe and appropriate disposal" (APA, 2013, p. 798).

Record-Keeping and Artwork

The inclusion of artwork, like other confidential materials, within distance supervision can become "confusing and cumbersome" (Orr, 2010, p. 109) in part due to the constant passage of documents. Supervisors and supervisees must be "committed to secure practices for sharing client artwork without compromising client confidentiality" (Brandoff & Lombardi, 2012, p. 94) and "agree upon ethical handling of and transmission of confidential information prior to beginning distance supervision" (Orr, 2010, p. 109). While images of the artwork can be safely transmitted and viewed, the ability to intimately experience and interact with the art is limited. For instance, subtle pressure points, slight smells of the art materials, the tactile impression and weight of the art, and the ability to view the art from a similar perspective as the artist are more easily lost. This requires the supervisee to have a heightened ability to describe and express the senses that can be conveyed by video and still photo. One method for conveying these details includes photographing or videotaping the artwork and sharing it with the supervisor in advance, not simply holding it up during a videoconference. We encourage supervisees to take photographs of the piece as a whole along with detailed photographs to capture nuances of the piece. Finally, the materials and dimensions should be noted when sharing client artwork or supervisee response artwork, as digital images can flatten artwork, making it difficult to comprehend the scale of a piece. By photographing or videotaping an artwork, it allows the supervisor to zoom in and out of an individual image or to press Pause.

Takeaways

- Distance supervision can be an exciting and groundbreaking opportunity, and, simultaneously, confusing.
- Distance supervision is complex and its own art, it is not simply a different form of supervision.
- Disadvantages of distance supervision include the reliance on technology, specifically a HIPAA-compliant platform, and the inherent disruptions requiring contingency plans.
- Advantages of distance supervision include increased options for better supervisory fit and specific clinical expertise, and decreased professional isolation.

Practice Prompts

Why Pursue Distance Supervision?

Before jumping blindly into the depths of distance supervision, explore personal and professional motivations for pursuing this approach. Fold a piece of paper in half and create a collage that addresses:

- On one side, your attraction to distance supervision; and
- On the other side, how your skills as a supervisor or supervisee transfer to videoconferencing.

Videoconferencing Rehearsal

Identify one HIPAA-compliant videoconferencing program based on our suggestions in this chapter or on your own.

- Conduct a mock supervision session with a fellow art therapist. Practice artmaking, sharing of art, and discussing a case.
- What differences do you notice between in-office supervisions, video-conferencing with friends, and attending a webinar? What similarities to you find?

Camera Shy?

Create artwork exploring any hesitations or concerns about being on camera and any other related technological insecurities.

- Determine how identified issues may impact "showing up" in session.

Do Your Research

Conduct research on the legal and ethical liabilities related to your jurisdiction, licensures, and certifications for distance supervision.

- If you already have a potential distance supervisee or supervisor in mind, perform the same research on their location.

References

Abbass, A., Arthey, S., Elliott, J., Fedak, T., Nowoweiski, D., Markovski, J., & Nowoweiski, S. (2011). Web-conference supervision for advanced psychotherapy training: A practical guide. *Psychotherapy, 48*(2), 109.

APA. (2013). *Guidelines for the practice of telepsychology.* Washington, DC: Author.

ATCB. (2018). Code of ethics, conduct and disciplinary procedures. Retrieved from www.atcb.org/resource/pdf/ATCB-Code-of-Ethics-Conduct-DisciplinaryProcedures.pdf

Baker, D. C., & Bufka, L. F. (2011). Preparing for the telehealth world: Navigating legal, regulatory, reimbursement, and ethical issue in an electronic age. *Professional Psychology: Research and Practice, 42*, 405–411. doi:10.1037/a0025037

Barnett, J. E., & Kolmes, K. (2016). The practice of tele-mental health: Ethical, legal, and clinical issues for practitioners. *Practice Innovations, 1*(1), 53.

Behnke, S. (2005). The supervisor as gatekeeper: Reflections on ethical standards 7.02., 7.04, 7.05, 7.06 and 10.01. *Monitor on Psychology, 36*(5), 90–91.

Bhat, C. S. (2005). Enhancing Counseling Gatekeeping with Performance Appraisal Protocols. *International Journal for the Advancement of Counselling, 27*, 399–411. doi:10.1007/s10447-005-8202-z

Brandoff, R., & Lombardi, R. (2012). Miles apart: Two art therapists' experience of distance supervision. *Art Therapy, 29*(2), 93–96.

Center for Substance Abuse Treatment. (2009). *Clinical Supervision and Professional Development of the Substance Abuse Counselor.* Treatment Improvement Protocol (TIP) Series 52. DHHS Publication No. (SMA) 09-4435. Rockville, MD: Substance Abuse and Mental Health Services Administration.

Cooper, S. E., & Neal, C. (2014). Consultants' use of telepractice: Practitioner survey, issues, and resources. *Consulting Psychology Journal: Practice and Research, 67*(2), 85–99.

Dawson, L., Harpster, A., Hoffman, G., & Phelan, K. (2011). A new approach to distance counseling skill development: Applying a discrimination model of supervision. Retrieved from http://counselingoutfitters.com/vistas/vistas11/Article_46.pdf

Fish, B. J. (2017). *Art-based supervision: Cultivating therapeutic insight through imagery.* New York, NY: Routledge.

Glueckauf, R. L., Maheu, M. M., Drude, K. P., Wells, B. A., Wang, Y., Gustafson, D. J., & Nelson, E. L. (2018). Survey of psychologists' telebehavioral health practices: Technology use, ethical issues, and training needs. *Professional Psychology: Research and Practice, 49*(3), 205–219.

Kanz, J. E. (2001). Clinical-Supervision.com: Issues in the provision of online supervision. *Professional Psychology, Research and Practice, 32*(4), 415–420.

Lustgarten, S. D., & Colbow, A. J. (2017). Ethical concerns for telemental health therapy amidst governmental surveillance. *American Psychologist, 72*(2), 159–170.

Luxton, D. D., Nelson, E.-L., & Maheu, M. M. (2016). Telesupervision and training in telepractice. In D. D. Luxton, E.-L. Nelson, & M. M. Maheu (Eds.), *A practitioner's guide to telemental health: How to conduct legal, ethical, and evidence-based telepractice* (pp. 97–107). Washington, DC: APA. doi:http://dx.doi.org/10.1037/14938-009.

Orr, P. P. (2010). Distance supervision: Research, findings, and considerations for art therapy. *The Arts in Psychotherapy, 37*(2), 106–111.

Rios, D., Kazemi, E., & Peterson, S. M. (2018). Best practices and considerations for effective service provision via remote technology. *Behavior Analysis: Research and Practice, 18*(3), 277–287. doi:10.1037/bar0000072

Rousmaniere, T. (2014). Using technology to enhance clinical supervision and training. In C. E. Watkins & D. L. Milne (Eds.), *Wiley international handbook of clinical supervision* (pp. 204–237). Chichester, UK: John Wiley & Sons.

Schank, J. A. (1998). Ethical issues in rural counseling practice. *Canadian Journal of Counseling, 32*, 270–283.

Thomas, J. T. (2007). Informed consent through contracting for supervision: Minimizing risks, enhancing benefits. *Professional Psychology: Research and Practice, 38*(3), 221–231.

Warren, J., Morgan, M. M., Morris, L. N. B., & Morris, T. M. (2010). Breathing words slowly: Creative writing and counselor self-care – the writing workout. *Journal of Creativity in Mental Health, 5*(2), 109–124.

Appendix A
Process Note

Purpose

The intention of an art therapy process note, also known as a process recording, is to provide art therapists with an in-depth method to recall how a specific session unfolded. The process note illustrates interactions and interventions in a way that enables therapists to delve deeper to understand exactly what occurred. It can be completed as a form of self-study, explicitly completed for a supervisor, or part of an educational program. The process note is *never* part of a client record.

Format

The format differs depending on the audience, which is primarily the art therapist and their clinical or campus supervisor. The following format is designed for an audience such as an off-site supervisor and can be adapted for audience and setting.

Structure

Client and Session Essentials
- Client name: *(pseudonym and/or identifying code)*
- Client age: *(not birthdate)*
- Session date:
- Session format: *(individual, dyad, or group, etc.)*
- Session type: *(scheduled, crisis, drop-in, etc.)*
- Attendees: *(indicate type and number of participants – clients, interns, supervisors, etc.)*

History and Context
- Background: *(bio-psychosocial information, medical and psychological history, etc.)*

- Session plan: *(goals and objectives, etc.)*
- Session number: *(e.g., Session 6, if client is receiving ongoing art therapy)*

Client Presentation

A concise yet factual description of the client's presentation in session.

- **Appearance**
  - ○ Overall appearance:
  - ○ Hygiene, etc.:

- **Client Interaction**
  - ○ Behavior: *(general conduct, speech, and tone, etc.)*
  - ○ Receptiveness: *(client response, engagement with art therapist)*
  - ○ Nonverbal communication: *(body language, physicality – near or far, etc.)*
  - ○ Verbal communication: *(speech, tone, significant discourse, superficial patter, pressured speech, etc.)*

- Artmaking: *(involvement with artmaking/materials, developing, and final artwork, etc.)*

Art Therapist Presentation

A succinct but authentic self-account of the art therapist's presentation in session.

- **Appearance**
  - ○ Overall appearance:
  - ○ Presentation:

- **Art Therapist Interaction**
  - ○ Behavior: *(general conduct and level of professionalism)*
  - ○ Receptiveness: *(art therapist response, engagement with client, etc.)*
  - ○ Nonverbal communication: *(body language, physically near or far, involvement with artmaking/materials, etc.)*
  - ○ Verbal communication: *(significant discourse, superficial patter, pressured speech, etc.)*
  - ○ Artmaking: *(introduction and management of the artmaking process, involvement with artmaking/materials, response to client and/ or therapist's developing and final artwork, etc.)*

Sequence of Events and Narrative of the Session

This is a step-by-step recounting of the session punctuated by verbatim dialogue and the art therapist's professional response. The art therapist's response includes subjective personal reactions that would be inappropriate in a progress note or other types of clinical documentation other than a process note. Expressing and addressing countertransference and other feelings about the art therapist's performance and reactions is the aim. The therapist writing the process note expands on the artmaking process observations, not only from the client's selection of materials, images, and reactions to the art therapist's interventions, art process, and product but the art therapist's responses to the client's choices.

Reflection and Understanding

This portion is dedicated to integrating the previous sections of the process note with objective reflection of the art therapy interventions, the artwork, the art therapist's use of self, and the art therapist's internal discourse and countertransference.

Art Therapy Interventions

Provide an in-depth analysis of the art therapy interventions utilized – in what ways were they engaging, productive, challenging, or maybe off the mark and not well received? Were the materials offered time-, age-, and developmentally-appropriate?

Artwork

Explore the role artmaking and the artwork held in the session. Identify repetitions and variances in how the art was utilized within the session and across the treatment history. Document the art through original artwork or a photograph.

Art Therapist's Use of Self

How did you engage and acknowledge your professional role to positively impact the session?

Art Therapist's Internal Discourse and Countertransference

This portion is an opportunity to review the art therapist's use of interventions, self, and professional interactions.

Summary

Comprehension of Session

This section is significant as it contains the art therapist's ability to follow and highlight the totality and complexity of the session. The therapist writing the process note identifies key themes, lessons learned, and insights on improving performance and understanding.

Goals

Include aspirations and goals for the art therapist in addition to the client.

Appendix B
Case Presentation Guidelines for Group Supervision

Background Information

- Identify and describe the location where art therapy is taking place – is it a non-profit, hospital, community-based organization, community center, educational institution, prison, etc.? What is the focus – adult, child, family, or community? More group-based than individual work? What is the average length of stay or amount of time a participant is involved in treatment?
- Describe the format of treatment provided for participants (i.e., group, family, individual, group centered, etc.).
- Describe the treatment team and other significant professionals and their specific roles (e.g., nurses, educators, physical therapists, psychiatrists, psychologists, social workers, other creative arts therapists, lawyers, peer advocates, chaplains).
- Describe the role of art therapy within the treatment team or professional group and site or program. How is art therapy used and facilitated for clients?

Presenting the Case Itself

When presenting the client/patient/participant/consumer/member/artist or group, be aware of confidentiality: use a pseudonym, do not present exact admission or discharge dates, a date of birth, or other explicit identifying information. Note whether the information was obtained through previously logged client documentation or through current client disclosure. Describe the artwork as you see and experience it, including but not limited to transference/countertransference or other inter-relational observations including somatic sensations (body-based) and relational dynamics.

Individual cases

- Identity of the individual, including age, sex, race, ethnicity, sexual orientation, developmental level, and any other psychosocial markers and intersections of identity.

- Precipitant for admission or reason for involvement at your placement.
- Client's story/presenting problem.

  ○ Receive information on how the client perceives their world.
  ○ Attend to presenting issue from client's perspective, not therapist's.

- History: include all areas relevant to client.

  ○ Milestone and developmental history.
  ○ Discuss psychiatric history, including previous psychiatric diagnoses, admissions, prior psychiatric and other prescription drugs, and treatment history.
  ○ Previous mental health treatment history, including art therapy, and related outcomes of success.
  ○ Medical, substance abuse, and trauma history.
  ○ Pinpoint pertinent history and locate any gaps or discrepancies as reported.
  ○ Reference family dynamics and involvement as well as relationship history.
  ○ Education, occupational, and military history.
  ○ Incarceration or legal system involvement.

- What are the treatment goals of this individual?
- Pertinent history or gaps in the history of the client, as you know it.
- Mental status and current medications.

  ○ Depiction of client's presenting status – appearance, mood/affect, speech and expression, body language, incidence of hallucinations or delusions, presence of suicidal and/or homicidal ideation, drug or alcohol use, etc.
  ○ List all current psychiatric and other prescription drugs.

- Locate client in a social, historical, and cultural context highlighting any experiential differences from the situational majority that impacts role in the community/world.
- Art therapy assessment

  ○ Describe formal elements, voiced associations, behavioral observations, and assessment synopsis of art.
  ○ Assess and identify client's strengths, assets, supports, and coping skills that could play a positive role in meeting treatment goals, while denoting potential risks and barriers that could adversely impact goal achievement.
  ○ Social functioning, coping strategies, defense mechanisms employed.

- Diagnosis

  ○ Explanation and reasoning for diagnosis.

- Treatment history, including art therapy, with brief psychiatric history if applicable.
- Treatment plan and course of treatment.

  ○ Apply theoretical orientation and hypothesize about the nature of the identified problem(s). Describe the role of art therapy within the treatment.

  ○ Develop long-term goals with supporting short-term goals and art-based interventions for each identified problem(s). Although site-specific, long-term goals are generally achievable by the end of treatment, and short-term goals are often achievable in three months.

- Forecast

  ○ This is essentially a summary of the case conceptualization that would support or create barriers for success.

Group cases

- Why does this group exist? Why are these individuals grouped together?
- Provide a map or drawing of the group room, with seating arrangements of the participants, including facilitator(s).
- What are the age range, developmental-level range, and identity range of the group?
- What are some of the interchange, communication, possible conflicts, and/or peace-keeping you are witnessing and observing? Is the individual verbal and behavioral content of the group members the same or different than the artwork or artmaking observed as a "group"?

Remember!

- Cover the signature(s) or name(s) written on all artwork that you bring to supervision.
- Ensure that you have written consent to present any and all artwork that you bring to supervision.
- Ethical concerns, legal matters, and referrals: be mindful of legal and ethical requirements. Make sure all needed consents and releases have been signed; dual relationships addressed; safety plans created – e.g., IPV (intimate partner violence), DV (domestic violence), suicidal/homicidal ideation, etc. – and that all required mandated reports are filed. Recognize, manage, and follow through on all needed referrals.

Appendix C
Disclosure Statement Worksheet

Description of formal training and education. Consider where and when you received your highest clinical degree, the unique aspects of your education, and any other formalized training. If you have relevant other degrees (e.g., a PhD in a non-clinical field) and they inform your supervision practice, describe how they influence your work if applicable:

_____

_____

_____

Identified areas of competence and services provided (e.g., addictions counseling; career counseling; eye movement desensitization and reprocessing, or EMDR):

_____

_____

_____

Relevant academic training or professional experience in demonstrating competency in clinical supervision:

_____

_____

_____

Description of model or approach to supervision, including the role of the supervisor, objectives and goals of supervision, and modalities (e.g., tape review, live observation):

_____

_____

_____

RESOURCES

Description of philosophical and/or theoretical approach to supervision:

_____

_____

_____

What evaluation procedures do you use in the supervisory relationship?

_____

_____

_____

What makes you unique?

_____

_____

_____

Other things to consider?

_____

_____

_____

Appendix D
Sample Supervision Disclosure Form

Professional Disclosure Statement and Agreement for Clinical Supervision

Explain your experience here. Include the following: your licenses (and corresponding licensure number), credentials (with corresponding credentialing numbers), and professional organizational memberships.

Areas of Expertise

What are your areas of practice? What do you do well?

Supervision Services Provided

Do you provide individual or group supervision? Do you provide other services, such as consultation for organizations? How will you establish goals? How will you evaluate your supervisees?

Supervision Philosophy and/or Theoretical Orientation

Narratively describe based upon theory and/or practice. Consider providing citations in case your supervisee is unfamiliar with the terms you are using.

Fees

Describe here, including different types of supervision (i.e., individual, dyad, or group). You must also note if your fee is $0.

Affirmation of Adherence to Codes of Professional Practice

What codes do you adhere to? Include any professional body you are credentialed or licensed by.

Grievances

How should a supervisee make a complaint? Would you like to try to resolve the concern first before they contact the professional organization? Include the name of the organization, address, phone number, and email address.

References

You may want to cite articles that speak to your theoretical orientation or areas of expertise. Consider articles, books, or other sources that your supervisees would find useful to better understand your supervision practice.

I have fully read this supervision disclosure and have had all questions answered by [*Your Name, Degrees, Credentials, Licenses*]. *You may also want to note any additional considerations here. For example, social media, gift giving/receiving, record-keeping (will you provide the supervisee a list of dates they attended?), etc.*

_____   _____   _____

Supervisee Name Printed   Supervisee Name Signed   Date

Mailing Address: _____

Email: _____

Phone: _____   OK to text: Yes   No

Place of Work: _____

_____   _____

Your Name, Degrees, Credentials, License(s)   Date

_____

Your Work Address

_____

Your Phone Number

_____

Your Email

_____

Your Website

Appendix E
Sample Artwork Release Form

I allow/do not allow [*insert art therapist's name*] to use, display, screen, and/or photograph my artwork for the following purposes:

(Yes/No) Publication
(Yes/No) Presentation
(Yes/No) Educational Purposes

If consent is provided, I understand my confidentiality will be protected at all times and I will only be identified by a pseudonym unless otherwise noted below in the *Additional notes* section. Identifying details will be removed from any descriptions.

I understand that signing this form is not a requirement for art therapy and will not affect my participation in therapeutic services in any way.

Signed: _____ **Date:** _____

Print Name: _____

Parent or Guardian Signature (if applicable): _____

Parent or Guardian Printed Name (if applicable): _____

Witness: _____

Contact Info

Phone # (circle: mobile/work/home): _____

Email Address: _____

Mailing Address: _____

City: _____ **State:** _____ **Zip Code:** _____

Additional notes: _____

Appendix F

Guidelines for Giving Feedback to Case Presentations in Group Supervision

Listen to and observe the presentation of case material. What feelings arise in you when you hear this case?

Questions

Identify any additional material you may like to know about the case. You may have additional questions about the case or the artwork presented before making comments. Questions may be about the individual, such as psychosocial markers that were not explicitly raised, how materials were presented, etc.

When focusing on the art productions, make observations or ask questions regarding:

- Developmental level.
- Manifest or latent imagery or forms.
- Possible conflicts or client goals manifested.
- Group Dynamics indicators, if applicable.
- Any possible diagnostic questions or imagery and form anomalies.
- Inter-relational observations.
- Materials – what was used? How were the materials used (e.g., with force)? What materials were offered to the client? Do not assume that the client did or did not choose the art materials if this was not made clear by the presenter.
- Time – how long did the piece take to be created? Did some elements of the art get worked on for different amounts of time?
- Space – if the artwork is on paper, is the entire space used or is it concentrated to a certain area (e.g., top, center, corner)?
- Content.
- Title.

Glossary

AATA Founded in 1969, the American Art Therapy Association (AATA) is a 501(c)(3) professional, and educational organization dedicated to the art therapy profession.

ADDRESSING framework Created by Pamela Hays, ADDRESSING reminds clinicians to pay attention to age, developmental and other disabilities, religion and spiritual aspects, ethnic and racial identities, socioeconomics, sexual orientation, indigeneity, national origin, and gender identity.

Administrative Component of supervision that includes the business aspects of supervision, such as evaluation, disciplinary procedures, and scheduling of supervision.

Advanced therapist A developmental phase of a clinician, one who possesses solid clinical decision-making abilities. Advanced therapists are also more experienced clinicians who are flexible as well as accepting of multiple perspectives and of themselves.

Agent status Identities that hold power.

Arts-based supervision Supervision model where theory and practice are unified by integrating the supervisee and supervisor's artmaking process, response art, and related discussions as a way to more deeply understand the clinical work and countertransference.

ATCB The Art Therapy Credentials Board (ATCB) protects the public by maintaining national art therapy standards through credentialing (i.e., ATR-P, ATR, ATR-BC, ATCS) and maintaining ethical standards.

ATCBE Acronym for the Art Therapy Credentials Board Examination, the national board examination administered by the ATCB. This exam qualifies a Registered Art Therapist (ATR) for board certification and licensure in some states.

ATCS Acronym for the Art Therapy Certified Supervisor credential granted by the ATCB. Certified Supervisor status requires several components, including professional experience supervising clinicians or graduate art therapy students, having received expert supervision themselves, and undergoing supervision training. The ATCS can only be held after first obtaining the ATR-BC.

ATR Credential granted by the ATCB indicating that the individual is a Registered Art Therapist. Registration requires several components, including professional work experience that has been supervised by a qualified professional, post-graduation from a master's program.

ATR-BC Credential granted by the ATCB indicating that the individual is a board-certified, Registered Art Therapist. Board certification is achieved after the passing of the ATBCE. The ATR-BC can only be held after first obtaining the ATR.

ATR-P Credential granted by the ATCB indicating that the individual is working towards being a Registered Art Therapist, with the "P" indicating "provisional". ATR-Ps have graduated from a master's program and are practicing art therapy under a qualified supervisor.

Back-up supervisor An alternative and previously identified supervisor who is available when an on-site supervisor-of-record is not available for clinical or site-specific guidance and decision making.

Broaching The act of purposefully bringing up matters related to culture into the clinical session.

Campus supervisor Employed and selected by the academic institution, the campus supervisor is an instructor (e.g., professor, adjunct faculty) who provides classroom-based supervision within the academic setting. Their focus is largely on client care, art therapy interventions, and application of clinical theory within the internship placement.

Case conceptualization Case conceptualization is not a single act but originates at intake and is maintained throughout treatment to better understand and organize client information. The supervisor guides the supervisee through this framework to interpret client observations within psychological concepts and art therapy theory, in order to guide treatment and monitor progress. Art therapists often have the additional visual elements and artmaking processes to consider.

Case presentation A case presentation is an oral or written presentation to better understand and organize client information by communicating all critical client elements and the conceptual reasoning, and proposing case-related questions as well as clinical justification to an audience.

Code of ethics Created by state licensure and credentialing bodies to guide practitioners and safeguard the general public. Noncompliance has disciplinary consequences.

Confidentiality "Confidentiality is the ethical concept, in most states it is the legal duty of the therapists not to disclose information about a client" (Corey, 2013, p. 41).

Credentials Documents or other certificates that are proof of qualifications, typically granted by a professional regulatory body to regulate the practice of a specific discipline, field, modality, or specialty. For art therapists, credentials often include degree held (e.g., MA), and national or state-administered qualifications. While the term is broad, for the purposes of art therapists *credentials* are often referred to when discussing the designation granted by a professional regulatory body to regulate the practice of a specific discipline, field, modality, or specialty. For art therapists in the United States, the credentialing body is the ATCB.

Critical race feminism   Rooted in critical race theory and a range of feminisms focusing on issues of power, oppression, and conflict.

Cross-disciplinary supervision   When the supervisor and supervisee are not trained in the same field or discipline. For example, when the art therapist is supervising a school-based counselor or a psychologist supervising an art therapist.

Cultural competency   Often described as the obtainment of awareness, knowledge, and skills to work with groups of people across cultures.

Cultural humility   Coined by Melanie Tervalon and Jann Murray-García, seen as an ongoing process which can be an alternative or complement to cultural competency.

Developmental Model of Supervision   Introductory, Intermediate, Proficient, and Advanced Therapists are the four phases identified for this supervisory approach. Supervision is adjusted to identify the supervisee's developmental phase and changing needs.

Disclosure statement   see *Supervision Disclosure Statement.*

Distance counseling   Professional relationship between the therapist and client(s) where counseling interactions (sessions, communications) are facilitated through the use of synchronous or nonsynchronous videoconferencing or other technology and do not occur in person.

Distance supervision   Professional relationship between the supervisor and supervisee(s) focused on increasing the supervisee's professional skills and expertise where supervisory interactions (sessions, communications) are facilitated through the use of synchronous or nonsynchronous videoconferencing or other technology and do not occur in person.

Dual relationships   What occurs when there is overlap between a personal and professional relationship that moves beyond the therapeutic or supervisory relationship.

Duty to warn   An art therapist's legal responsibility, as a mental health care professional, to notify individual(s) of potential harm by a client.

Dyad supervision   when one supervisor is supervising two clinicians in a supervision session.

E-counseling   See *Distance counseling.*

E-health   Information and communication technologies are utilized to deliver or enhance health services and information to improve healthcare, increase access to healthcare information, and provide resources to better manage personal health.

Educational   Component of supervision that includes the ability to interact with clients, and is learned by teaching and sharing knowledge, proficiencies, approaches, theories, ethics, and values. For art therapists, education also considers how the artmaking process and expression is utilized and impacts clinical work.

Feminist Multicultural Supervision Focuses on power and power dynamics between the various relationships involved in treatment – supervisee/therapist–client, supervisor–supervisee, and supervisor–supervisee–client–society.

FERPA The Family Education Rights and Privacy Act (FERPA) is a federal law allowing a child's parent(s) or guardian(s) to have access to the child's educational records. The law also permits parents to potentially have records revised, and to have some level of power over the disclosure of data that is personally identifiable.

Group supervision Group supervision is more than three clinicians meeting together with a supervisor to discuss clinical work and related matters. Distinct from individual supervision, group supervision benefits from the feedback and dynamics of multiple clinicians in the supervision session.

HIPAA The Health Insurance Portability Accounting Act is a federal privacy law intended to protect an individual's health information while permitting the exchange of needed health information and encourage.

Individual supervision When one supervisor is supervising one clinician.

Informed consent The right of clients "to be informed about their therapy and to make autonomous decisions pertaining to it" (Corey, 2013, p. 40) and that "results in the patient's authorization or agreement to undergo a specific medical or mental health intervention(s)" (Hodgson et al., 2013, p. 30).

Integrated Model of Supervision This approach often combines orientation-specific theory (e.g. cognitive behavioral, psychodynamic) with developmental foundations and additional elements for a more eclectic, yet intentional method.

Interdisciplinary supervision See *Cross-disciplinary supervision.*

Intermediate therapist A developmental phase of a clinician that marks some experience working with clients, but still requiring active guidance from a supervisor.

Intersectionality Term coined by Kimberlé Crenshaw, a legal scholar who noted that the intersections of identities, particularly race and gender, are often ignored and looked at as independent factors (i.e., women are white, men are Black).

Introductory therapist Beginning-level therapist who often desires highly structured supervision.

License Typically granted by a state governing body or agency to regulate the practice of specific professions.

Managing up This approach shifts the traditional top-down management dynamic empowering the supervisee to consciously identify deficiencies in the supervisory relationship and actively create and implement strategies to get their needs met.

Off-site supervision Supervision which occurs outside of the location where clinical work is taking place. Often times, off-site supervision is contracted, meaning that the supervisor and supervisee agree to meet. The supervisor and supervisee are not employed by the same site and therefore will not have similar institutional knowledge of the place of work.

Online counseling See *Distance counseling.*

On-site supervision Supervision which occurs where the clinical work is taking place. The supervisor and supervisee are employed by the same site and therefore may have similar institutional knowledge of the place of work.

Orientation-Specific Model of Supervision A supervision approach clearly defined by and based on a specific psychotherapy theory that provides the framework for the supervision process.

Peer consultation group Peer consultation groups can occur for professionals or during training, and may happen on- or off-site. These leaderless groups generally meet on a regular basis to discuss a range of topics, such as challenging clinical work, self-care, the impact of privilege and difference, and ethical concerns.

Privileged communication The communication between two parties that the law deems confidential and cannot normally be disclosed by force.

Process note Also known as a process recording, the note provides structure for supervisees to share with a supervisor what was experienced objectively and subjectively during and after a session. Includes: presenting information and history, observation and description of the art therapy process, art therapist's reflection on inner process, interpreting and assessing the session, and summary/goals.

Professional disclosure statement See *Supervision disclosure statement.*

Proficient therapist A developmental phase of a clinician who possesses competent clinical decision-making skills and self-awareness about their limitations.

Racial/Cultural Identity Development Model (R/CID) A five-stage development model aimed to identify how minority groups view themselves, others like them, other minorities, and the majority population.

Self-reflection The ability to explore personal positionality, emotionality, and vulnerabilities as well as professional competence and clinical assumptions, etc., to enhance ethical practice and art therapy proficiencies.

Site supervisor Primary supervisory contact providing clinical supervision and location-specific leadership art the internship site. Main liaison between internship site and academic institution.

Social media All formats of electronic communication, including social networking websites, applications, blogs, and other platforms designed to create and share content such as text, videos, information, audio, and photos with online communities. Some well-known examples include Facebook, Instagram, Snapchat, and Twitter. Individuals, small businesses, large corporations, and causes, among many other types of enterprises, utilize social media.

Supervision agreement See *Supervision Disclosure Statement.*

Supervision disclosure statement This form, also called a *supervision contract or agreement*, establishes the supervisory relationship. It includes logistical information on the supervisor, such as fee schedule, cancellation policy, location of practice, credentials, and the bodies or parties who maintain ethical oversight, including how to resolve conflicts should they occur. Contracts also contain the supervision philosophy and act as a point of discussion for the supervisee to learn about the supervisor's way of working. Parallel to informed consent for clients. This contract may or may not include goals.

Supervision of supervision A supervisory relationship where supervisees are seeking supervision to become better supervisors.

Supervisor-of-record This is the primary on-site supervisor who is ultimately responsible for supervision, supervisee development, and client care.

Supportive Component of supervision that emphasizes work-related stress as well as supporting the supervisee's emotional responses.

Target status Aspects that lack power or hold subjugated meaning.

Technology-assisted counseling (TADC) See *Distance counseling.*

Technology-facilitated supervision See *Distance supervision.*

Telecommunications technologies Common designation for science and technology of communications by cellular telephone, radio, television, etc., to transmit encoded information such as images, sounds, or computer data.

Telehealth The application of technology to augment health care services, health education, and public health, and provide virtual medical health services.

Telemental health See *Distance counseling.*

Telephonic supervision Term for distance supervision delivered via the telephone system.

Telepsychology Alternative term for distance counseling. See *Distance counseling.*

Title protection Acts created to protect consumers by restricting use of titles to those who have fulfilled the requirements (e.g., a license) to call themselves a certain type of professional.

Videoconferencing Audio and video data is transmitted through computer networks, allowing conference participants to communicate from remote locations.

WRID White Racial Identity Development model created by Pamela Hays.

References

Brown, K. W., & Ryan, R. M. (2003). The benefits of being present: mindfulness and its role in psychological well-being. *Journal of personality and social psychology,* 84(4), 822.

Corey, G. (2013). *Theory and practice of counseling and psychotherapy.* Belmont, CA: Brooks/Cole.

Hodgson, J., Mendenhall, T., & Lamson, A. (2013). Patient and provider relationships: Consent, *confidentiality, and managing mistakes in integrated primary care settings. Families, Systems, & Health,* 31(1), 28.

Index

Page numbers in *italics* refer to figures, page numbers in **bold** refer to tables.

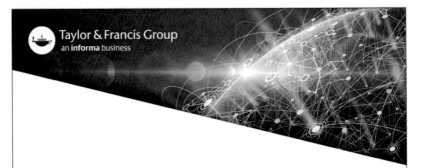